"Rupert Hayles has written [...]ership
or lay, will consider invalua[...]ight or emotional intelligence
and what it brings to spiritual leadership is something I have not seen as
yet to this date. Read it and you will be blessed and be brought into a
new level of understanding and dependency on God."

    — Elder Maurice Waddell
        Chief Operating Officer,
        New Birth Missionary Baptist Church

"Rupert Hayles' book on *Emotional Intelligence and the Church*
provides penetrating insight into perhaps the most important arena of
understanding in church life today. Hayles brings his extraordinary
perspective as a church leader, thinker, and practitioner to this subject.
Too many leaders and congregations are derailed by unhealthy
emotional patterns – this book is a road map toward emotional health
and fruitfulness for Christ's kingdom."

    — Rev. Dr. Mac Pier
        President, The New York City Leadership Center

"In *'Practical Strategy: Emotional Intelligence and the Church,'*
Rupert Hayles offers a way of understanding the central connection
between emotional intelligence and the religious and spiritual
communities. It is an important contribution and one worth
exploring."

    — Marcia Hughes,
        President, Collaborative Growth and Author -
        The Emotionally Intelligent Team

"I have known the Hayles for many years and they give out to others
out of their own experiences. *Emotional Intelligence and the Church*
is a culmination of life experiences, life understanding and life direction
from this wonderful couple. The knowledge imparted in this book will
not only help the Church, but will develop anyone who desires to grow
as true children of Christ."

    — Rev. Derrick Greene
        Senior Pastor, Christ Church of Elizabeth

"As Christians, we aspire to be like Christ relating to others by the fruit of the spirit. Rupert Hayles, through emotional intelligence, is able to provide a link between assessing yourself and determining where you transformation. The result is introspective searching; Psalm 139: 1-24, with humility and dependency on God. The content of this book will bring an understanding of personal change that will transform your life forever."
— Rev. Gordon Goutremout
      Founder and President, Cross Roads Soul Care

"Rupert Hayles does a masterful job of explaining Emotional Intelligence in a way that is clear, compelling, and applicable. His method of explaining the concept, relating it to the Fruit of the Spirit and utilizing real life case studies sets his work apart from others. It is a tremendous read and one that would be beneficial to all leaders, whether they operate in the social sector or corporate realm. I highly recommend it."
— Todd W. Hall, Ph.D., Biola University
      Professor of Psychology
      Director, Institute for Research on Psychology and Spirituality
      Editor, Journal of Psychology and Theology

"Rupert Hayles' *Emotional Intelligence and the Church* provides practical insights and "how tos" for enhancing relationships and leading in the church context. He has built his work on the best of the research on emotional intelligence and extended the application into the church community. You will find suggestions for all of the mission critical challenges of leading your congregation."
— Roger Pearman, Ph.D.
      Founder and President, Leadership Performance Systems

"Rupert, a social sector strategy consultant, has come alongside Cathedral International in our strategic change process. He understands people and process and this work, *Emotional Intelligence and the Church*, will help any organization understands the importance of emotional intelligence and its connection to our spiritual growth and development. The book is a treasure which every leader should have on his bookshelf. Read it, be challenged and be changed!"
— Bishop Donald Hilliard, D. Min.
      Senior Pastor, Cathedral International Church

EMOTIONAL INTELLIGENCE

AND THE CHURCH

BE TRANSFORMED BY THE RENEWING OF YOUR MIND

EMOTIONAL INTELLIGENCE

AND THE CHURCH

RUPERT A. HAYLES, JR.

Foreword by Jim Mellado
President of Willow Creek Association

BE TRANSFORMED BY THE RENEWING OF YOUR MIND

BRIDGE
LOGOS

Alachua, Florida 32615

Bridge Logos
Alachua, FL 32615 USA

Emotional Intelligence and the Church
by Rupert A. Hayles, Jr.

Excerpted Information with Permission: Copyright © 2010
Multi-Health Systems Inc. All rights reserved. In the USA,
P.O. Box 950, North Tonawanda, NY 14120-0950,
1-800-456-3003. In Canada, 3770 Victoria Park Ave.,
Toronto, ON M2H 3M6, 1-800-268-6011. Internationally,
+1-416-492-2627. Fax, +1-416-492-3343.

All Scripture quotes are from The Holy Bible, New International
Version, 1984, unless otherwise noted.

Printed in the United States of America

Library of Congress Control Number: 2012937508
ISBN 978-0-88270806-5

DEDICATION

⟨⟨⟩⟩

I would like to thank God for giving me the courage to complete this subtle piece of material He has placed in my heart.

I dedicate this work to Maryann Conti. Maryann is one of the godliest people anyone could ever meet. Her personal journey is filled with emotional challenges and triumphs. She has survived growing up with manic-depression, trichotillomania, and mental institutionalization. Through this entire journey, God has delivered her. Maryann came into my life at a time when I struggled with the emotional dimension. She was able to help me walk through this.

With her experience and her long journey of pain, she has helped many people who have come into her path. She lights up the room because she understands not just intellectual matters, but emotional matters others would subconsciously dismiss. She has a keen ability to discern that which is not obvious. She believes intellect doesn't make a person, but rather it is one's connection to other human beings that makes us better people.

I dedicate this book to my wife, partner, and friend—Maryann Conti Hayles.

ACKNOWLEDGEMENTS

Numerous people have had their parts to play in this book. I would like to thank the Reverend Gordon and Emily Goutremout from Cross Roads Soul Care. With his unique expertise, Gordon, was able to conduct interviews and gather critical and credible feedback from participants that were the basis for the many cases in this book. To all the subjects in the book (who remain nameless) and who at times were willing to undergo the grueling sharing of private information so the Body of Christ could learn from personal experiences, I have much appreciation. To the folks at Leadership Performance Systems, Roger Pearman and Leap Enterprises and Rita Hummel Crowe, I am humbled by your participation.

To my writers who were able to capture interviews and convert them into skeleton cases and to John Castagna, I thank you for your diligence and your hard work.

If it were not for Carole Leflore, my extremely gifted writing executive assistant at the church, who endured all the changes, phone calls, and printing of documents, I would be lost. She is a treasure and her ability to see what needs to be said, even though it is not said in the proper way, is a gift.

To Dr. Dick Thompson, whose company is the publisher of TESI - Team Emotional and Social Intelligence measuring instrument, and my first instructor in the field of emotional intelligence, my gratitude is beyond words.

To Marcia Hughes, who co-developed TESI-Team Emotional and Social Intelligence, your work is appreciated and I hope will have a lasting effect on the world around us.

I am thankful for the folks at Multi-Health System, where Dr. Steven Stein is the president. I appreciate your approval of the use of your definitions in this work to ground others in the meaning of the emotional intelligence scales and subscales.

A sincere special thanks to Dr. David Ireland, who was able to give me the opportunity and support to start the Center for Emotional and Spiritual Development, and his support as my pastor to continue to do great works for God.

"Once I understood the nature of work, it helped me relax and be more generous. I learned that people get frightened if asked to change their worldview. And why wouldn't they? Of course people will get defensive; of course they might be intrigued by a new idea; but then turn away in fear. They are smart enough to realize how much they would have to change if they accepted the idea. I no longer worry that if I could just find the right words or techniques, I could instantly convince people. I know many people who've been changed by events in their lives, not by words they read in a book."

— Margaret Wheatley, Leadership and the New Science

TABLE OF CONTENTS

FOREWORD

———

I (Jim) grew up in seven different countries around the world…
mostly in underdeveloped regions. No matter where we lived,
my family was always deeply involved in local church ministry.
Some of these churches had dirt floors and a handful of members—
others were much larger with hundreds of members. Today I
attend Willow Creek Community Church in South Barrington,
Illinois—a mega church with incredible resources. Whatever the
size and whatever the resources, God always met me and used
each faith community to grow me up in Christ. For me, the
most meaningful positive memories in life were connected with
my church. Even though my wife Leanne had a very different
reality growing up in essentially one church, many of her most
transformative experiences were also connected to her church
experience.

Given that background, I'm not surprised that both mine
and Leanne's primary callings in life are focused around helping
churches realize their full redemptive potential. This is in spite of
earning degrees, between the two of us, in engineering, business,
education, and leadership. Like our pastor Bill Hybels always
says, "There is nothing like the local church when the local church
is working right!" That's certainly true from our experience. But
we also know that when the church isn't working right, it has
the potential to create painful experiences for those who attend.
Unfortunately, sometimes the church works against the very
mission it was created to fulfill—making disciples of all nations.
The difference is found in the quality of its leaders. How skilled
and knowledgeable are they? How committed and experienced
are they? Most importantly, how Christ-like are they? This book
deals with an often ignored but critical aspect that more often than

not impacts Christ-likeness and determines the long-term success of a leader in a church setting.

One of the many blessings that comes with leading the Willow Creek Association is getting to meet a wide variety of incredible church leaders around the world. I met Rupert Hayles while on a Global Leadership Summit trip to New Jersey. We were expanding into the Northeast region and, as is the norm, we travel to visit churches we consider to be on the cutting edge. Christ Church was one of those churches and is overseen by senior pastor Dr. David Ireland (who has served on the Global Leadership Summit faculty). Rupert serves in the capacity of Chief Operating Officer of Christ Church. He and I have very similar backgrounds. We are driven. We try to defeat obstacles that are placed in our way. We are passionate to see God be what He really is in every person's life. Leanne and Maryann, Rupert's wife, have similar experiences in the ministry that led us to some interesting conversations about service to God and service to people.

The questions we addressed in our numerous conversations and that are addressed in this book are: How do we serve and lead others in a healthy way when we are on a healing journey ourselves? Are there processes in place that can help a leader understand what their emotional blindspots are and then provide transformation strategies to help him or her deal with them them along the way? What do you do when ministry leaders seem oblivious to their shortcomings and the church suffers because of it? How do you handle things when that person is you? How does a leader engage a healing process without that healing process becoming an undue distraction to the staff or congregation?

This is what Emotional Intelligence and the Church is about. It's a powerful topic and one that requires brutal self-awareness, honesty, and courage to confront some of the painful truths that will help us come to terms with some of the deep "whys" behind our behaviors.

This book is an insightful, thoughtful, vulnerable, and holistic look into Rupert's journey of self-discovery and healing. He and Maryann provide numerous examples from the Bible, their own experience, and from other modern day leaders to help us better understand the problems and potential solutions to the emotional shortcomings leaders often have that go unchecked. They will help us examine the impact emotional intelligence has on creating a culture and environment that fosters spiritual growth and maturity in the context of a local church. They combine the latest knowledge of emotional intelligence, deep spiritual sensitivity, and personal experience to bring us a road map and strategies to equip churches to become the healing agents God intended them to be— for leaders, staff members, and their congregations. Their passion to see every local church realizing its fullest potential is evident throughout. If you want that for youself and your church, and if you want others to experience your life-giving leadership, I encourage you to read this book with a courageous outlook that is open to follow God's healing journey for you—wherever it leads.

Jim and Leanne Mellado
President, Willow Creek Association
Ministry Director, Willow Creek Community Church

PREFACE

—◇◈◇—

As servants of Christ we are called to be exemplary citizens in the world around us. We are called to be people who are separate and different from the world. But how can we be different? Do we get up the day after conversion and say, "Lord, it is time for me to act differently, be different, and demonstrate I am a perfect person in the sight of Christ." It is a process that requires us to examine our spiritual wellbeing, align our lives to God, and not just our spiritual lives, but our natural, practical existence as well.

As Socrates once said, "Know thyself!" It is my belief that in order for us to be different, we must know ourselves. How do we know ourselves? We know ourselves by examining our inner being, understanding the environment in which we operate, and by being aware of ourselves, and how our emotions affect others. We know ourselves when we do not allow the way we feel—the way we emote, the way we understand how others are feeling, why they do what they do, how they do what they do, and the way in which they do what they do—to determine our behavior in certain situations.

To know thyself necessitates reflection. It requires us to go deep within our inner being and understand why we behave in a certain manner. Is the way we behave driven by our past, our experiences, our beliefs, and our upbringing? I will dare to say it takes a combination of all of the above; however, there are specific things that are more dominant than others.

Over the past months and years, I have been in deep reflection, wondering why I do what I do; wondering why I say what I say; wondering why I react the way I react. It does not matter whether I'm a Christian or not. What matters more to me is that being a child of God I should be aware of how I view and how I am being viewed. The following books come to mind: *Blink* and *The Tipping Point* by Malcolm Gladwell; *Emotional Intelligence* by Daniel Goleman; *Emotional Intelligence and Your Success* by Steven J. Stein and Howard E. Book; *Primal Leadership* by Daniel Goleman, Richard Boyatzis, and Annie McKee; and *The Emotionally Healthy Church* by Peter Scazzero. These books address issues related to knowing oneself, knowing the environment, knowing people, and understanding how we make critical decisions that can affect not just ourselves, but the world around us.

There are many in this field of study who will ask, "What is the author's authority for writing this book? Does he have a Ph.D.? Is he a counselor or therapist?" To be frank, I am not. I have long believed and have seen genuine validity in the statement "A man with an argument has nothing over a man with experience." I speak from the stable of experience more so than argument. I have lived what is written in this book and the topic has aligned my second call in life, which is to see the Body of Christ be emotionally healthy and the Church to be what God wants it to be. I am by no means an authority on the subject; however, I am an authority on the experience. I have now dedicated my life to research (Ph.D. candidate at Regent University), live, share, and teach this subject for the remainder of my existance.

This particular writing is one based more in experience than one based on theological and theoretical research and understanding. If the reader is looking for quantitative and qualitative analysis dealing with emotional intelligence, then there are a countless books that address the topic, particularly some of those named above. This book deals with the practicalities of how and why we behave the way we do. This book deals with how and why we react or engage in situations that could exert tremendous harm on others, and even on ourselves. This book discusses serious psychological and emotional issues people cope with and how, if they are not handled properly, they are brought into and create havoc in the church or workplace. This book is based upon painful experiences, identified issues, and struggles within ourselves, as well as how we confront problems, deal with and address them so we can be better stewards of what God has given us. And how He has led us to be better for His enjoyment.

As you read, you'll realize the most interesting thing about the book is how it is organized. Actual cases of real people in real circumstances dealing with current issues in our church and our workplace are used. First and foremost is the heavy reliance on case studies. As an MBA student from one of the top business schools in the country, I have learned the best way to teach is not to rely on theory, but to give an understanding of real-life circumstances and situations that can yield fruitful outcomes.

Thus, from a directional standpoint, I have made the decision to include cases of individuals who suffer from low self-esteem and how they recover; cases of deep anger and a total lack of empathy from senior leadership and how that can lead to a deepening morale crisis on the job; how individuals people-please to ensure success, but at the same time lose track of who they are and the impact their behavior is having on the family; a case of the effect of emotional tone-deafness and the traumatic blow it can have on the people who love and serve us. Further, there are cases dealing with individuals who have sincere psychological trauma in their lives and how these traumas manifest themselves in subtle ways, which, if left unaddressed, can have a major impact on workers around them.

Besides the cases, the book will focus on emotional intelligence, spirituality, emotional quotient, and intelligence quotient. It will bring to the forefront the need for congregations and workplaces to address the issue of emotional intelligence and the consequence emotional intelligence will have on the success or failure of an organization.

From visiting churches, experiencing churches, and observing churches prior to writing this manuscript, I have come to realize that many people within our churches often focus on the spiritual dimension without focusing on the emotional aspect of others. At times, leadership believes that if someone is "in-tune" with God, then there should be no need for determining or considering why that person should behave or act in a certain manner contrary to Scripture. This is somewhat of an ignorant and naïve way of looking at the world because we live in many dimensions. We are spiritual beings with a natural existence. Hence, it is becoming increasingly more evident that we need to address the natural component to help enhance our spiritual development. Many elders, ministers, deacons, leaders and lay people have focused primarily on spirituality to the detriment of emotionality. I do not advocate we focus exclusively on the emotion, but it has become clear to me that the lack of focus on the individual's emotional wellbeing has cost us greatly.

I hope after reading this book you will appreciate the fact that there's more to how we operate than ensuring the work gets done and that we are spiritually in alignment with God. I trust there will be a renewed focus on the emotional aspect of life and how it can greatly impact, either positively or negatively, the general outcome of any situation, whether it is in the church or the workplace.

PART I

The Basis for Change

CHAPTER ONE

CHANGE:
WHY IT IS ALWAYS YOU?

. . . .

It was a brisk fall day in November and the organization for whom I was a senior executive was about to embark on one of their most ambitious goals ever. We were putting on the greatest event our organization's parent company had held in its twenty-year history—exciting to say the least. I was emotionally charged up driving to the palatial Crystal Plaza in preparation to meet all the dignitaries, families, and friends of the organization. As the leader of the group I realized there were many activities that needed to be done prior to officially starting the event. I relied heavily on my assistant Cheryl, who was my heart and soul. She was the person who would make sure all the plans were executed and she was responsible for ensuring that everything would be done par-excellence. This is what was expected. I was so excited.

Ten minutes prior to my arrival at the Plaza, I called her on the phone. I requested all the information we had agreed upon to be ready for me at the front desk. I said to her, "Cheryl, please have the documents for me when I pull my car up to the front door." I could tell she was nervous and concerned. She said to me, "I'm sorry. I don't have the documents. I've been working on the registration all day and even though we are a half hour away from the official start of the event, we are not fully prepared." I felt the blood in my veins begin to percolate as she spoke of the impending nightmare and ultimate disaster. I felt as though I was experiencing an out-of-body experience. I seemed to be leaving my natural body, looking down at myself as I screamed at her, "I've told you numerous times to be prepared. I will not have any of this nonsense. Your behavior reflects badly on me, on our leadership, and our organization. You have disgraced me."

She started to cry. I said, "Why are you crying? Was it something I said? How dare you do this now when we're at this most critical moment?" The only thing I believed I could do was to hang up and start trying to devise strategies for the containment of what was about to happen.

Strangely enough, this also was the beginning of my journey into understanding the emotional component of my life—the before I do what I do, how I do it, the manner in which I execute things, and how my actions might impact others. Needless to say, the beginning of the event was a disaster. Nothing worked as planned. I was furious. Our guests had arrived and there was no registration information for them to get into the event. There were no nameplates or table settings and the list of attendees was in table order instead of alphabetical order. Those around me tried to calm me down and tell me everything would be okay. I, however, was inconsolable. All I knew was this event had taken us over one year to plan and was getting off to the most dreadful start, with the expectation that it would be going downhill shortly. Dignitaries arrived and were shuffled to on-the-spot table assignments. I remember distinctly having someone from the media, who was an adversary, being assigned to the table with one of my most cherished donors. What a night!

Throughout the evening, I reflected on what could have been done to ensure this disaster could have been prevented. Deep within myself, I knew that Cheryl had done the best job she possibly could. In my heart, I knew I was right because a few days before, I had reminded Cheryl about what we needed to do to ensure a successful event. I had even offered her additional assistance, but she, at that time, refused and said, "Rupert, I am okay. All is well." However, in my mind, I felt if only she had listened to my instructions things would have ended in a better place.

Later that night as the event ended I saw Cheryl. We hugged. I guess the hug was more a reflection of us consoling one another for just getting through the evening. Weeks later, I was informed that Cheryl had had a major breakdown the night before the event. She had a panic attack shortly after I had hung up the phone with her earlier in the evening. She had actually refused to come to the event because she knew it was going to be one big disaster. The only reason she eventually did make an appearance was at the insistence of one of her closest friends.

My role as chief operating officer of a mega church and my role as president of the affiliate organization kept me quite busy. I quickly internalized what had occurred at the event and concluded it was all Cheryl's fault. I hastily moved on to my next priority, which ironically, was a mission trip to the Dominican Republic just a few weeks later. I was traveling with the senior pastor of our church, Dr. David Ireland. It was a one-week, short-term trip. As we departed for the Dominican Republic, I sensed Dr. David had something he wanted to discuss with me. I have internal radar and have the uncanny ability to sense when folks are uneasy or are uncomfortable around me. I have antenna that tells me when things are not going as planned or as projected. Although I felt that way boarding the airplane, I did not, however, know exactly when Dr. David was actually going to speak to me. But I did know for sure he had something to say.

The trip to the Dominican Republic was to hold leadership-training sessions and many days and hours were spent speaking to large crowds of people about leadership development. It wasn't until the final day, in the final hour, that I received a call from Dr. David. He requested I come to his room because he had something very important to talk to me about. While going up to his room in the elevator, I kept wondering in my mind and heart what it could possibly be he want to talk to me about? Of course, at the very beginning of the trip my intuition told me something was wrong and Dr. David would be discussing something important with me. I wondered if this was it. Is he going to fire me or relieve me of my duties?

When I got to his room, he asked me to sit on the couch and then he told me why he wanted to speak to me. He said, "Rupert, it is important when you are dealing with people that you ensure they feel respected. It is important they feel cared for and that they feel loved. It has come to my attention that Cheryl feels she has been insulted, ridiculed, and made to feel like less of a person than she really is." Dr. David continued, "Cheryl's friend and co-worker, Carmella, called my office crying and told me Cheryl did not feel like working at the church or the affiliate anymore. Carmella stated that you insulted Cheryl so badly it had left her feeling inferior."

Dr. David said, "You know, Rupert, there is one thing about Jesus I can say and it is this: no matter who He was speaking to, that person never felt less than who they were. It didn't matter if Jesus was speaking to a Pharisee, to a beggar, or to a king—that person never felt belittled. You need to apologize to her."

I immediately became defensive and told Dr. David that the failure of the event was all Cheryl's fault. As we continued our dialog, however, it became clear to me I had contributed significantly to what had occurred. I informed Dr. David I was stressed and I was trying to do the best I could with what I had. Tears welled up in my eyes as the pain, pressure, and emptiness of my soul came to light.

It was at that very moment, I realized I needed to change. I realized it didn't matter what others do. What does matter, however, is how I react, and what I do about it. Deep within my heart and soul I felt confused and conflicted. I felt frustrated because I knew I was trying to do the very best I could with what

I had. Dr. David, the wonderful pastor that he is, began to pray for me. I recognized in that very moment I would never be the same again. Deep within me, I could feel my emotions scatter. I did not know what to feel—a host of feelings arose in me. I felt anger, pain, shame, guilt, stress, anxiety, and unhappiness—all at the same time. All I knew was something was going on deep within me I could not explain. I could not vocalize it. It was not an intellectual exercise, nor was it spiritual. It was something else. Even though it was an issue of right and wrong which, for the most part, is an ethical and spiritual consideration, I still felt in my heart something existed within me that needed to be cleansed and rooted out. I could not articulate it. But I did know I had to change.

On the return flight from the Dominican Republic to the United States, I was reading one of Dr. Ireland's books, *Journey to the Mountain of God*. As it happened, I met a wonderful stewardess who noticed I was reading Dr. Ireland's book. She asked me if I knew Dr. David Ireland. She was thrilled when I introduced her to Dr. David. She told me she was currently reading a book entitled *Abba's Child*.[1] She showed me the book and as I began to read it, I found the words in the book expressed what I was feeling. The sovereignty of God was amazing to me in that He would allow me to be on an airplane and have someone give me the very book that expressed what I was feeling. The book spoke about having an impostor in your life, someone or something that takes the place of you in certain circumstances. When we get angry, our impostor comes out. When we get afraid, our impostor comes out. At times our impostor protects us. At times, however, our impostor masks who we really are. After that flight, I delved deeply into the book and it helped me to understand and learn why I was the way I was and what I needed to do in order to be a true servant of God.

Over the next few weeks, I thought about who I really was. One specific item the Holy Spirit kept dirtecting me to address was the issue of anger in my life. At times I would have serious outbursts that were sometimes uncontrollable, but yet here I was—a child of God. How could I be angry and simultaneously be a child of God? How could I have rage and be a child of the King? These things did not make any sense to me. One thing I did know was I needed to apologize to those I had hurt in the past and to make a significant change from deep within. The time for dealing with this imposter was at hand.

It was the morning of Tuesday, December 5, 2006, when I spoke to my staff about what I felt and what I had been going through. Every Tuesday morning, the entire staff would gather for chapel, a time of praise and worship and Bible study. I requested five minutes after Bible study so I could address the staff. Dr. David did not know what I was about to say, but he did know I wanted five minutes so I could share information with the staff about the incident that had occurred with Cheryl and also about the bigger issue I was dealing with in my life. I stood up in front of the entire staff and began to tell them how I felt. I knew this would be difficult, but in my heart I knew it had to be done. I wrote my thoughts and comments out that morning because I knew if I tried to just say it without written reference, my emotions would probably take over and I would not be able to finish what I needed to say. I said the following:

WORKING ON OURSELVES

Greetings,

Let me say that this has to do with how I might have responded to each of you over the past days, months, and years. I wrote this because it might be too difficult to say it all.

I have been in deep contemplation these past days and weeks. It is important for me to make sure my heart is always pure. For those of you who know me, you know I apologize a lot. It is essential to me to make sure I apologize to keep my heart pure. This time is so appropriate as we are coming to the end of the Journey to the Mountain of God.

I have been reading a book entitled *Abba's Child – The Cry of the Heart for Intimate Belonging* by Brennan Manning. When I read it, it gave me such clarity about who I am and what I need to do.

You see, at times we put up personas to mask who we really are. This mask—I call it *imposter*— is good for us at times, in that it protects us. But it can also be a terrible thing to have because sometimes we use the imposter to protect us and not show who we really are. Let me read a passage from Manning's book, which refers to Simon Tugwell's book, *The Beatitudes*:

"And so, like runaway slaves, we either flee our own reality to manufacture a false self which is mostly admirable, mildly prepossessing, and superficially happy. We hide what we know or feel ourselves to be (which we assume to be unacceptable and unlovable) behind some kind of appearance which we hope will be more pleasing. We hide behind pretty faces that we put on for the benefit of our public. And in time we may even come to forget that we are hiding and think that our assumed pretty face is what we really look like."

To all of you, I have been an imposter—hiding behind the fact that I might have a problem with anger and also with performance. I have hurt some people by the way I speak to them and the way I connect with them.

Some of you have experienced my speaking harshly to you, allowing you to feel intimidated, allowing you feel like you're not worth anything.

Pastor David spoke in the Dominican Republic last week and I can hear these words so clearly: "Jesus never let anyone feel less than themselves. He never let anyone feel like they were nobodies."

To some of you, I have done that and I am truly sorry. Some of you have experienced the anger, harshness, and at times, the way I have stretched you for performance reasons rather than to show you that I care.

As I look around, I am not afraid to mention names. This list is not exhaustive; however, it gives an indication of the number, type, and extent of the people who have been hurt by my actions.

Karen Sweeting – I am sorry

Minister Karen – I am sorry

Gerald Whitaker – I am sorry

Libby Hill – I am sorry

Pastor Anthony Franklin – I am sorry

Cinda Gaskin – I am sorry

Kelvin Co – I am sorry

Selesteen Filmore – I am sorry

Sandra D'Costa – I am sorry

And for those who work closely with me
Deborah Kendell – I am sorry

Rondell Walker – I am sorry

I am sorry for how you are made to feel when you haven't accomplished things or you haven't listened to what I have asked you to do."

I have to learn how to appreciate people. I have to learn how to accept them for where they are and where they are not.

The interesting thing is I am not only here to talk about how I might have spoken to someone, but also how I am perceived. I am perceived as being difficult, not wanting to let go, managing without giving people a chance to breathe, and being hard on people.

It has also even been said that I am manipulative. Well, it doesn't really matter what has been said. What matters is that I am taking ownership of it, apologizing, and furthermore getting help by speaking to someone who can help me flush these things out.

I am a human being. I am not perfect. I make mistakes. I no longer want to hide behind a mask or be an imposter. I want to be me. The real me. I have no intention of being Pastor David. As much as I love you, pastor, I have no desire to be you because all I want to be is me. You're the greatest pastor I know, but I don't want to be you. I want to be who God has called me to be.

Folks, I want to appreciate you for who you are. I want to be me, who can say to someone they are not doing something correctly, but say it in the right tone. Me, who can be a strategist and say things that people don't interpret as being manipulative.

Matthew 5:48 says, *"Be perfect, therefore, as your heavenly Father is perfect."* Another interpretation says, *"Be ye*

compassionate as the Lord your God is compassionate." I
need to be more compassionate and accept you all. I am
not ashamed to tell you that I am not perfect...all I want
is to be like Jesus. I will seek help. I am not ashamed to
say that. Why? Because I am just admitting my human
frailties.

An interesting title I saw for a book the other day was
Leading with a Limp. I have a limp and I will ask God to
help me. Pastor David spoke about sustainable pace and
I need to do this in order to be able to sustain and endure.

Finally, I wrote a letter to myself yesterday I would like to
read because I believe it captures my heart.

Dear Imposter,

How are you today? I greet you today because my God
said that this will be the easiest thing for me to do. What
I consider difficult, God considers simple for me because
His Word says all things are possible to them that love
Him. I have been dealing with you for quite a while. In
times past, I have been able to gladly accept you because
you make me secure. You spur me on to do things I could
not have dreamed, but sadly enough you made me feel
at times as if I am the only person that matters—to the
detriment of others.

Well, now is the time to have a discussion with you. You
have made me lash out at people when I didn't need
to. You have made me someone who holds people up
to standards God has not ordained. You have made me
control people to get a desired outcome, only to make
them tired, exhausted, and resentful.

You need to be humbled. You need to be brought under the arm of Jesus. You need to be brought under the rule and Lordship of Christ. These people whom God has given me to lead mean so much. I would rather die than to hurt them by my actions, so I will go no further without asking God to deliver me from your antics. Yes, at times, you might act up. At times you might rear your ugly head when things are not going right, but that is okay. You're my limp. You're my imposter. I not only accept you, but I subject you to the Lordship of Christ.

God will do a great work in me. I will overcome and you know that neither you nor I will get the glory. He will because He is the champion of my life.

So staff, kindly forgive me. I will seek help because God knows I want to be more like Him every day.

By stating this, I embarked on a wonderful journey of restoration and the discovery of who I really am. I began to investigate why I behaved in a certain way. I began to ask myself the question, "If I am a child of God, how can I show and control my emotions rather than having my emotions control me?"

Closing the Section

1. Think back on the things you have done. Things that bother you. Things you hope you hadn't done or times you wished you hadn't displayed a particular kind of behavior.

2. Ask God to show you why this occurs.

3. Close your eyes and meditate for a minute; then open your eyes.

4. Pray the following: "Dear Lord, you created me. You know everything about me. Lord, I know that others might not

appreciate me or my behavior, but one thing I do know, Lord, is that you love me. Please show me now the things that could be detrimental to me in my development as a person and as a son or daughter of yours. Reveal it to me now, Lord. Amen"

5. Write down what God has revealed to you.

CHAPTER TWO

YOUR HISTORY AND YOUR FUTURE

....

E d Smith, noted founder of Theophostic Prayer Ministry, once said, "Ninety percent of what we do is based on our experience in history." He went on further to say that the way we react to things is determined by what occurred in our past. Throughout my life journey there is one thing that has been a constant struggle with me. That struggle has been in the area of anger. Sometimes when I get angry it makes me feel as if there is a growth in my body, and if I had the opportunity to pull it out, I would be a better person. Now if I pull this anger out, it would be like pulling an organ out of my body and getting rid of it.

Strangely enough, though, in Ephesians 4:26, the Apostle Paul, writing to the church at Ephesus, stated we are to be angry but sin not. If I look at the verse it is clear that anger is a part of us. This is an emotion that our heavenly Father has given us, but Paul warns us that we should not sin when we engage this emotion. So when I struggle with anger, what does that mean to me or how do I interpret it? It means the anger that exists in me is not something I can pull out of myself. It is something I need to have as a regular part of my physical makeup given to me by my Creator, God. However, with adequate impulse control I should be able to manage the anger in an emotionally healthy way, so I do not cause enmity between God and myself or enmity between myself and my brothers and sisters.

From my earliest childhood, I have always struggled with this thing inside of me. At times I have ignored the feeling. Anger would lead to rage. Rage would lead me to being out of control. But where did this anger come from? Why does this thing deep within me cause me to struggle so much at times? I have been a born-again Christian for decades, but yet I struggle with the issue of anger. I would contemplate, "How then can I be born-again, Spirit-filled, and responsible for the operations and administration of a mega church in the Northeast, and still struggle with anger?" This makes no sense.

If I am holy and sanctified, then I should not have to struggle with this emotion, which at times takes over. It should just disappear once I am born again and commit my life to Christ. Right? Absolutely not! That kind of remark is naïve and ignores the dimension in which we operate. Before I discuss dimension, let me continue with my thought process as I began to figure out how to deal with this emotion. Knowing where I am now at this stage in my life and where I have come from as I look back, I've concluded that my anger can be attributed to heredity. Or is it heredity? Doesn't saying *heredity* offer an excuse—or does it help me to understand my history and what character flaws or attributes are inherited? And if this anger is hereditary, does that mean I have inherited something from my father I will never be able to get rid of?

My dad was such a hard worker. He had six children, five boys and one girl. He worked tirelessly for his family to ensure we were taken care of and we wouldn't be without. He was not an educated man, nor was our mom an educated woman. I was born in an urban area, the youngest of six children. From an early age, I recognized that my father was never home due to his work. I remember during my teenage years that my dad would work three jobs in a given day at times to ensure that our family stayed together.

My dad traveled quite a bit when I was young—from the Caribbean where I grew up and lived, to London, England and to New York City, to earn enough money to support his family and to pay for his children's educations. I sensed my dad worked really hard; however, I felt that deep down inside he expressed great animosity to other people because he had to work so hard. One thing that was evident in our lives was that the presence of racial discrimination existed, as much as my parents asked us to embrace diversity. (Racial discrimination is the ability to formulate conclusions, whether good or bad—usually bad—about someone based on their race or ethnicity.) I believe the fact that my father had to work so hard to provide for his family led to the deep-rooted anger he expressed at times. This anger would normally manifest itself or become more pronounced during nights or bouts of continuous drinking and socializing.

I happen to be a hard-working individual, who does my best to be the best. I have a competitive energy within me that caused me to compete in everything. This competition during my life has led me to a fear of failure. This fear of failure is good in that it allows me to be competitive to the point where others' opinions do not matter. *Others do not matter* syndrome is clearly demonstrated in my outbursts of anger. When I look back, the smallest thing, at least they seem small now, would lead me to have repeated outbursts at others.

I never understood why I would feel the way I did. A simple trigger such as ensuring that the car was parked properly, picking up the laundry on time, telling my co-workers and subordinates to perform a task, when not accomplished, would lead me into outright rage.

This rage that lives inside me was not so evident in corporate America. I spent decades at Prudential, Cytec Industries, and Merck Pharmaceutical. It was not until I came on board at the church that God started to highlight these character defects in me. When one enters the world of ministry, it is no longer about you and what you do, but it is about others—working with them and ensuring that God's will be executed through you.

My dad took a similar path by working hard for his family. I did the same. However, it has become clearer to me recently that the things I feel within me are not just learned behaviors, but are behaviors I have observed throughout my life in my own family, from one person to another.

An example of this anger outburst came clearly to me when I was speaking to Jack, the son of a friend of mine. Jack was thirteen years old at the time and I thought I needed to mentor him to ensure he became a good and upstanding citizen. One day when we were going to the bookstore, he told me he did not want to read the book on character development I had recommended to him. This book, I thought, was exceptional for any young man. The book would help him grow into the fullness of his character.

As Jack and I went to the store, he kept on telling me, "No, Rupert, I do not want the book." I repeated, "Jack, it is good for you. It will help you to grow." He restated his refusal to read the book. I could feel my temperature rising as I was being challenged by a teenager. The more he insisted on not reading the book, the more I insisted he should read it.

Needless to say, I said to Jack, "You're worthless, you know. You have no clue that what I am doing is good for you. As a young man you will need this." I interpreted his disobedience as a challenge to my authority. I started to scream at him. Soon enough, his mother came by and saw me in a rabid rage directed at her beloved child. That marked a glaring moment in my life as my anger reached a fever pitch aimed at a teenager who had disobeyed me. The consequence was deep, as it ended the relationship between Jack, his mother, and me.

The question I asked myself numerous times after that moment was why did I become so enraged? Why did I find it necessary to rail against someone who was obviously much younger, less experienced, and less developed than I? Why did I see the need to lash out at him and not consider what might have been going on in his life that would cause him to not respond to me as I wanted him to?

To this day I wonder. Now, some twenty years later, I recognize it was part life and part family experience that had caused me to behave that way. My dad at times would react the same way toward me as I did to Jack. He would scream at me and sometimes hit me. Hitting was acceptable back then. I am not questioning that at all. What I am questioning is, why was he so angry with me that, at times, he would go into a rage? I could see that the rage I exhibited obviously had to do with my past. But greater than that, it had to do with my father and all the life experiences he had gone through; and these experiences he had passed on to me. It took until I reached forty-one years of age for me to recognize these character flaws.

If you or someone you know suffers from rage, the first thing to do is to recognize that some of what you experience and the potential causes are the same.

Closing the Section

1. Meditate on the phrase, "Lord, is there any character flaw in my life you need to alert me to? Is there anything you do not want to see in me?"

2. Write each item down God has revealed to you.

3. Close your eyes and meditate for a minute; then open your eyes.

4. Pray the following: "Dear Lord, I recognize I am indeed not perfect. There is only one perfect Person and Lord, that is you. Father, at this time I ask you to show me character flaws or character deficiencies that have prevented or hindered your full work in me. Lord, I put this under your authority and

ask you to help me. Lord, continue to show me the emotions I need to address. Bring them to the forefront. In Jesus' name, Amen."

5. Review what you have written down and make any necessary alterations.

Note To Reader: Chapters 3 through 7 focus on the nuts and bolts of emotional intelligence. It is highly recommended you peruse these chapters, but do not get lost in them. For those who understand emotional intelligence, you may go to chapter 8 immediately.

PART II

Background on
Emotional Intelligence

CHAPTER THREE

BACKGROUND
OF INTELLIGENCE

. . . .

Before we begin to look at emotional intelligence, it is important for us to define intellectual quotient, or IQ. IQ is what is referred to commonly as cognitive intelligence. It is the ability to plan, organize, execute, employ words, understand, bring together, and to interpret factual matters. For over one hundred years, most academicians and, for the most part, all individuals have focused on cognitive intelligence as the means to an end for all that we do to determine one's level of intelligence. Not to mention, cognition is recognized in most cases as the mark by which we are judged intellectually and, in many regards, how our futures are determined.

It was in the early 1900s that two gentlemen—Alfred Binet and Theodore Simon—developed the first known intelligence test. Binet was a psychologist by occupation and Simon was a psychiatrist. The school system in Paris asked these gentlemen to develop a test in which children could be categorized and structured according to their ability to succeed. This would be based on their current level of development and also project their future possibility of success. The intent was to get rid of those individuals who did not fit a certain criteria; i.e., those who did not seem to fit the means by which success or potential success could be measured.

Binet believed three fundamentals were required for a child, or anyone for that matter, to succeed. The three things were: 1) judgment, 2) problem-solving and 3) reasoning. Binet proposed if they could measure these children along these three guidelines and further correlate his findings to the level of growth and intellectual development, they could propose an indicator—a measure or a number—that could be used to represent a person. The test was created and administered in Paris.

In 1910, Henry Goddard met with Alfred Binet who had left Paris a few years earlier. Goddard was a psychologist and educator and both men further refined and developed the test for wider use. Lewis Ternan from Stanford University further modified the test and it was at that time the term Stanford-Binet[1] test was developed and coined. It is what we know as the IQ test today.

IQ tests were not only used in school, but also in places of employment, for personal assessment, interpersonal interaction, and many other applications. The use of the IQ test became more and more prevalent as time went on. Eventually, it became the sole indicator of someone's success or failure. But with its success, questions were raised as to the validity of the test and whether it could be used as a sole instrument to determine someone's success. By the late 1950s, psychologists, sociologists, psychiatrists, and others began to debate the relative importance of such a single factor as a predictor of someone's future.

Even though there was constant questioning, there were those who believed the test was relevant and that, absent any other instrument that could prove or disprove its relevancy, it made absolute sense to continue the utilization of such a tool. A firestorm over the use of these tests erupted in the late 1980s with the publication of the book, *The Bell Curve*.[2]

In summary, the book's implied conclusion is that race has a strong correlation between one's IQ and his or her relative success or failure in life. The firestorm that resulted from opponents of the book gave renewed energy to those who believed the use of

IQ unfairly classified people. These same opponents were against the use of IQ in everyday society. As this opposition began to develop, new means of classifying and measuring one's success came into being.

Closing the Section

1. Meditate on the phrase: "Lord, since you have made me and created me, is there anything that you would like to tell me regarding my intellectual capabilities?"

2. Write down each item God has revealed to you.

3. Close your eyes and meditate for a minute; then open your eyes.

4. Pray the following: "Dear Lord, I know that you are Lord and Savior. You made the heavens and the Earth. Precious Lord, I thank you for making me who I am. I thank you for the abilities you have given me. Lord, I do not receive any language or any thought that says that I am not qualified. You made me. You made me in your image and for that I am thankful and I know, Lord, that you will utilize my intellect to bring you glory. I thank you. In Jesus' name. Amen."

5. Review what you have written down and make any necessary alterations.

CHAPTER FOUR

HISTORY OF
EMOTIONAL INTELLIGENCE

· · · ·

In the early 1980s, a survey of some of the most prominent and influential American corporate leaders was done with the primary focus being to identify what qualities successful leaders possess that would cause others to follow them. The qualities rated the highest were: 1) honesty, 2) discipline, 3) good interpersonal skills, and 4) hard work or diligence. It is clear none of these qualities were the result of one's intellectual capacities, but were deemed *soft* skills. A conclusion can then be drawn that these same qualities, listed in the corporate studies, can apply to church as well as para-church organizations. What does this mean? If IQ does not determine someone's final success, then there must be other factors that help determine what one can do to improve one's standing in life.

Emotional intelligence according to Reuven Bar-On is "...an array of non-cognitive (emotional and social) capabilities, competencies, and skills that influence one's ability to succeed in coping with environmental demands and pressures."[1] Further, Peter Salovey and Jack Mayer define emotional intelligence as "...the ability to perceive emotions, to access and generate emotions so as to assist thought, to understand emotions and emotional meanings, and to reflectively regulate emotions in a way that promotes emotional and intellectual growth."[2]

The aforementioned gentlemen, Reuven Bar-On, Peter Salovey, and Jack Mayer, are giants in the field of emotional intelligence. If it were not for their work, the field of study would not be what it is today. In addition to these men, there have been others such as Daniel Goleman, Edward Thorndike, R.W. Reeper, and more who have contributed significantly to the field of emotional intelligence.

Emotional intelligence is a field that, surprisingly to me, has existed from the eighteenth century. Former writers and researchers at the turn of the century came up with, investigated, and had input into this field. It was not termed *emotional intelligence*, but rather had other labels that, in retrospect, are synonymous with this field. In 1870, Charles Darwin, though his beliefs are contrary to Christian belief in God, created the first writing on the subject of emotional intelligence, but his focus was on its application and use in the area of survival and adaptation.[3]

As the field continued to develop, other researchers looked for alternatives to the Stanford-Binet IQ test. In 1920, Edward Thorndike discussed the term *social intelligence*. Though the term is synonymous with emotional intelligence, it wasn't until the 1940s that David Wechsler discussed the need to have emotional measurement included in any intellectual assessment, which at the time was the Stanford-Binet IQ test. In 1948, a researcher by the name of R. W. Leeper[4] gave importance to the term *emotional thought*, which he was convinced at the time contributed to our cognitive processes.

Ideas in the emotional intelligence realm dramatically increased in the 1970s and 1980s. In the early eighties, Howard Gardner wrote about having not just one intelligence, but multiple intelligences. The groundbreaking book that brought the attention of emotional intelligence to worldwide prominence was the publication in 1995 of *Emotional Intelligence: Why It Can Matter More Than IQ* by Daniel Goleman.[5] I have not yet discussed Reuven Bar-On, Peter Salovey, or Jack Mayer, whom I have previously termed as giants in the field. Most of their significant work occurred in the late 1980s and early 1990s, when emotional intelligence was not fully recognized, but without their breakthrough work in the field.

The term *emotional intelligence*, though known to others in 1995 with Goleman's groundbreaking publication, was coined in 1990 by John (Jack) Mayer of the University of New Hampshire and Peter Salovey of Yale University.[6] They solidified a definition and with David Caruso developed a test for emotional intelligence called the MSCEIT — Mayer-Salovey-Caruso Emotional Intelligence Test. This test is not self-reporting such as that of the Reuven Bar-On, which focuses on will. This test is based on ability.

Reuven Bar-On, an American Israeli, has worked as a clinical psychologist since 1972, when he completed an MA in clinical psychology at Pepperdine University in California. He furthered his studies at Rhodes University in South Africa in the late 1980s. His interest in the field was spurred on by the many questions he had that drove him on a quest to study emotions and intelligence, questions such as, "Why is it that some who are so intellectually gifted tend to end up as failures in life?" and "Why do some people have greater emotional connections than others?" Questions such as these were the beginning of Dr. Bar-On's quest to understand the field, and what it takes to further determine if there can be a fundamental measure that can be created to capture anyone's emotional intelligence level.

From his quest, Dr. Bar-On is the one noted with creating the term *emotional quotient*. He coined the term *EQ* (Emotional Quotient) in 1985 to describe his approach to assessing emotional and social functioning. This term first appeared in his doctoral dissertation, which was sent to the Rhodes University Library in addition to two internal readers at Rhodes University, South Africa, and one external reader at the University of Witwatersrand in South Africa. He created the Bar-On Emotional Quotient Inventory (the EQ-i®) in 1997, which is the first test of emotional intelligence to be published by a psychological test publisher. The EQ-i® passed the one million mark worldwide five years after its publication, making it the most popularly used EI measure. The use of the Bar-On EQ-i® will be used as the basis of measure in this book and we will discuss the components of the EQ-i® test and assessment in upcoming chapters.

As we delve further into the book, we need to understand that both IQ and EQ play a role in our successes and failures. However, it would appear recently, through research, it is EQ that has obviously a greater predictor of ultimate success than IQ. According to Stein and Book, "One can make the argument that in order for us to take advantage of and flex our cognitive intelligence to the maximum, we first need good emotional intelligence. Why? Because regardless of how brainy or intelligent we may be, if we turn others off with abrasive behavior or are unaware of how we are presenting ourselves or cave in under minimal stress, no one will stick around long enough to notice our high IQs." [7]

Closing the Section

1. Meditate on the phrase, "Lord, can you reveal my emotions to me?"

2. Write each item down God has revealed to you.

3. Close your eyes and meditate for a minute; then open your eyes.

4. Pray the following: "Precious Lord, you are my God. You have made me. You have made me human with an intellect, but you have also made me human with emotions. Lord, it was in your design that I would have emotions and I would demonstrate them to myself and to my fellow man. Lord, help me to utilize the skills you have given me so I can control my emotions and demonstrate my emotions to myself and my fellow man in a

God-like manner. Use this book to help me to be a better person for you in mind, body, and soul. In Jesus' name. Amen."

5. Review what you have written down and make any necessary alterations.

CHAPTER FIVE

THE BRAIN AND OUR EMOTIONS

. . . .

We are physical beings fashioned by our Creator to do things according to His will and purpose. We are physical entities that operate in many dimensions. We operate in the spiritual, the emotional, and the intellectual. All of these dimensions are expected to operate in kind or in sync with each other. All of these dimensions are expected to be catalysts to help us attain a holistic and wholesome life. Each is intermingled and each enables us to operate as a full unit rather than as separate interdependent silos—whether emotional, physical, emotional, or intellectual.

To further understand how we operate, we must take a look at the brain, which is the center for all our functioning, whether cognitive or emotional. The brain gives us the ability to understand, analyze, and determine things, whether abstract or concrete. The brain allows us to decipher things real and unreal. The brain lacks emotion. This might sound like an oxymoron, but the brain has no emotion. The brain, for all intents and purposes, is broken into two discernable parts. Daniel Goleman refers to it as the capacity to do *high road* and *low road* functioning.[1] The high road function is the part of the brain system that focuses on the analytical. It is the part of the brain that focuses on discernment and arriving at astute conclusions and precepts, which help us as human beings make right and wrong choices. The low road, on the other hand, is the part of our system that focuses on the emotional. It is the part of the system that focuses on love, hate, anger, care, empathy, personal relationship, stress, tolerance, and other emotional connections. To deal with the low road and high road function, we should look at the brain. Before we do so, I must make it clear this book is not a book on the medical dynamics of the human brain. However, it is important, if we are going to focus on emotional wellbeing, that we understand where these things come from and what part of the body regulates them.

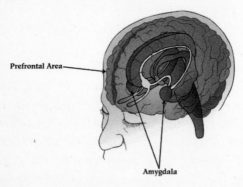

The systems in our brain responsible for cognitive and emotional functioning are completely separate, but are intermingled. There are two parts of the brain that are of great importance to our discussion: 1) the amygdala and 2) the prefrontal areas.

Our analytical brain works in concert with our emotional brain to ensure that we are balanced individuals. In times of crisis, however, our emotional brain takes over and overpowers the analytical brain. The emotional brain, driven by the limbic portion of the brain, takes over all brain functioning in times of emotional threats. It is at this time the brain shuts down the analytical functioning and makes a decision to either a) stand its ground, b) run away from a situation, or c) like a deer in the headlights, remain and freeze. The center and key point for all the emotional decisions and functioning is what we call the amygdala. The amygdala is the part of the brain that triggers us to act on impulse. It is the part of our system that works to protect us from possible harm. Understanding the key to the amygdala will help us understand what is happening to us in times when we feel threatened, times when we feel hurt, and times of severe trauma.

Have you ever had the thought, "This leader makes me so mad, I feel like just storming out. I feel like literally punching him in the face"? The dynamic of spiritual maturity will help in implementing impulse control in order that you don't actually end up strangling a leader or your own pastor. However, it is not only your spiritual wellbeing that is going to help in overcoming the need to act upon the emotion that arises, it is also your emotional control and an understanding of who you are, where you are, and what you are that will help determine your ultimate reaction. It is a combination of spiritual maturity and impulse control that will help you through such a situation.

Utilizing the prefrontal area of the brain will help analyze the situation to determine from an analytical point of view what to do. Your emotional center, the amygdala, will help you to decide between *fight* or *flight*, and your spiritual maturity will help determine if this is the best course of action at a given moment.

The prefrontal area is the brain's center for executive decisions. Imagine *Star Trek*'s Starship Enterprise and the control room that overlooks the landscape of the entire universe. What is at the front of the Starship is the prefrontal area. It is in this location that critical decisions take place and are executed. In times of severe crisis, however, automatic triggers from the amygdala send signals to the prefrontal area to help determine what should be done. Just as on the Starship Enterprise, the prefrontal area takes in information from all areas of the ship and analyzes the information to determine what needs to be executed.

It must be noted, however, that during times of severe crisis when time constraints are a factor, the amygdala might send a signal to the prefrontal area, but due to the nature or the severity of the possible action, the prefrontal area can delay or even ignore an emotional response. For example, "He is my pastor, I cannot punch him." He is your spiritual leader and you're accountable to him before God.

Closing the Section

1. Write each item down God has revealed to you.

2. Close your eyes and meditate for a minute; then open your eyes.

3. Pray the following: "Precious Lord, you're my God. You have made me with emotions, with spirituality, and with intellect. Father, let not my emotions get ahead of my spirituality. Father, let not my intellect get ahead of my spirituality. Lord, let not my emotions drive me. Dear Lord, I ask you to meld all three dimensions together so I can be a better person to serve in and for your Kingdom. In Jesus' name. Amen. "

4. Review what you have written down and make any necessary alterations.

CHAPTER SIX

FACTORS WITHIN
EMOTIONAL INTELLIGENCE

. . . .

There have been many practitioners in the field of emotional intelligence since the late 1980s. One of the most prominent in the field of EQ has been Howard Gardner of Harvard University. Gardner was one of the first psychologists to challenge the notion that IQ was the standard by which all intelligence should be judged and measured. He developed Project Spectrum, a program of Tufts University, a curriculum that focuses on multiple intelligences rather than on a single method of measuring one's potential success.

Gardner believes there is more than one way to measure someone's potential for success. There is a fundamental belief that if we administer the same test to everyone, we will be able to normalize the measure and assume if one gets a 110 on an IQ test and another gets 120, the person who measures 120 is more likely to be successful in life. Right? Not necessarily so.

Gardner's 1983 book *Frames of Mind* came out in stark contrast to the belief that IQ was the sole measure of success. Gardner believed there was more than one way to determine success. He believed it could range from IQ to verbal and math understanding, as well as interpersonal skills and musical and artistic ability. While Gardner's book was being discussed and coming to the fore, Reuven Bar-On was investigating and determining that there must be certain triggers, if you will, that lead to full understanding and calculation of emotional intelligence.

According to the book *Emotional Intelligence* by Daniel Goleman there are some basic groupings that can be used to determine someone's emotional effectiveness and level of emotional intelligence. Goleman went on to state that there are five main domains under which emotional intelligence can be defined according to Peter Salovey and John Mayer, as discussed earlier in chapter 4.

According to Salovey and Mayer:[1]

1. **Knowing Your Emotions**: Recognizing feelings as they occur. It is the ability to monitors one's feelings moment by moment and be able to understand what is going on within one's own body. In other words, to be able to take and monitor your own emotional temperature. This is one area that appears to be simplistic at first blush, but is fundamental to understanding and directing one's life. Not to know what we're feeling leaves us completely exposed and unable to process what is happening to us.

2. **Managing Emotions**: Effectively being aware of your emotions and managing them to know how to react during certain situations is a laudable feat. It is not only necessary to know what you're feeling, but also to be able to process what you're feeling and determine effective measures to deal with the varying environmental triggers.

3. **Motivating Oneself**: To be able to determine feelings and to adapt critical, motivational systems to enable one to determine future success and avoid failures is one of the critical components of emotional intelligence. To clearly understand how to institute impulse control while at the same time using that ability to display empathy to achieve a goal is an outstanding factor within the emotional intelligence sphere.

4. **Understanding Others:** This by far is the most critical component of emotional intelligence, not only from a physical dimension, but also from the aspect of the spiritual realm. To be able to put oneself in another's shoes is the most significant and critical component of living the life of someone who follows Christ and wants to be like Him. It was Christ, after all, who put himself in our shoes and took on our sins.

5. **Handling Relationships:** This component can be tied closely to managing emotions and understanding others. To be successful in life requires us not to work at such speed so as to ignore those critical relationships that are necessary in order to be successful.

CHAPTER SEVEN

REUVEN BAR-ON AND EMOTIONAL INTELLIGENCE

. . . .

Throughout my studies, it was critical that I understood exactly how to measure this ideology that is called emotional intelligence. Previously, I mentioned that Howard Gardner of Harvard University was able to refute the idea of a single intelligence. While debunking the singular measure of IQ, he presented the case for multiple intelligences. If that is the case, however, there has got to be a way to measure the effectiveness of EQ. What are the components? How do you determine what is more effective than the other? Is there a singular measure that tells me what is good and what is bad?

Reuven Bar-On has been investigating the same thing and was able through his research to come up with a significant test that answers the questions listed above in addition to the following: Why is it that some people possess greater emotional intelligence than others? Why are some who are intellectual giants such fervent failures when it comes to life successes? He developed the EQ-i® test that comprises 133 questions, and is a self-reporting tool. The test gives information on three different levels:[1] 1) How one is doing as a whole compared with the overall population, 2) How one is doing in the five main component areas listed below, and 3) How one is doing in the sub-components listed below. The test focuses on the following:

1. **Self-perception** – This facet of emotional intelligence addresses the inner self.
   a. Self-regard
   b. Self-actualization
   c. Emotional Self-awareness

2. **Self-expression** – This is an extension of Self-perception and addresses the outward expression or the action component of one's internal perception.
   a. Emotional Expression
   b. Assertiveness
   c. Independence

3. **Interpersonal Skills** – Understanding our relationships and how we interact with the environment around us.
   a. Empathy
   b. Social Responsibility
   c. Interpersonal Relationships

4. **Decision-making** – The Decision-making Composite scale addresses the ways in which one uses emotional information.
   a. Problem solving
   b. Reality testing
   c. Impulse Control

5. **Stress Management** – The ability to withstand stress without losing control and falling apart.
   a. Flexibility
   b. Stress Tolerance
   c. Optimism

Note: Previously, the EQ-i® included happiness as one of the fifteen components of emotional intelligence. Happiness is an indicator of emotional health and well being. It is characterized by feelings of satisfaction and contentment, and by the ability to enjoy the many aspects of one's life. Happiness combines self-satisfaction, general contentment, and the ability to enjoy life.

Below are the definitions that are adopted from EQ-i® Bar-On Emotional Quotient Inventory Technical Manual:[2]

Self-perception Component – Understanding our inner selves and how we function.

- *Self-regard:* The ability to respect and accept oneself as basically good. Respecting oneself is essentially liking oneself. Self-acceptance is the ability to accept one's perceived positive and negative aspects as well as one's limitations and possibilities.
- *Self-actualization:* The ability to realize one's full potential. This component of emotional intelligence is manifested by becoming involved in pursuits that lead to a meaningful, rich, and full life.
- *Emotional Self-awareness*: The ability to recognize one's feelings. It is not only the ability to be aware of one's feelings and emotions, but also the ability to differentiate between the feelings. To know what one is feeling and why you are feeling that particular way, and to be able to discern what caused the feeling.

Self-expression Component – It assesses one's propensity to remain self-directed and openly expressive of thoughts and feelings, while communicating these feelings in constructive and socially acceptable ways.

- *Emotional Expression:* The ability to openly express one's feelings verbally and non-verbally.
- *Assertiveness:* The ability to express feelings, beliefs, and thoughts and defend one's right in a non-destructive manner. It is the ability to express feelings, the ability to express beliefs and thoughts openly, and the ability to stand up for one's personal rights without being a

doormat or without acting out in an aggressive manner. It is therefore neither being aggressive or passive but in the middle between these two extremes.

- *Independence:* The ability to be self-directed and self-controlled in one's thinking and functioning and to be free of emotional dependency. Independent people are self-reliant in planning and making important decisions.

Interpersonal Component – Understanding your people skills. How one interacts with those around them.

- *Empathy*: The ability to be aware of, to understand, and to appreciate the feelings of others. It is being tuned in or being sensitive to what, how, and why people feel the way they do.
- *Social Responsibility*: The ability to demonstrate oneself as a cooperative, contributing, and constructive member of one's social group. This ability involves acting in a responsible manner, even though one may not benefit personally.
- *Interpersonal Relationships:* The ability to establish and maintain mutually satisfying relationships that are characterized by intimacy and by giving and receiving affection. Mutual satisfaction includes meaningful social interchanges that are potentially rewarding and enjoyable.

Decision-making Component – This reveals how well one understands the impact emotions have on decision-making, including the ability to resist or delay impulses and remain objective in order to avoid rash behaviors and ineffective attempts at problem-solving.

- *Problem-solving:* The ability to identify and define problems in addition to generating and implementing potentially effective solutions. It is multi-faceted in nature and includes the ability to go through a process of sensing a problem, defining and formulating the problem as clearly as possible, generating as many solutions as possible, and making a decision to implement one of the solutions.

- *Reality Testing:* The ability to assess the correspondence between what is experience and what objectively exists. It involves a search for objective evidence to confirm, justify, and support feelings, perceptions, and thoughts.

- *Impulse Control:* The ability to resist or delay an impulse, drive, or temptation to act. It entails the capacity for accepting one's aggressive impulses, being composed and controlling aggression, hostility, and irresponsible behavior.

Stress Management Component – Your ability to withstand stress without losing control or coming apart.

- *Flexibility:* The ability to adjust one's emotions, thoughts, and behavior to changing situations and conditions. It refers to one's overall ability to adapt to unfamiliar, unpredictable, and dynamic circumstances and situations.

- *Stress Tolerance:* The ability to withstand adverse events and stressful situations without falling apart by actively and positively coping with stress. It is the ability to weather difficult situations without getting overwhelmed.

- *Optimism:* The ability to look at the brighter side of life and to maintain a positive attitude even in the face of adversity. Optimism assumes a measure of hope in one's approach to life.

For future reference, I will use the terminology and definitions from Reuven Bar-On's work to refer to categories and components of emotional intelligence. It is, however, not my intention to state that Mr. Bar-On's work is the sole work and reference material on emotional intelligence, but his test and measurement instrument is the one that I refer to and utilize in my own experiences and one that I find to be of tremendous benefit.

PART III

Biblical Approach to Emotional Intelligence

CHAPTER EIGHT

EMOTIONAL INTELLIGENCE IN PRIOR DAYS

. . . .

In Luke 2:52, the Bible states, *"And Jesus grew in wisdom and stature and in favor with God and men."* This text is important because it gives a biblical position that we are not to be complete in one area of our lives to the detriment of another. The context of the passage is it highlights how Jesus grew from a little boy to a young man. During a trip to Jerusalem when He was twelve, He went to the temple courts and sat with the teachers and listened and asked questions. His parents did not know where He was and when they did find Him, they asked Him why He was not traveling with them from Jerusalem. Jesus' response was to inform His parents that He was about His Father's business.

The verse in Luke 2 states clearly that Jesus grew in wisdom and stature. Wisdom represented knowledge and understanding. Stature represented his presentation and development before man. The passage depicts Jesus as being total man and total God. His growth was in the area of physical, spiritual, intellectual, mental, and social areas. His physical growth represented his stature; His spiritual growth represented His favor with God; His intellectual growth represented His increase in wisdom, and His social growth showed His growth in favor with man. Jesus was complete. He grew emotionally, spiritually, and intellectually.

One interesting sidebar is that Jesus grew and developed over time. The timeframe in which the Scripture captured Jesus' growth was over an eighteen-year period of time. He developed. I must mention that in order for us to develop completely, it will take time. There have been too many one-hit wonders in God's Kingdom where men and women—or priests, kings, and queens, according to Douglas Weiss in his book *Kings and Priests*[1]— mistakenly conclude that since they have a title, they have arrived. Even Jesus himself had to grow and develop. We grow and develop spiritually, we develop intellectually, and the same expectation exists for us in the emotional realm.

Did emotional intelligence exist in prior days? Did the concept of emotional intelligence exist during the time of Adam and Eve, the time of Christ's death, burial, and Resurrection and even until today? Raising such a question could also raise such questions as: Did God exist during the time of Adam and Eve? Did God exist while His Son was being crucified? The fact that something exists and is operating in us, even if we don't recognize it, does not deny the existence of that fact. The thing we now call emotional intelligence, could have been termed something completely different in the past. But that does not negate the fact of what it is or isn't.

We further need to ask ourselves the question, Did emotions exist from the creation of time until now? The obvious answer is yes, but the terminology and the interpretation of what we see does not deny the fact that it does exist. Throughout the Bible from the beginning of the Scriptures in Genesis1:1: *"In the beginning God created . . ."* until the end in Revelation 22:21 *" ... the grace of the Lord Jesus be with God's people. Amen,"* emotions ran rampant.

My prayer to God upon the writing of these words was, "God, if you see how emotions affect our very lives, why is it so difficult for us to accept that they are an important part of our lives and if so, where is it in Scripture?" The base revelation, however, is that God operated in the emotions. It is not strange that in Paul's writing in Galatians 5:22-23, the Fruit of the Spirit is based on emotional characteristics rather than anything intellectual, physical, or spiritual, although the foundation of these characteristics reveals the spiritual dimensions of God.

From the beginning of time when God created Adam and Eve and He put them in the Garden, His purpose was to have them stay in the Garden forever and not eat of the fruit of the Tree of the Knowledge of Good and Evil. When God discovered that they indeed had eaten of the fruit, he asked of the woman, *"What is this you have done?"* (Genesis 3:13). God knew they had not only eaten of the fruit, but their eyes were now open to good and evil. One can conclude they now could see not only themselves, but also the very essence of who they were in the spirit and in the natural.

Their eyes were open as to how to operate in the flesh. God wanted Adam and Eve to communicate what they had done and what the possible result of their actions would be. Within that very moment there was fear, anxiety, concern, sorrow, gloom, despair, guilt, and regret. Adam had not only disobeyed God, but he had followed his wife into sin and, by so doing, had brought forth the downfall of all mankind.

I ask myself this question: *If I were Adam, how would I feel?* The mere fact that he had caused the entire creation to fall must have been devastating to Adam. How did Eve feel? I would dare say that she must have felt worse than Adam. The fact is that Adam had an excuse, although not an acceptable one. Eve basically listened and allowed herself to be tempted by the serpent, and that led to her downfall. Further, instead of Adam blaming Eve and Eve blaming the serpent, what would have happened if Eve and Adam had expressed to God how they felt about what they had done?

What if Adam had asked God to forgive him? What if Adam and Eve had said to God, "We have committed a sin of enormous proportion, God. Can you forgive us?" We will never know because they never did. God seeks expression of how we feel, not a defense of our actions. Adam and Eve, through the devastation they experienced, did not state how they felt, but instead blamed each other for the destruction that had been created based on their actions.

As we get into this topic, I bring up Adam and Eve because we as creatures fall. We make mistakes, big ones—mistakes that cause family and whole genealogies utter devastation. We should not be alarmed, however, but be comforted; it happened in the Garden of Eden. The question is not that we have done wrong. The question is not that we have expressed our emotions in ways that have hurt others. The question is, what do you do with the unbelievable actions that have been committed through misguided emotions?

In the following few pages, we will recount some of the emotionally charged situations in the Bible. Bear in mind the list of accounts in the Bible that fit this description are numerous. My intent is to document a small number of these situations and add commentary to them as they relate to the subject matter of emotional intelligence. The intent is not to conclude whether a situation was handled correctly (of course we only want to make right conclusions), but rather to convey the emotions that were expressed and how the emotions could have been handled differently to lead to a more desirable outcome.

In order to help with the analysis, a table is referenced in Appendix – Synopsis of Emotional Intelligence Situations in the Bible. This appendix captures emotional situations chronicled in the Bible from Genesis to Revelation. Emotions are expressed within the table that are attached to the circumstance documented in the passage. In addition to a commentary on the particular passage, I have projected what the potential Emotional Intelligence (EI) components are that are related to the story in the passage. The EI component is derived from the Reuven Bar-On emotional intelligence measurement instrument. (The reference to Bar-On's EI components is in chapter 7.)

The potential lists of emotions by major categories are anger, disgust, enjoyment, fear, love, sadness, and shame. This categorization is derived from Daniel Goleman's work reference in *Emotional Intelligence: Why It Can Matter More than IQ.*[2] The major categories have subcategories of emotions that further express the feelings outlined in a particular encounter or situation. The subcategories of emotions are as follows:

- *Anger:* outrage, resentment, animosity, hostility, and irritability.
- *Disgust:* contempt, aversion, distaste, and repulsion.
- *Enjoyment:* happiness, bliss, delight, thrill, and satisfaction.
- *Fear:* anxiety, concern, fright, wariness, and nervousness.
- *Love:* acceptance, friendliness, trust, affinity, and agape.
- *Sadness:* grief, sorrow, gloom, melancholy, loneliness, and despair.
- *Shame:* guilt, regret, contrition, and chagrin.
- *Surprise:* wonder, amazement, and astonishment.

Simeon and Levi: Genesis 34

During this period of time, Jacob had just returned from meeting with his brother Esau, to whom he owed a great deal. He had stolen the birthright from Esau and, prior to this passage he had reconciled with him and lodged in the city of Shechem in Canaan. Jacob had a beautiful daughter named Dinah who was violently attacked by Hamor's son Shechem. At that time, Shechem was infatuated with Dinah. He, however, did not see fit to go the prescribed course of seeking Jacob's permission to have his daughter in marriage. Instead, Shechem attacked her when she was alone, violated her, and slept with her.

After this grievous act was commited, Jacob discovered it, but instead of telling his sons Simeon and Levi, he decided to wait until they returned from the fields. By the time his sons returned from the fields, Hamor and Shechem approached Jacob, Simeon and Levi. Hamor requested they give Dinah in marriage to his son Shechem.

Simeon and Levi conceived a plot. They agreed to the request, but on one condition. The condition was the men of Hamor's house should be circumcised. Hamor, his son Shechem, and the rest of his men all agreed to be circumcised. During this period, three days after the circumcision as the men were recovering, Simeon and Levi attacked the men of Hamor's house including his son and all the men in the city and killed them all. They then plundered everything from the city including flocks, herds, and donkeys.

Upon hearing of this, Jacob was angry and incensed. Though Simeon and Levi had done the right thing in avenging their sister, they had done the wrong thing in terms of how the deed was carried out.

The list of emotions involved in this text is numerous. There is outrage, resentment, anger, disgust, and repulsion from Jacob, Simeon, and Levi at the great wrong that had been done to Dinah. There was fear, anxiety, concern, and nervousness on the part of Hamor when he found out that his son had perpetrated such a heinous crime. There was the fear, anger, shame, and sadness Dinah felt from the pain of being raped and disgraced. Jacob was fearful about what might occur to him and his family because of the retaliatory actions of his sons Simeon and Levi.

From an emotional intelligence perspective, we cannot deny these emotions. Emotions are a key part of who and what we are. To deny these emotions can be counterproductive to health. Dinah was hurt. She had suffered grieviously at the hand of Hamor. In her hurt, she suffered through possible depression and the feeling of being abandoned and isolated by her family. To enter into a sexual relationship in those times, without the formality of marriage, was tantamount to sacrilege. She had to suffer through the shame of not understanding why this had occurred, but also dealing with sharing the news with her family.

Empathy on Hamor's part would have led to understanding the feelings that Dinah would go through from the experience of being violated. The fact that it was customary in those times to ask a woman's family for her hand in marriage does not negate the norm that consent also was needed prior to engaging in any sexual act.

I would summize that Jacob was fearful, initially upon hearing of this sin against his daughter. He was fearful because he knew the potential of this situation getting out of control was very real. The fact that his sons might seek revenge was very real. His fear came to fruition when Simeon and Levi attacked the city and killed all the men in it.

There were many violations of emotional intelligence concepts. There was failure of emotional self-awareness on Shechem's part. He did not understand his emotions and the impact of those emotions on others. There was also a failure in the area of empathy. He failed to put himself into another's shoes. He did not put himself in Dinah's place to understand the pain he was going to cause her. There was a failure of impulse control, not to wait until the appointed time to ask Jacob for permission to marry Dinah. There was failure on Simeon and Levi's parts in the area of impulse control and stress tolerance.

The brothers did not react well to the stress of finding out their sister had just been raped. According to Daniel Goleman, their low road functioning, mentioned in chapter 5, took over, and all rational sense disappeared as they began plotting revenge for what had happened. Finally, there was a failure on Shechem's part in the area of reality-testing. He felt Jacob's family would just accept the fact their sister had been violated and they would give into the request of marriage to solve the problem.

Have you seen yourself in any of the things related in the passage above? It happened more than two thousand years ago and it still happens today. Dealing with emotional upheaval is not new. How we deal with it is indicative of how we understand ourselves and others around us. In the passage in Genesis 34, it is obvious that the issues were not dealt with properly. The greater question is, have we completely learned and accepted the fact that as Christians, we can be serving Christ and have the same misdirected emotional reactions to things that occur in our lives?

Closing the Section

1. Has there been a time when you have done wrong? Have there been times when others have done you wrong?

2. Ask God to give you insight.

3. Close your eyes and meditate for a minute; then open your eyes.

4. Pray the following: "Dear Lord, You know I am not perfect. There are things I have done that were not representative of you. Lord, as you have shown me these flaws, accept me as I am. Allow your Holy Spirit to direct me in this area. Lord, I recognize that I need your help, but also, Lord, lead me to those who can give me practical help so that I can become the person you want me to be. In Jesus' name. Amen"

5. Write down what God has revealed to you.

Moses' Anger: Exodus 32:19; Numbers 20:1-13

It is hard to believe that because of our emotions, we can be preventing the things God has promised to do in our lives. Moses is the perfect example of a leader who could not control his anger. His anger drove him to a point where he was denied entrance to the Promised Land with the Israelites.

There are two significant instances in the Bible where Moses demonstrated his anger. In the first instance, Moses and Joshua had ascended the mountain to meet with God. While he was away, he left Aaron in charge of the people. Much time passed and the people began to wonder where Moses was. While they wondered, they approached Aaron with the request to *"Come, make us gods..."* (Genesis 32:1) so they could worship. There was a longing in the people for their leader. This longing created a void in their hearts for the things of God. Instead of seeking God, however, they asked for idols to be made.

The result was that Aaron acquiesced to their demands and built a golden calf. Then he built an altar and announced a festival for the following day, which included sacrifices, offerings, and fellowship offerings. The Lord, knowing this, told Moses to return down from the mountain to deal with the situation. God, himself was angry and asked Moses to leave the mountain. It is important to note God's intention was to destroy the people for bowing down to idols. Moses asked the Lord not to harm to the Israelites, but to relent, and He did.

When Moses returned from the mountain, he heard singing and observed the people dancing. It is at that point that Moses' anger burned. He threw down the tablets that he had brought from the mountain and broke them. He took the calf that was made and ground it to powder, threw it in the water, and had the Israelites drink the water. He asked for those who supported Almighty God to come with him. The Levites came with him and he instructed them to go throughout the camp and kill all who were involved in this festival celebration to the gods. The result was three thousand were slaughtered on that day.

The anger demonstrated by Moses was a justified, righteous anger. He had spoken to God and asked Him not to kill the people. He knew God's anger could have a more significant effect on the people than his own anger. It is certain that Moses felt outrage, hostility, and resentment against the people for what they had done. His emotions were justified. The Bible states, *"Be angry, but sin not."* God gives us justification to be angry, but requires us not to commit sin in the process.

In the text, Moses was angry and, from the perspective of being righteously angry, he made a decision to eliminate those who had committed sin against God.

Numbers 20:1-13 gives an example of anger that leads to sin, which ultimately prevented Moses from entering the Promised Land. In this instance, the Israelites were in constant complaint because they were in the Desert of Zen and did not have any water to drink. They complained to Moses and Aaron about the lack of water. They even began to look back on where they came from and question the wisdom of taking them from Egypt to a place where there was no water.

Needless to say, Moses and Aaron were upset and went to the Tent of Meeting to seek the Lord regarding the complaints the Israelites had directed against them. God's instruction to Moses at the time was for him to take his staff and go in front of the Israelites and speak to the rock in front of them and water would pour from the rock.

Moses again took God's instruction to the people. He gathered the people, but instead of following the instruction of speaking to the rock, Moses got upset, disgusted, angry, resentful, and hostile to the group. He struck the rock twice after condemning the attitudes of the Israelites who had complained about the lack of water. This very act prevented both Moses and Aaron from entering the Promised Land.

One might ask, "What is the difference between speaking to the rock and striking the rock?" We might never know the answer to this. One thing is for certain and that is God gave specific instructions to Moses to *speak* to the rock. He was not supposed to hit it. He was not supposed to strike it. He was supposed to speak to it. I dare to speculate as to what was going through Moses' mind. He was frustrated. He was tired of hearing complaints from people who should have known better. He was resentful of these people who did not carry the mantle of leadership, but complained when leadership did not deliver what they wanted. From an emotional intelligence perspective, there was a failure of Moses in two major areas—stress tolerance and impulse control.

Moses' failure to handle the stress of constant complaints from the people caused him to miss the promised destination. Managing stress means that you do not fall apart due to environmental pressures. If Moses had been adequate in the area of impulse control, he would have been able to resist, delay impulses, and defer any drive or temptation to act. It is stated that people with good impulse control are less impatient, not over-reactive, and do not lose control or become angry.

It is obvious from Moses' actions that he failed significantly. It is not tragic that Moses lost control. It is not against God's law for us to get angry. God himself was angry. What is indeed tragic is the consequence of not controlling our emotions. The consequence of Moses losing his temper and disobeying God's instructions was that he lost out on the most significant passage of the Israelites in their trek from Egypt to the Promised Land.

Anger can be controlled and contained. Your anger doesn't have to get the better of you and cause you to miss out on the promises of God. I am sure Moses had no intention of using the staff to hit the rock. He was a servant and a man of God. He followed instructions; however, the basic emotional dimension was short in this area. In chapter 11, we will address the three primary dimensions in which we as humans operate: 1) the intellectual, 2) the spiritual, and 3) the emotional. Moses knew how to do things. He used his intellect with God's help to migrate from Egypt. He was a man who could get things done. Further, Moses was a spiritual being. His relationship with God was indescribable. The fact that he was completly adjusted on the spiritual and the intellectual levels did not relieve him of his responsibility for emotional control. That loss of control ruined his earthly destiny.

Closing the Section

1. Pause for a moment. Think of times when you have been so angry that you did things that you regreted.

2. Ask God to give you insight.

3. Close your eyes and meditate for a minute; then open your eyes.

4. Pray the following: "Dear Lord, you know who I am. God, you made me to be a spiritual, intellectual, and emotional being. I surrender all these dimensions to you. Lord, I ask you to give me wisdom, tools, and techniques to be used to help me within the emotional realm. God, let me not be like Moses, whose emotional failure led to his being barred from the Promised Land. Lord, I do not want to lose out on my destiny because of my emotions. Show me what I need to do. It is this I ask in Jesus' name. Amen."

5. Write down what God has revealed to you.

David's Emotion: 2 Samuel 18:31-22 & 19:1-8

King David is known as a man after God's own heart. He is one who is known to embody the very character and indwelling of the Lord. David was an emotional being. He was one who was known to sing wonderful praises to God as he worshiped Him endlessly by playing his harp. David was also a man who was a warrior of warriors. He fought and killed bears and lions, but his claim to fame was his slaying of the Philistine Goliath. So not only was he a worshiper, he was also a warrior. He was not only right-brain, but he was also left-brain.

For all intents and purposes then, David was a well-rounded individual who expressed his emotions in many forms. He was moved to lust for Bathsheba and committed sin by not only sleeping with her, but also arranging for her husband Uriah to be killed.

One example of David's emotion on display was related to the death of his son Absalom. The background of the story focuses on two of David's sons, Absalom and Amnon, and his daughter Tamar. Amnon had fallen in love with Tamar, even though she was his sister. He desired to sleep with her; however, such an act was forbidden in all of Israel. Amnon insisted, and through the advice of Jonadab, David's brother, he conjured a plan to have Tamar visit him as he lay in bed pretending to be sick. His plan called for the house to be empty of everyone except for him and Tamar. Once they were alone, Amnon took advantage of her and raped her, even though she insisted it was forbidden and should not be.

Left in shame, Tamar went to live with Absalom. It is noted that Absalom never forgave Amnon for this act, even though he decided it was in his best interest not to speak of the situation that had occurred with his sister. Absalom was shrewd and he asked King David to allow him and Amnon to go on a journey. Absalom's plan was to have Amnon killed on the journey, and he accomplished this with the help of his men.

Following the killing, Absalom fled from David for many years and it was through the behest of Joab that King David allowed his son Absalom to return to him in Israel. Upon Absalom's return, however, he set another plan in motion. This time his plan was to overthrow King David and take over the throne. He did this through manipulation, fear, and caustic planning. He convinced all around that he should have been judge over the people. Further, he sent his messengers throughout the camp to state that he was now the king. Upon hearing of this, King David fled with all his advisors, including Joab, who was the one who initially requested that Absalom come home.

While King David fled, Absalom planned to not only take over the kingdom, but also to slay his father David. A great battle ensued. In spite of the fact that David was fearful, concerned, and wary of his son, he did not want to see his son injured. In spite of the fact that his son wanted to kill him, David did not want his son hurt. David's nature is representative of God, in that even when others hurt Him by what we do, He still loves us, no matter what.

While riding on his horse on his way to kill David, Absalom's hair got caught in a tree. As he was hanging from the tree, Joab thrust his javelin into him and killed him. Joab had killed someone who was near and dear to King David. He had killed his son.

When messengers came to David to inform him of the battle, David was fearful of the news. He wondered if the battle had resulted in his son's death. The first servant who came to him only told him that the battle was won by David's men, but when there was an inquiry as to what had happened to his son, the servant stated there was confusion and he didn't know. The next servant made it completely clear to David that his son Absalom was indeed dead.

David's reaction turned from fear, anxiety, and concern to grief, sorrow, despair, and gloom. His emotional state when told the news was not of elation about the fact that the battle was won. It was sadness that his son, who was seeking to kill David, was now dead. Can you imagine the emotion? It is said there is nothing worse than for a parent to lose a child. The mere anguish from this kind of loss is beyond expression.

I can only imagine how God feels when one of His creations— man, woman, or child—is eternally lost. The anguish God feels when someone has lived his or her life on this Earth and then, through failure to recognize Almighty God, leaves this world without reconciling with Him, must be painful. David was reacting to the death of his son as God would when one of us dies without knowing Him. He created us, He knows us, He loves us, and He does not want harm to come to us.

Reality Testing and Impulse Control

At times, we have to process emotions while simultaneously dealing with the situation at hand. Even though our situation may be dire, proper emotional processing is required for us to manage effectively during the circumstances. In David's situation, stress tolerance was required as his son Absalom searched for him. How did he deal with the fact that someone was seeking to kill him? Was he empathetic to the cause of his son? Empathy is to put ourselves in the shoes of another. It does not require us, however, to be completely blind to the fact that someone wants to hurt us. I would also suggest that some might conclude David's reaction to his son's death was not good from a reality testing perspective. Reality testing involves understanding your surroundings and what is happening to you. It means putting a proper perspective on our situation and circumstances. It means to experience events as they are, not as how we want them to be. The fact that David was upset at his son's death, a man who was trying to kill him, did not faze him. He still hurt because the son he loved was dead.

David demonstrated impeccable impulse and self-control throughout his dilemma with his son. David could have easily bypassed his advisors and just gone to battle with his son. A man's normal reaction is to have an immediate and, in our mind, justifiable reaction to those who threaten him. David decided to hold firm. He decided not to do anything stupid. He decided to be shrewd and strategic in how he approached the situation of someone trying to kill him. I often wonder if I am able to not be impulsive when someone hurts me. Can I correctly assess the situation before reacting? Can you do the same?

David's sorrow led Joab to confront and rebuke him. Joab felt David should have been happy that the very enemy of his soul, whether family or not, was now dead. David should be celebrating for this reason. From a reality perspective, Joab was correct. From a spiritual perspective, he was not. Grace causes us to forgive those who hurt us or put us in great danger.

I will address David's circumstance and put it into perspective as it relates to you and me. There are times when others commit great and, in our minds, unforgivable sins toward us. There are times when it seems no matter what someone says or does to us, our actions can be justified. Regardless of the circumstances, our emotions sometimes drive our reactions, rather than godly principles. The fact is our godly principles and our emotions should be aligned so that we can process what is going on in our environment. No one I know is completely perfect. We are all growing and learning about ourselves every day. We are learning intellectually. We are learning and growing spiritually and we are learning and growing emotionally. These three dimensions are seldom aligned naturally. It takes prayer and intentional action to align these dimensions.

Finally, was David correct in grieving? Yes. He was hurting because his son was dead. Was David correct in being fearful when Absalom was seeking to kill him? Yes. He was exhibiting the same emotions any of us would exhibit if we were in his situation.

Closing the Section

1. Pause for a moment. Think of times when others might have done something to you that you thought was reprehensible. What was your reaction?

2. Ask God to give you insight.

3. Close your eyes and meditate for a minute; then open your eyes.

4. Pray the following: "Dear Lord, as I saw how David dealt with stressful circumstances, please create in me a heart that knows how to handle hard, gut-wrenching situations. Father, I want to be more like you in all my talk, my reactions, and my deeds. Help me, Lord, not to be reactive in my flesh, but that in all my reactions, you will govern my actions. Father, if there be things in me that I do not see, show them to me. Not only show them to me, Lord, but create situations wherein

others might be able to help and assist me so I can become more like you. Thank you, Lord. Amen."

5. Write down what God has revealed to you.

Elijah and Depression: 1 Kings 19:1-5

The passage begins with King Ahab telling Queen Jezebel of the great defeat and deaths of the prophets that occurred the previous day at the hand of Elijah. These prophets were not godly men, but were prophets who worshipped the idol Baal. Jezebel swore, and through a messenger, told Elijah she would kill him in similar form and fashion, just the way he had killed the prophets of Baal.

What precipitated this outburst by Jezebel to kill Elijah? The background can be found in the three previous chapters. Ahab was anointed king of Israel shortly after his father Omri died. Ahab married Jezebel, who worshipped and served Baal, which was a representation of a god, but not the true God. Because of this, Elijah informed Ahab that a drought was to come upon the land for years. As Elijah had prophesied, so was the word perfected and the drought began.

By the third year, the drought had increasingly worsened. The more the people continued in their worship of Baal and denial of the true God, the worse their circumstances became. By the third year of the drought, God commanded Elijah to present himself to Ahab. Now ever since the proclamation of the drought by Elijah, Ahab had been trying to kill Elijah. He wanted to silence him. During this time also, Ahab's wife, Jezebel, was determined to wipe out any of God's legitimate prophets.

When Elijah met with Ahab, Elijah informed him that it was the sin of Ahab and his family that had caused the tremendous drought upon the land. That led to a challenge by Elijah to Ahab. Elijah asked all the prophets of Baal, four hundred and fifty of them, and all the prophets of Asherah, four hundred of them, to meet on Mount Carmel for a challenge. The challenge was for two bulls to be killed and put on a wooden altar at Mount Carmel. The false prophets were to call on Baal. Elijah would call on the Lord God. The God that responded with fire to burn up the sacrifice would be called the true God.

The false prophets went first. They called upon Baal, but there was no response. From morning until evening, there was no response. When it was Elijah's turn, he made certain everyone knew his God was indeed the true God, so he had water poured on the altar and created a trench around the altar and filled it, too, with water. He called on God, and fire from Heaven consumed all that was on the altar, the water, the stones, the wood, and everything on the ground.

The people fell on their faces and worshiped God. Seeing this tremendous victory from God, Elijah called for all the prophets of Baal to be executed. The people who once worshiped the god that was not real were killed. This cleared the way for Elijah to call upon God to send rain and end the drought.

Ahab returned to his home and informed Jezebel of all that had occurred regarding the prophets of Baal. She was outraged and immediately sent a messenger to put a death sentence on Elijah's life.

Elijah had just experienced a significant victory. He had experienced a victory in the Lord that was like none other. He had seen and heard of prophets of God being routed and killed by Jezebel. But through the demonstration of God on Mount Carmel, he felt vindicated. He felt happy. He felt overjoyed. He felt he was the victor. He felt God had demonstrated His supernatural power and that would silence the naysayers. It would put an end to the foolishness of Jezebel. He was sadly mistaken. As soon as Jezebel got word, she did not become humble. She did not become contrite and apologize for the error of her ways. Instead, she asked that the person who orchestrated this demonstration of God's supernatural power be killed.

Immediately Elijah experienced fear, anxiety, concern, and fright. It is quite natural that during significant times of victory, when our hopes are high in terms of how we expect people to behave and react, we are often surprised. Elijah was surprised. I do not think he was so much surprised by Jezebel. I believe he was more surprised by God. He was surprised that God was allowing someone who was unholy, unrighteous, and undeserving to threaten his life.

This very fear and anxiety caused Elijah to flee. He went into the desert to flee the potential harm that would come to him. He searched for meaning in what had happened. He searched to find out why this had to happen to him. He searched for meaning in the midst of victory and melancholy. At some point during this entire ordeal, Elijah took the focus off God and started to focus on himself. It is natural. He was only human. The implication is that God will be God. He can do whatever He will. He can orchestrate whatever He sees fit to get the glory. Elijah started to focus on the great things he had done and his expectation was that God would grant him favor—Jezebel would repent. He saw the people of Israel had repented, so why not Jezebel?

From a psychological perspective, Elijah was experiencing depression. He was depressed because after such a great victory, he expected something different. He expected joy, but instead he experienced fear, anxiety, and fright from the potential danger that still existed for him. From an emotional intelligence perspective, his stress tolerance levels and impulse control levels were high. He needed to manage his emotion. The only way to manage his emotion was to flee. He had to run. He had to seek refuge in the desert. If you or I had a threat on our lives, it would be a stressful situation. We would seek to find ways to temper the feelings that we were experiencing.

It is typical for us humans to expect honor to be bestowed upon us when we have done something incredible. It is clear in this case that this is not what God had planned for Elijah. God's treatment for Elijah's depression was rest, food, and drink, which He provided for him. That, however, did not address the conundrum that Elijah faced. How could this happen? From an emotional intelligence perspective, he was assertive. He did what was asked of him. He did exactly what he was instructed to do.

When we feel disillusioned, depressed, gloomy, melancholy, lonely, and despairing, God's answer is to rest, eat, and drink. We cannot try to move forward with the normal daily routine without taking time to assess where we are. Elijah went to the desert as a manner of assessment. He was confused and he needed clarity. To get clarity, he needed to be alone. Being alone was not an antidote to Elijah's depression. It was a prescription for his current state— he needed to be alone to understand what had just occurred.

We can learn much from Elijah in this circumstance. At times, when we are confused, hurt, and don't quite understand what is happening to us, we need to take the time to go somewhere in solitude. We need to converse with God. We need to ask the *what and why* of our circumstance. It is important to note that asking God the what and why of our circumstance should not be demanding, but merely asking for true understanding.

In the desert, God did approach Elijah (see 1 Kings 19:10-15). He tried many different approaches to get to Elijah. He tried to speak to him through a great wind, an earthquake, and even fire. Elijah did not move. Twice he remonstrated with God that he had done all that was asked of him, and still he was put in this predicament where his life was threatened. He challenged God. It was not until God's soft voice sounded to him and told him to move on, that he did. Interestingly enough, God did not specifically answer him. He instructed him to go and anoint three people, one of whom was his successor.

It is extremely important that we do not put ourselves in a place of self-importance before God. In Elijah's case, God did not answer; He instructed him to move on. You and I will wrestle with things at times. God will answer us, but He also wants us to be humble and follow His agenda because He knows what is good for us.

Closing the Section

1. Pause for a moment. Think of a time when you have done something you thought was great, only to see God do something you did not expect. How did you feel?

2. Ask God to give you insight.

3. Close your eyes and meditate for a minute; then open your eyes.

4. Pray the following: "Dear Lord, at times I have done things I know and believe you have ordained for me to do. I have done them with my expectation being singularly focused on me and not on you. Forgive me, God. May you use me continually in the future and may my focus be on you only and you always. Thank you. I ask this in Jesus' name. Amen."

5. Write down what God has revealed to you.

Jesus' Distress: Mark 14:32-36

Prior to Jesus' going to the Garden of Gethsemane, He had spoken with Peter regarding the fact that he would deny Him that night. Jesus—the all-knowing God, the Son of God, the One who was, is, and is to come—knew what was going to happen to Him in the upcoming hours. Jesus told Peter he would deny Him three times that night before the rooster crowed.

After the rebuttal by Peter, Jesus and the disciples headed for Gethsemane. He knew that soon He would be crucified. He knew that in a little while He would be taking on the sins of the world. Interestingly, Jesus took the disciples with Him to pray.

There was a progression in Jesus' distress. He took all the disciples with Him. They were the closest people to Him. During this time of distress, He wanted the people who were closest to Him to be with Him, as He prepared for that which was to come. The *first progression* was to invite the disciples to pray. He wanted people around Him who understood the seriousness of the present circumstance and He wanted them close by. All eleven disciples— absent Judas who was on his way to betray Him—were with Him. He progressed so far and left eight of them at the gate. The eight were close to Him. They understood Him. They loved Him. They cared for Him. They wanted the best for Him. He wanted them to *pray*.

The *second progression* was to take Peter, James, and John with him. They went deeper into the Garden with Him. At times, you will need to leave the masses and bring a small group of people with you. These people are your confidantes, the ones whom you trust even more deeply than everyone else. The smaller group with Jesus understood about Christ more deeply than the others. They shared in His anguish and His pain. This does not refute the fact that the eight didn't. It just means that this smaller group presented more of a focus for Jesus. His instruction to them was to *watch*.

The *third progression* was to be alone. Jesus left the three— Peter, James, and John—and went a bit further into the Garden. This is symbolic that He alone would have to bear the sins of the world for us. He would have to carry the darkness and bear the burden that was to come—His Crucifixion. The pain was agonizing. The anguish was unbearable. Jesus was completely man, but yet He was completely God. He suffered and hurt like anyone else. In Genesis, it states that God made man in His own image. It didn't matter that Jesus was in Gethsemane alone. He was alone because it was the will of the Father for Him to prepare for Calvary.

Even though Jesus was purely God, He was purely man. As a man, He experienced emotion. He experienced grief, sorrow, gloom, melancholy, loneliness, and despair. These emotions are all a subset of sadness. He felt sad. Jesus was distressed and troubled and His soul was overwhelmed with sorrow. He was sorrowful because He knew that within hours He would begin the journey that would lead to His death. He knew the journey was not going to be uneventful. It was going to be hard. It was going to be challenging. It was going to be difficult. He was going to be beaten. He was going to be mocked. He was going to be spat upon. Prospects such as these would cause anyone to experience the emotions Jesus was feeling.

Sadly enough, as Jesus bore all the sins of mankind on the Cross, He felt the whole burden of those sins in His body. He did not desire to go to the Cross. He had asked God if it were possible, could He, the Father, remove the cup from Him. The cup was threefold: bearing the sin penalty, separation from His Father, and death. His inquiry to God was basically, *Is there any other way this can be accomplished without my having to go through this?* Was there any way, other than the Cross, that the God of the universe could find so Jesus did not have to go through this impending turmoil? As God is all-powerful, could He have used another way? The fact that the Father did not even answer was indicative there was no other way for man to be saved, but through His Son, Jesus, and the Cross.

Stress tolerance and impulse control are the key components of emotional intelligence in this circumstance. It was a stressful time for Jesus. He was distressed. The stress level of anyone who is about to experience death should be considerably high. It is possible we may never be in a situation that is potentially life threatening, but consider the situation Jesus found himself in. He wondered if there were any way He could bypass the hurt to come. His general mood was affected. Jesus, the most positive of men, was sad. He was not happy. He sought solace from His Father and He did not receive it.

How difficult is it for us to face impending hurt? How do we react when we are hurt? From an emotional intelligence perspective, research shows that one cannot be empathetic when one is hurt. But Jesus showed empathy while He was hurting. The fact is that Jesus *was* empathy. He was the Person who took our place on the Cross. Do we demonstrate the emotions Jesus showed in Gethsemane? Is it okay to demonstrate those emotions? If the Creator can show those emotions and we are made in His image, then of course, you can demonstrate the same thing.

Stress is a normal part of life. We have a right to show our emotions, but we also have a responsibility to control them. Jesus demonstrated that you could experience stress, feel pain, feel overwhelmed, and yet, at the same time, leave everything up to God—knowing that God's will is the ultimate decider. We will all feel pain and hurt. The key is to seek God's input as to why we feel it, why it is happening to us, and to ask God whether it is His will that we go through it. Allan E. Nelson, in his book *Broken in the Right Places: How God Tames the Soul,* said "To be broken means to be reduced to submission; tamed."[3] Pain does that to us. At times we will go through pain, but that pain might be God humbling and taming us.

Closing the Section

1. Pause for a moment. How do you react when going through pain? Do you ask God why it is happening? Do you ask if it is His will?

2. Ask God to give you insight.

3. Close your eyes and meditate for a minute; then open your eyes.

4. Pray the following: "Dear Lord, as you have reminded me of painful times now and to come, God, I pray that you will give me the character and the spirit to involve you in my pain.

Father, I know that your will is paramount in my life. Help me to surrender to you. Help me to give everything to you, even my pain, and show me, Lord, through my pain, what you would like me to learn from my experiences. I ask this in Jesus' name. Amen."

5. Write down what God has revealed to you.

Anguish After Denial: Matthew 26:74

The stage is set. Jesus has been taken from the Garden of Gethsemane. He has been brought before the Sanhedrin. As Jesus was being taken, one of the twelve followed close behind. It was Peter. He followed Jesus at a distance. He followed Him close enough to hear the activities that were going on. He followed Jesus to the courtyard of the high priest.

Peter had seen his Lord being taken away. He wanted to hear the proceedings. He wanted to know what would occur. Peter had an interest in knowing what was going to be the outcome. He might have had a subconscious interest because prior to Jesus being taken away, He had told Peter, *"Before the rooster crows, you will disown me three times."*

In Matthew 26:31-35, Jesus predicted what would happen with Peter as it relates to his very denial of any association with Christ. Jesus quoted Scripture to His disciples that stated, *"Strike the shepherd and the sheep will be scattered"* (Zechariah 13:7). Jesus reminded the disciples that it is written and must come to pass that they will scatter after He is crucified. Peter's response to Jesus' proclamation was, *"Even if all fall away on account of you, I never will"* (Matthew 26:33). Jesus then told Peter that this night before the rooster crowed, he would deny Him three times. Peter challenged Jesus by stating, *"Even if I have to die with you, I will not deny you"* (Matthew 26:35, NASB). The remainder of the disciples said the same.

As Peter watched Jesus before the Sanhedrin and He was charged, based on the words of the people, with blasphemy for acknowledging that He was the Christ, Peter observed what happened. At the time this was occurring, Peter was not consciously aware of the promise he had made to Jesus. He was not aware that he had promised Him earlier that he would never deny Him.

It is typical for us to make promises to Jesus—to our God— only to break them later. It is interesting to note that even though God knows we will break our promises, He loves us anyway. At times people make promises that mean so much. They make promises they will swear upon, for any person or in any circumstance, and they believe they never will fail in that promise.

Imagine, if you will, being there with the King of the Universe, being there with Jesus, the Christ, being there with the Son of God, being there with the One who had discipled you and taught you everything about Christ and the love of God. Imagine making a promise to Him. It would be a promise you would want to keep. It would be a promise you would want to uphold. Of course people make promises to friends, relatives, and others, but that is different. Peter was making a promise to God himself.

There were three intensity levels of the denial. The first denial was a *circumstantial* denial. It contained an emphatic denial not of Christ, but of what the young girl accused him of: *"You also were with Jesus of Galilee"* (verse 69). This denial was of the circumstance the girl was talking about. Peter's denial was that he did not know what she was talking about. He did not understand if what she was saying was actually true. He did not state that what she was saying was false, but rather that he was not aware of it.

The second denial was a *personal* denial. Another young lady stated, *"This fellow was with Jesus of Nazareth"* (verse 71). Peter's response was, *"I don't know the man!"* (verse 72). He denied any association, any relationship, any connection with Jesus himself. He denied the very personhood of Christ. He was adamant about the denial. He declared with an oath that he did not know nor had he ever associated with Christ.

The third denial was a denial of *accusation*. The crowd went up to Peter and said, *"Surely, you are one of them, for your accent gives you away"* (verse 73). Peter's response to the accusation that he was one of Jesus' disciples was, again, a personal denial when he said, *"I don't know the man!"* (verse 74). Circumstantial, personal, and accusational denials were all borne by Peter. He denied the circumstance of Christ. He denied the person of Christ, and he denied the association with Christ and the accusations that were being laid upon him by the multitude.

The emotions Peter felt were outrage, resentment, hostility, and irritability. These are all associated with anger. Further, Peter felt shame. He felt guilt, regret, contrition, and chagrin. Additionally, he was grieved, sorrowful, lonely, and in despair. All these emotions occurred once the rooster crowed. He felt severe grief for what he had done. The emotions were real. They demonstrate the humanness of Peter.

As humans we tend to hide our feelings. We tend to block out and not show who we are and what we are experiencing. The Bible states that upon hearing the rooster crow, *"And he went outside, and wept bitterly"* (verse 75). The New Living Translation states, *"And he went away, crying bitterly."* Peter was profoundly sad for what he had done. He had made a promise to the Creator and now he had disowned Him—the very person he promised he would not deny.

Did Peter feel self-actualized—the ability to realize your personal capacities? From an emotional intelligence perspective, he felt the contrary. Other emotional intelligence dimensions that were affected were his general mood, self-regard, stress-tolerance, and even his impulse control.

If Peter could experience these emotions and his emotional intelligence could be affected based on his responses to the current environment, then we all can and will be affected by our circumstances. The question is not will we be affected; the question is how will we respond to situations wherein we have caused grief or been affected by grief? Peter was a man; he grieved, cried, and wept bitterly. In today's society, men are called to be strong, at times not to show emotions, not to cry because it demonstrates weakness. Peter was one of the Twelve. He cried. He showed emotion. He showed that when things hurt, he had to process those emotions. He did not bottle it. He did not contain it. He did not try to show that he was a man and need not cry.

It is clear that Peter's high road function had completely failed. His low road, emotional processing, had taken over and was generating his responses to the circumstances within and without. We all experience emotion, whether we are born-again, churchgoers, or unchurched; it does not matter. We all experience emotion. Peter did and he had to process it. He hurt and he cried. When was the last time you hurt and you cried? If one of Jesus' disciples can cry, so can you.

Closing the Section

1. Pause for moment. Are there things that hurt you? Are there people that hurt you? How do you feel? Process your emotions.

2. Ask God to give you insight.

3. Close your eyes and meditate for a minute; then open your eyes.

4. Pray the following: "Dear Lord, help me to be like Peter, not to deny you, Father, but to be a human and process my emotions. Let me not be afraid, Lord, to show my emotions. Teach me, Lord, to have a heart that is open. Father, help me to be open with those who are my family, my friends, my church, or in my home—and teach me to be more like Christ.

Teach me to show my emotions because you have made me in your image. Thank you. I ask this in Jesus' name. Amen."

5. Write down what God has revealed to you.

CHAPTER NINE

FINAL NOTE ON BIBLICAL APPROACH: THE PSYCHOLOGICAL & THE SPIRITUAL

· · · ·

It is extremely important from a theological and psychological perspective that we remain clear as to what emotional intelligence is. Emotional intelligence does not counter growth in the spiritual. Emotional intelligence does not contradict the spiritual. I have heard in the past that when we—the Church—discuss emotions, we are speaking of the psychological, which for some comes in stark contrast to the growth of one's spiritual dimension. Alan E. Nelson in his book *Broken in the Right Place* states, "Many Christians languish in their spiritual walk because of psychological barriers, preventing God's Spirit from bringing about the maturity and manifestations He desires."[1] His research and book focus on the process of being broken. Being broken means that we admit our shortcomings, that we run to God to seek solace, and to ask Him for help in bringing us to a place of complete surrender where we can allow Him to make us into what He wants us to be.

It is important to refer to Alan Nelson's book because the process of looking at the emotional dimension is one that requires us to remove our guards, whether they be psychological, theological, mystical, or whatever one wants to call it. It is important we remove the barriers so we can see God work through the myriad of tools

He has given us to better understand ourselves and why we do what we do.

God made man in His own image (see Genesis 1:27). He created us with feelings, thoughts, and ideas. He created us with the same makeup as His. This means He created us with the same emotional dynamic He has. It would be foolhardy of us to consider that since we enter the sanctuary of a church we are supposed to throw away the basic makeup of who we are or to deny a part of ourselves. God in His infinite wisdom gave us this characteristic to better understand each other and in so doing, we are able to eliminate misconceptions and misunderstandings that can be derived from us not acknowledging that fact.

The psychological is as important a part of who you are as your physical existence. One does not survive without the other. The emotional is driven by the psychological, but not to the detriment of the spiritual. The spiritual requires a surrender of all things whether physical, intellectual, or psychological to God so He can make us into who we truly are and what we truly should be.

Sometimes within the Church there is an over-reliance on spirituality to the detriment of other aspects of human existence. I do not say the following to disparage those who are not trained in the area of theological understanding or in the understanding of the spiritual dimension, but consider the following exchange: "Hey, I have this problem with controlling my feelings and reactions to other people." "Well then, what you need to do is pray about it and seek God and He will deliver you." I do not for a minute want to suggest that dedicating things to God—our struggles, our fears, our life concerns—does not matter to God. Actually, He cares about them more than we do.

The above response, however, is a naïve one. It implies that all things are solvable solely through our reliance on God and His almighty power. I often wonder why God gave us physicians, psychologists, doctors, lawyers, and other professionals. It can be said He bestows great knowledge on men and women so they

FINAL NOTE ON BIBLICAL APPROACH

can put practical solutions and steps in place to deal with all the maladies of our existence. It does not replace God and His great power, but can help in our journey. It, in essence, creates a structure wherein we can seek advice from professionals and talk to them about the various situations we experience.

From a biblical perspective, it is apparent that emotions are to be expressed. It is clear that God made us in His image. If we are made in His image, that means we take on the character of God. It also implies that what He experiences and feels, we feel.

Now then, does emotion exist in the Bible? Should we care about emotions? Why does it matter? If God made man in His own image that means man should then experience what God experiences. God experiences anger, love, and hurt, and His Son Jesus Christ experienced pain, frustration, suffering, and as the Bible recounts, He even wept. If God and His Son can experience such varied emotions, then who are we to deny His command to be like Him?

Too often we see that men, unlike women, tend not to show their emotions. They would rather appear strong. They would rather not cry or shed a tear because, in our civilization, crying is a sign of weakness. However, if it is a sign of weakness, then I am happy to be as *weak* as Jesus, my Savior. He demonstrates the very emotions that others tend to suppress because of their personal experiences, family backgrounds, or even their lack of accurate information.

EMOTIONAL INTELLIGENCE, THE CHURCH, AND MODERN SOCIETY

. . . .

David Kinnaman starts his book, *UnChristian: What a New Generation Really Thinks About Christianity and Why it Matters,* with the following statement: " 'Christianity' has an image problem."[1] The fact is an image problem can easily be fixed by instituting a clear method of communication to ensure that which creates an image deficit can be developed thoroughly. That which needs to be projected can clearly and succinctly be brought forward to address the shortcoming in perception. This is easier said than done because the basic definition of Christianity spreads across all denominations and could include people from all sectors of society, various countries, and groups of people.

How do you manage the image of an entire religion? Better yet, who is responsible for ensuring the religion and those who belong to the various subsects of the religion are projecting the right and necessary image? Jesus' basic tenet of the Church is that His Church will include those who follow Him and who share the gospel with those who are lost. Believers who are called by His name, therefore, should project a true image of Him to whom they owe their salvation. Christ's followers are called to demonstrate the very character, mannerism, depth, position, and attitude of the One who is their Savior.

Why does image matter? It matters because those on the outside looking in are very skeptical of the image that is portrayed when it is contrary to the very word that is being communicated about a Christ-follower. Image matters because those who look on us as examples also look to us to display the very nature of Christ. If we are to win others to Christ, it is the character and image they see of Him in our lives that will draw them to Him. Image, by definition, means a reproduction or imitation of the form of a person or thing; exact likeness; a tangible or visible representation; a person strikingly like another person.

In Genesis 1:26 the Bible states, *"Then God said, "Let us make man in our image, in our likeness."* In Matthew 5:48, Jesus said, *"Be perfect, therefore, as your heavenly Father is perfect."* This is a tall order! God created us in His exact likeness. Then He instructed us to act and behave like Him. Therefore according to Kinneman, if this is the case, then the very image that should be projected of who Christ is through His followers is flawed because the medium (us) through whom Christ is being projected is flawed. It does not truly reflect who He is. It does not truly reflect the very persona of Christ, which is love, joy, peace, patience, kindness, goodness, faithfulness, gentleness, and self-control. If indeed these characteristics were lived out in us, the perception and image challenges that Kinneman alerts us to would not be so severe. It is, however, clear that a perception and image problem exists. As I scour the information and news landscapes, I am no longer surprised as to why the image challenge exists. A few of these image problems are presented below. The names have been changed to protect the church and those who are affected.

Back to Africa

In July 2000, Pastor Richard Carose and the leadership of his church made the decision to leave the United States and relocate permanently to Africa. The genesis of the decision was that the laws in the United States were too severe and in direct opposition to the religious practices that Pastor Carose and his group so passionately, though erroneously, believed. Consequently, the group moved from northern New Jersey to Kabal in Africa, leaving behind family members who objected to the move and who decided not to go. Left behind were the families that were torn apart when fathers decided to leave their wives and children and instead went to Africa to be with the church and its leadership. Left behind were broken lives and broken spirits.

Those who had not gone struggled with feelings of guilt and abandonment, but soon began to gain clarity and peace regarding their decision not to move to Africa when reports of turmoil and gross ethical failures began to surface in the group. The healing process was long and difficult for many, due to the fact that the moral failure and departure from basic spiritual truth that had existed covertly among the leadership and selected members in the church for so long were so severe.

Many had to take a long, hard look at their spiritual beliefs, which over the years had become distorted by the teachings and practices imposed on the members by Pastor Carose. They had to come to a place of recognition where they could finally reject the erroneous and harmful manipulations of that church and return to basic, wholesome biblical truths. Others never fully recovered from the experience at Pastor Carose's church, but instead, sadly, began a downward spiral into depression, loss of self-esteem, and ultimately into self-destructive behaviors. The un-Christlike image that Pastor Carose and his leadership projected to the congregants marred and, in some cases, totally destroyed the healthy image they had of themselves and of God. For many, it was a long and painful journey to recover the healthy self-image and the sense of peace and acceptance with God.

Anger Management in the Pews

The headlines were jarring. On August 22, 2007, "Bishop Attacks Prophetess in Parking Lot." It didn't matter what the magazine or newspaper was. What mattered is this story had risen to national notoriety due to the fact this was a bishop of a major non-denominational church, and the prophetess in question was a nationally recognized leader who taught in national and international conferences.

Let us be clear. The intention of relating this story is not because the author is agreeing with the details of what happened. The intent is not to recognize that either the bishop or the prophetess was right or wrong, although it is easy to assess blame and responsibility on both parts. What is interesting to note is that emotional intelligence plays a major part in our lives, whether we are Christians or non-Christians. It is more important to note that, in the secular as well as the non-secular environment, if an emotional intelligence shortcoming exists, the issue surrounding these lapses will only be intensified as the organization grows bigger and bigger. It is important to note that either the bishop or the prophetess might have emotional shortcomings and if they are not dealt with, the consequences can be dire, and worse yet, can lead to major undermining of the religious order and Christians around the world.

According to a news report on WSB-TV[2] in Atlanta, the bishop related the following events at a major news conference:

On June 3, 2007, his wife, the prophetess, announced to the entire congregation that she was no longer returning to the church in which she and the bishop were pastors. On June 5, 2007, the church staff received a fax cancelling a major international event by the prophetess, and in the fax it indicated the bishop and the prophetess were separating. On June 14, 2007, a cease-and-desist letter was sent to the world headquarters detailing the need to remove the prophetess' likeness, pictures, or anything with her name on any product.

On August 3, 2007, the church duplicated over 5,000 DVDs for an event being sponsored by the prophetess. On August 16, 2007, the prophetess came to the bishop's office to seek reconciliation and expressed her desire for them to continue working through the issues in their marriage. On August 20, 2007, both the bishop and his wife, the prophetess, spent time together working toward healing in their marriage. On August 21, 2007, they met at a hotel to discuss the prophetess' personal upcoming projects, but the cease-and-desist letter needed to be rescinded first.

No one knew the content of the conversation exactly, but things spiraled out of control and the end result was the bishop was charged and arrested for attacking his wife, choking her, and causing her bodily harm. He was charged with aggravated assault and terrorististic threats.

To anyone who understands the inner workings of the church world, it is clear that emotions are brought to bear in more situations than not. What led to the out-of-control rage? Why did a respected bishop and an internationally known prophetess appear on the front page of local newspapers exhibiting the same actions that are more characteristic of rock stars?

This prophetess has been on the national and international stage for decades. The bishop has been a nationally known speaker who grew a church from nothing to over 3,000 members. Were there things in the past that could have identified the need to address emotional issues well before they overflowed onto the national scene?

Fox News Atlanta reported the bishop was accused by past parishioners of engaging in acts that led to the physical harm of the chief financial officer of the organization. According to reports, he and the CFO engaged in a verbal altercation, which led to the CFO being body-slammed by the bishop. When the CFO was taken to the hospital by fellow employees, they contacted the prophetess. Instead of having the CFO enter the emergency room, they agreed it was best to not have the media involved and to take care of treatment outside of the public space.

The fact that this was not the first incident related to the bishop is not the issue. The bishop is credited with building a great church and he, obviously, was a successful minister. He was by definition the symbol of Christian accomplishment. He had built a church, and with his wife's help, he had grown the church significantly. They had taught and trained many in the ministry, and yet he had not dealt with the issues that led to the downfall of his church. Shortly after the announcement they were separating, the church attendance dropped from 3,000 to 300. This situation came to a head shortly thereafter during a conference when local sheriffs showed up at the church to evict the bishop and conference attendees.

Utilizing the 360° dimension model in a later chapter, it is clear that the bishop had shortcomings in the emotional realm. The model highlights the many dimensions in which we operate: spiritual, emotional, intellectual, and physical. Clearly, the bishop was smart, in that he was able to manage a mega church with over 3,000 people. He operated in the physical realm because we are spiritual beings having a natural existence. Clearly he was a spiritual person who attended Bible school, fasted, prayed, and labored to build a church of such note and with such strengths. It is sad, however, to see the blind spot that existed in his makeup, one that he had refused to deal with over the years.

The interesting thing about God is He will bring things to our attention that we need to deal with, adjust, and change. He will deal with them on very personal levels—levels where they are brought to us with little to no attention from others. If we fail to listen to what the Lord says, then that flaw will become more pronounced as our success increases. Unfortunately for the bishop and the prophetess, issues were not dealt with in a quiet, confidential manner, but instead they were brought out in the open for all to see.

In his March 21, 2008, conviction, the bishop was sentenced to three years of probation, 200 hours of non-church community service, and anger management counseling. The anger management counseling was a direct result of his explosive nature as well as his inadequacies in the emotional intelligence realm, which led to his downward spiral. Clearly, in the stress management sub-component of the Bar-On emotional intelligence scale, he suffered deficiencies in the realm of stress tolerance and impulse control. A more effective management of his impulses and his reaction to trying situations, whether conscious or subconscious, could have resulted in a more controlled reaction to his environment.

A period of continued failure to acknowledge he had a problem, or even needed help, culminated in the disastrous events of August 22, 2007. The question, therefore, is not that this happened, but rather how many others in full time Christian work are moving forward in their ministries without addressing the core realities their low level of emotional intelligence and emotional sensitivity are surely handicapping their service to God?

The sad end to this episode in Christendom is that the couple separated in May 2007, and divorced on June 21, 2008. The harm brought to the Body of Christ and to the many believers both past, present, and future is significant. Controlling and taming the emotions in spiritual servitude is necessary and required.

Emotional Tone-deafness

Pastor John was the spiritual mentor of Richard Martin. Even though Pastor John was a pastor, he also had tremendous experience in the field of finance, and actually had been president of a company before he took on the duties of the pastorate. Richard Martin had made financial decisions early in his life that were questionable, and which were creating a major strain in his life. Instead of dealing with it on his own, he went to Pastor John to see if the pastor could help him understand why he had made those bad decisions and to help him navigate the financial landscape he was now encountering. As he spoke with the pastor, he was expecting kindhearted, gentle advice from Pastor John.

Instead, he found Pastor John kept focusing on what he did wrong financially in the past, but could not connect with the emotional pain he was feeling now. Instead of futher elaborating on his circumstances, Richard shut down. He refused to go any further and instead decided not to engage Pastor John in any future counsel.

Emotional tone-deafness is the complete inability to understand what others are feeling. It is a lack of care, an inability to care, or a lack of regard for how someone might be feeling. It is similar to the term *alexithymia* or someone who is *alexithymic*, meaning someone who is completely lacking in the ability to express his or her feelings.

Various studies[3] indicate that empathy builds on self-awareness. The more understanding we have of our own emotions, the more empathetic we are and the more we can read the feelings of others. Actually, if you are tone-deaf, the question is whether you are aware of that fact and, if you are not aware of it, the tone-deafness will continue and you will hurt people unintentionally. The person who is emotionally tone-deaf, even though he or she is a Christian and a Spirit-filled believer, will try to behave in a way that is Christ-centered, but they will still face the psychological challenge that they are not aware of their own failing and the critical damage it can cause others.

In my discussion about this example with psychiatrist Devendra Kurani, he stipulated that the pastor is convinced that the approach he was taking was absolutely correct. Pastor John wanted to ensure that the process of assessment of the financial situation was done and clear. He wanted to ensure data and information clarity without the contamination of feelings and other emotions.

However, what was missing was the ability to see and understand what Richard was feeling. Richard would have preferred a balanced approach, an approach where the analysis was done as to what financial decisions he made were incorrect and why, but he also wanted to share how and what he was feeling. The end result is Richard felt almost blindsided by the analytical manner in which he was being counseled, as opposed to someone who was caring, loving, and mindful of what he was experiencing.

On the alternate side of things, the pastor felt Richard was basically incompetent for making such decisions, in light of the fact that these decisions would have created major strain on Richard's life.

The importance of understanding feelings in the execution of ministry operations cannot be overestimated. Too often, the thought process is if someone is in a spiritual or ministry role, they are without flaw. This is by definition a cult, and if anyone within the Church thinks that way, their theology is flawed. The fact that a senior leader believes he is always right, yet is completely deaf to the fact that emotion is a critical component in the delivery of that ministry, is something that can be observed in all levels of the clergy. It should not be. This further exemplifies the need to blend emotion within the ministry, rather than think the ministry can, in and of itself, exist without capitalizing on the emotional dimension.

Narcissistic Personality Disorder

There are leaders within our homes, our churches, our communities, our society, and our world who believe all things rotate and revolve around them and them only. In his book, *Primal Leadership,* Daniel Goleman[4] describes this type of person as a narcissistic leader. By definition this is an individual who believes that all matters, all states of affairs are conducted and come as a result of his or her own strength. There is no accreditation to others. There is no form of teamwork and effort that brings forth success. The reason for the significant growth in sales, growth in the company, growth in other leaders around them is attributable to them only. In the Church, this is the priest, the pastor, or the leader who has such a grandiose opinion of himself that he cannot see that others around him have contributed to the growth of the organization.

Within the Church, the mere fact that we are called to be God's creatures would surely render such a leadership style null and void in the spiritual and Christian environment. Is it possible for someone to be in love with themself so much they would use others toward their own goals; speak well of people to get them into their circle; manipulate their own way into other's lives for their ultimate purposes; be emotionally tone-deaf to the plight and desires of others; and be so caught up with their own spiritual desires that those very desires would lead to the mistreatment of those who are supposed to be their friends and part of their inner circle?

The question on the table is if you're a person who recognizes these blatant behaviors, can we hide behind them and rationalize ways to justify the behavior? The interesting thing is that the person who is behaving in such a way might be the greatest preacher, singer, songwriter, worship-leader, pastor, or prophet anyone could have experienced, but still have these flaws. In present day churches, these patterns of behavior exist and are accepted as the norm. They are rationalized as "Well, he is growing in the Lord and with time he will get better." The Apostle Paul spoke of the thorn he had that was never removed. I would venture to say the thorn he had did not result in his hurting people or he would have spent most of his ministry apologizing. He certainly didn't need to leave his work because of any pain he inflicted on others.

It is important to recognize someone could be living a perfectly normal and spirit-filled life and still be demonstrating the above-mentioned spiritual deficiencies. The question then is, "Are these spiritual deficiencies or are they emotional deficiencies?" In this case, the emotional deficiencies might be driving the spiritual growth. Or can we conclude that spiritual growth is devoid of emotional shortcomings? Is it possible for someone to have the *spiritual* dimension completely under control to the point that others who view them conclude they are a man or woman of God and yet, at the same time, there is a significant lack in their *emotions* and it is just accepted as the norm? That did not become clear to me until the term Narcissistic Personality Disorder was brought to my attention.

According to the World Health Organization in 1992, in ICD-10 "International Classification of Mental and Behavioral Disorders" states: "Narcissistic Personality Disorder (NPD) is a disorder in which a person has a grandiose self-importance, preoccupation and fantasies of unlimited success, a driven desire for attention and admiration, intolerance for criticism, and disturbed, self-centered interpersonal relations." A person has a personality disorder when the person's identity is driven by their habits—the habits then become the identity.

Sam Valkin, one of the world's leading experts on the subject, describes it as an all-pervasive pattern of grandiosity—in fantasy or behavior—the need for admiration or adulation, and lack of empathy, usually beginning in early childhood and presenting itself in various contexts.[5] Pathological narcissism is a life-long pattern of traits and behaviors which signify infatuation and obsession with one's self to the exclusion of others and the egotistic and ruthless pursuit of one's gratification, dominance, and ambition. It is rigid, maladaptive, persistant, and causes significant distress and functional impairment. Therefore, it is easy to conclude that Narcissistic Personality Disorder (NPD) is an extension of pathological narcissism. This disorder first appeared as a mental health diagnosis in the *Diagnostic and Statistical Manual* (DSM) in 1980.

The criteria for someone to be diagnosed with Narcissistic Personality Disorder according to the *Diagnostic and Statistical Manual of Mental Disorders* published by the American Psychiatric Association, is outlined below. It is important that at least five of the criteria be met before an official classification is given. As you review the list, I am sure you are thinking how this might apply to yourself or those who are in your world. According to the DSM-IV, the disorder begins by early adulthood and is indicated by the subject exhibiting at least five of the following:

1. Feels grandiose and self-important (e.g., exaggerates achievements and talents to the point of lying; demands to be recognized as superior without commensurate achievements).

2. Is obsessed with fantasies of unlimited success, fame, fearsome power or omnipotence, unequalled brilliance (the cerebral narcissist), bodily beauty or sexual performance (the somatic narcissist), or ideal, everlasting, all-conquering love or passion.

3. Firmly convinced that he or she is unique, and because of being special, can only be understood by, should only be treated by, or associate with, other special or unique or high-status people (or institutions).

4. Requires excessive admiration, adulation, attention, and affirmation—or failing that, wishes to be feared and to be notorious (narcissistic supply).

5. Feels entitled. He or she expects unreasonable or special and favorable priority treatment. He or she demands automatic and full compliance with his or her expectations.

6. Is *interpersonally exploitative*, i.e., uses others to achieve his or her own ends.

7. Devoid of empathy. Is unable or unwilling to identify with or acknowledge the feelings and needs of others.

8. Constantly envious of others or believes they feel the same about him or her.

9. Arrogant, haughty behaviors or attitudes coupled with rage when frustrated, contradicted, or confronted.

It is possible the reader might have experienced one or more individuals with at least five or more characteristics outlined above. Empathy is the crux of the gospel. Empathy is to place oneself in another person's shoes. Jesus came to take our place at Calvary. He decided to place himself in our shoes. If it is possible, then, to be devoid of empathy, how can you be someone who serves the Lord and loves His children? This question will be a constant when in the presence of someone who demonstrates NPD symptoms.

In the church, it can be manifested in areas where someone who is working with the narcissist sees circumstances that leave him or her concerned about the action that was taken by the NPD leader. A lack of empathy could be demonstrated by a lack of care for those who are in the congregation or, worse yet, a false sense of care for those in the congregation. It is difficult to separate heart from action and in this case it can be deduced that what one says, in the NPD leader's world, does not really add up to the action that is taken. Further, these actions can be contradicted in person because the NPD leader may have stated something publicly, but privately demonstrates a different act or statement.

Another demonstration of lack of empathy is a total lack or inability to relate to someone's feelings and needs. It can be demonstrated when NPD leaders begin to speak of themselves. When they do, they are the center of attention, but if the listeners were to interject or add something specific about themselves, NPD leaders will more than likely feel interrupted because the focus must be on them, even though the listener might have a genuine and valid point. Further, NPD leaders are unable to listen to or understand other people's feelings. In order to deal with the feelings of others, NPD leaders will tend to either 1) duplicate the feeling that is being thrust upon them, or 2) worse yet, replicate the action of the feeling without the feeling itself.

Due to this lack of empathy, according to Ashmun, "The biggest challenge and frustration with board members, elders, leaders, or staff members dealing with an NPD leader can be alleviated when people recognize that the leader lacks thinking (cognition) and feeling." They don't understand the meaning of what people say and they don't grasp the meaning of the written word either, because so much of the meaning of what we say depends on context and affect, thus the NPD leader only hears words.

The NPD leader can be verbally abusive and is concerned with what can be gained from others without context. It does not matter whether they are spiritually in-tune because lacking the emotional context without a spiritual manifestation, they will continue in this vein without reason and without thought. It is important for the NPD leader to be completely in control. The NPD leader will invest in those who make them look good. They therefore confuse love with want. The statement is made that "He is in love with those he is with." That clearly means the NPD leader only focuses on their own needs over all else. If you're with them and they enjoy your company, then they are the best at helping you, but once they recognize you are of no help to them, the most likely possibility is you will no longer be needed or wanted.

The NPD leader shows love in a different and awkward way. At times they love you so much they put you forth to others as some sort of trophy. The fact that you're put out there is not because the focus is on you, but more because of who you are as the trophy; you belong to them so by bringing you forward, the NPD leader is actually having the focus on himself because he has made this possible. At times you can be loved by the NPD leader, but as soon as something within the relational dynamic changes, you can be treated in a way that borders on outright abuse.

Further evidence of an NPD leader within your sphere is someone who says one thing, but then contradicts himself either by stating that he didn't say what was presented or, worse yet, he does not remember. The fact of the matter is that if the question of sincerity regarding truthfulness is brought up to the NPD leader, he is likely to question your accuracy about what actually occurred. The NPD leader is inflexible and, at times, authoritarian. They are sometimes classified as a *benevolent dictatorship*, because the manner in which they manage leads others to be attracted to them because of their outward persona. But once one is close enough to understand the environment, they are quickly turned off and it is important to leave as soon as possible.

NPD leaders demonstrate insincere emotion, immature conscience, and, at times, are hypersensitive to criticism. The leader will tend to want to stifle people, with the need to have every activity perfect. Even if there is a flaw in something that, for the most part, is excellent but not perfect, the NPD leader will require that it be adjusted, even if the adjustment will lead to embarrassment for the person who is responsible for the task. The research paper, "Narcissism in the Pulpit" by M. Swanson and Stan Wilson, Ph.D., gives a chilling account of how to deal with and encounter people who demonstrate NPD tendencies. In fact, there are specific actions required but not exclusive, that can be used as a deterrent when interfacing with someone who has NPD symptoms. They are:

- Limit the listening time or the time that you spend with the NPD leader. While doing so, remember to put in place proper exit strategies.

- Limit or contain the times you praise or give support. That only serves to bolster the ego of the NPD leader.

- Contain your input and ideas beyond what is required.

- Perform mental and emotional rehearsal due to potential defenses.

- Implement self-preservation measures so that your guilt responses do not overwhelm your need to preserve who you are.

- If possible, find a Christian counselor or someone to confide in, not to gossip with, but someone who can give you guidance.

- Document as much as pertains to meetings, plan adjustments, and directional changes as they relate to your performance.

- In *Crucial Conversations: Tools for Talking When Stakes are High,*[6] when having an important conversation, please ensure there are others present besides the NPD leader—someone that they trust, but someone who can confront.

- Be proactive at all times. There is a fine line between pro-action and fear. Do not be fearful, but remember God is in control.

- During crucial interaction with the NPD leader, it is advisable that you write out all communication prior to presenting it. Ensure that you have compared and contrasted all information that will be presented to ensure you have all the details and any possible blindspots that might occur. Prepare for a chess match and have all bases covered with written responses.

The NPD leader is someone who devours experiences, people, bodies of work, sound, entertainment, books and films. They are incapable of enjoying anything because they are in constant pursuit of perfection and completeness. To that end, be prepared that during most of your time with this leader you will be exerting energy that, for all practical purposes, you would prefer not to expend. To ensure you're in good graces with this leader, you will do that for now.

Many More Disruptions

As we complete this chapter, there are innumerable troubling matters within the news. These items can all be attributed to the lack of emotional intelligence or that which emotional intelligence will be able to solve. Actions on behalf of leaders within the Church cannot be solved with one over-reaching solution. However, the role of emotional intelligence as a tool can help minimize or even eliminate situations and circumstances that cause these disruptions.

In the news we hear of church leaders who fleece their flocks; leaders who, due to emotional shortcomings in their childhoods, rely on other leaders who also lack emotional intelligence to help them develop. The end result is that leaders who lack the basics of empathy are then multiplied. There are stories related to ministers who could not control their basic sexual urges and instead end up sleeping with members of the same sex—the result being they are excommunicated from the church they themselves have founded. In recent years, we have seen the rise and fall of such persons as Jimmy Swaggart, Jim Bakker, and Ted Haggard. There are stories of priests in the Catholic Church who took advantage of naïve and unassuming children for their own sexual pleasures, and we have seen the unconscionable non-action of the Catholic Church as it relates to the abuse of these children at the hands of priests. And the list continues.

In the case of the Catholic Church, one might find Stockholm Syndrome, where the victims relate more to their abusers than with the police or even their loved ones. The victim identifies with the abuser and becomes dependent on him due to the extreme mistreatment inflicted on them, and when there is a reduction in pain, the victim becomes more grateful to the captor than for those who are coming to the rescue.

In the history of our civilization we have seen moral lapses in the churches and society at large. A statement is made quite frequently that there are two reasons why leaders fall, "Money or Honey." This is amusing, but it has such a ring of truth to it that failure to pay attention could be done at one's own peril.

There is no reason why some of these actions occur. Our society is rife with such shortcomings from church leaders as well as servant-leaders. The interesting thing is the Church has been around for thousands of years. The realm of emotional intelligence is new, so how can something new be brought in to solve the ills of an institution that has been around for millennia? It can't and shouldn't. Much like the spiritual instructions outlined in the Bible, emotional intelligence is a tool that can assist us in dealing with the temptations of daily life and can help us goodhearted, Spirit-filled,

Christ-loving, well-meaning people to be more like Jesus. In Luke 2:52, the Bible states, *"And Jesus grew in wisdom and stature, and in favor with God and men."* He grew. He matured. He was well-rounded. He understood and mastered the dimensions in which he operated—spiritual, intellectual, physical, and even the emotional. Many of the stories cited above all started with men and women who, for all intents and purposes, wanted to do the right, proper, and biblically sound thing. The end result, however, is that due to some deficiency in their emotions they did not fare well. They could have if this dimension had been understood, respected, and appreciated.

Closing the Section

1. Pause for a moment.

2. Ask God to give you insight.

3. Close your eyes and meditate for a minute; then open your eyes.

4. Pray the following: "Dear Lord, your son taught us to ask for forgiveness. Here again, as I read this chapter, I could think of all the ills that we experience in the church environment. Lord, it simply points us back to you because neither I nor anyone in the chapter is perfect. Allow these stories to draw me closer to you and to rely on you now more than ever. Grant me the ability to accept your adjustment in my life so that I can become more like you. In Jesus name. Amen."

5. Write down what God has revealed to you.

PART IV

Our Current Disposition

CHAPTER ELEVEN

THE COMPLETE YOU – 360° DIMENSION

. . . .

"Know thyself!" This is a famous phrase of the ancient Greeks. If you do not know yourself, you are not capable or able to understand others. Is it possible to know oneself? I believe it is, but the idea of knowing oneself cannot be characterized as only knowing what upsets me, what makes me sad, or what makes me cry. To know one's self means to understand the major dimensions in which we as humans operate.

Over many years in the role as chief operating officer of a mega church, I have had the opportunity to hire people and sadly enough, experience the pain of having to release some of them from employment. Over time as I gained experience in my role, I realized more and more that most individuals were released not because they weren't smart enough or because they did not have the solid spiritual foundation necessary to work in this environment. Most of the people

PHYSICAL

SPIRITUAL
An individual's relationship with his/her creator

EMOTIONAL
An individual's non cognitive capabilities to cope with his/her environment

Our Being

Our Being

INTELLECTUAL
The ability to concentrate and plan, organize material, to use words to understand, assimilate and interpret facts.

PHYSICAL

were released for an emotional deficiency. After much research and investigation, I arrived at the conclusion that we operate in the three specific dimensions of the spiritual, intellectual, and emotional. My methods of hiring people have changed from looking for individuals who are strong and sound intellectually to looking for individuals who are well-rounded. This led me to develop three specific requirements that I look for in anyone that I hire: 1) spiritual depth, 2) intellectual acuity, and 3) emotional attunement. We will discuss these three criteria later in the chapter.

Understanding these dimensions and understanding the impact these dimensions have on our lives, and realizing if we are not careful and don't adhere to the principle of knowing oneself, we could easily have a deficit in our lives that could hinder us from being who God has called us to be. Before going any further, let's take a few moments and look at each of the dimensions specifically.

Spiritual dimension

As human beings we are created to serve our Creator. Most people have devised ways and manners in order to determine what it means to serve their Creator and specifically who their Creator is. In his book, *The Purpose Driven Life*, Rick Warren states clearly that why we exist and our purpose for being here has nothing to do with us, but more to do with the Person who created us. So from a spiritual perspective, the focus in this dimension is on our relationship with our Creator. According to Pastor Warren, "You were born by His purpose and for His purpose."[1]

The spiritual dimension has to do with my seeking God, my understanding God, my getting close to God, my understanding my purpose, why I am here to serve, and to seek Him. The ultimate purpose of man is to serve the Creator. It is to serve the One whom you and I were created for. Over our lifetime, we go through many different search processes. We try to determine what our ultimate purpose is. We try to determine what school we should go to. We try to determine what boy or girl we should go out with. We try to determine the job we should take. We try to determine the best company to work for.

In the end, though, none of it matters if we have not decided in our hearts *How will I serve the one whom I was created for?* Naturally this book is not one that goes into the many aspects of how to conduct a search and ultimately how to serve God. It is a foregone conclusion in the mind of the author that you have determined God is your ultimate Creator and the One to serve. If you have not made a decision for Christ, then let me pause and deal with that.

God sent His Son Jesus into the world to forgive us of our sins. The fact of the matter is we were born as sons and daughters upon this Earth, not as righteous, God-fearing individuals, but as individuals who are lost. God loved us so much He decided that He didn't want to force us to serve Him. Instead, He decided to give us our own free will. You have a choice whether to serve Him or to deny Him. It is that simple. To serve Him means to forget your past, connect with Him today, and live the rest of your life with Him.

Jesus wants to see you become part of His Kingdom. You can accept Him this very day, this very moment because He is there, just waiting for you to accept Him as your own personal Lord and Savior. If that is your desire, just say this prayer with me, "Heavenly Father, thank you for being my Lord and Savior. God, I have done things in my past that did not represent you, that demonstrated I was far from you. Today, Lord, I ask you to come into my life. Forgive me of all my sins and be my Lord and Savior from this day forward. I thank you in Jesus' name, Amen."

This prayer demonstrates the beginning of anyone's spiritual journey. As human beings, no matter who we are, there is a yearning for a spiritual connection with our Creator. This is the spiritual yearning we all have. This yearning also demonstrates we are spiritual beings who operate in the spiritual dimension of life. This means that spirituality has to do with a decision as to whether you will serve God or serve the enemy of your soul, the devil. One way or another, you will serve God or the devil. There is no option as to whether you will serve in the spiritual dimension. You can't say, "Well, I just decided today that this spiritual dimension is not for me, so I am just going to boycott it." The spiritual dimension means you will operate in it; but how you serve in it determines your ultimate destiny—Heaven or hell.

Intellectual dimension

INTELLECTUAL

Intellect is the power of *knowing*, as distinguished from the power to feel and to will. It is the capacity for knowledge and the capacity for rational or intelligent thought, especially when highly developed. Before we can focus on the intellectual, we need to focus on the driver of the intellect, which is the brain. God gave us this wonderful organ called the brain. The brain is one of the most complex parts of the body and one of the most essential in order to function. God gave us a brain so we can think, so we can make decisions, and so we can alter our course of action based on rational thought. Each of us has a brain. It is what we use to help us to become president of the United States, a senator, or the maintenance engineer at Sears.

This dimension of life catapults us from where we are to where we want to be. It is this dimension that helps us to assess where we want to be, and with thought, decisive action, and use of the emotional component of desire, we can reach our potential.

It is with the brain we devise cognitive thought. It is with the brain we determine, with thoughts and processes, the things we should do and the things we should not do. I am not saying the brain helps us to determine right and wrong. I believe, based on our experiences, that the brain gathers factual information and assimilates that information to help us determine the directions we should take in life.

Previously, the concept of high road and low road was brought into play. High road is defined as the part of the brain that does fundamental and rational analysis to help us determine, from an analytical perspective, what we should do, how we should do it, and when. The low road, on the other hand, manages our emotions and is the center of our emotional activity.

The brain is divided into two streams—both low and high road functioning, and we will be considering the high road functioning to begin with. The human brain, from a standard perspective, is roughly three pounds in weight. The difference between man and the non-human primates is the utilization and the development of our brains over that of primates. We have the ability to process things. We have the ability to think and to speak at a high level.

For ease of discussion, the brain consists of the *neocortex*, the top layer of your brain, which is the seat of thoughts, and the *limbic* system, used in focusing on learning and memory. As humans, since we are able to think and also are able to learn and gather memory, we have the ability to gather information from past experiences, analyze it, strategize as to what is best to do in a situation, and then to move forward in a specific direction. This does not mean that other species do not do this. They do, but from a scientific perspective there is a difference between analysis leading to action versus instinct leading to action. This is what separates humans from primates.

On a simpler level, the intellectual dimension in which we operate can be considered the physical dimension. It is amazing to me that God, who created us, is a God who is also intellectual. God created our environment and us in six days and on the seventh day He rested (see Genesis 1 and 2). Specifically, God created man in His own image as Genesis 1:27 states: *"So God created man in his own image, in the image of God he created him; male and female he created them."*

I bring this point up because just as God has created us in His own image, He expects us to behave and act like Him. He has an intellect. He didn't do everything all at once. Even if it was as an example to mankind, God created specific things on specific days to advise us that we cannot and should not try to do everything all at once. If our eternal God takes time to do things, why should we not do the same and follow His example? In Genesis 1, God created things in a phased approach. Day 1: He created day and night; Day 2: He created the sky; Day 3: He created the seas, the land, and vegetation; Day 4: He created the sun, the moon, and the stars; Day 5: He created birds and living creatures of the Earth and the seas; Day 6: He created man and woman; and on Day 7: He rested.

What a great depiction of God to be used as a depiction of mankind. We are created to be like our Creator. We are created to think like Him, act like Him, and be like Him. We are created with a desire to do things—just like God. The brain allows us to process things and to create things. When we learn, when we work, when we strategize, when we do things, it is God in us urging us to create and imitate His own handiwork that He created at the beginning of time.

Over time, mankind has created tools to measure the effectiveness of humans from an intellectual standpoint. The history of Intellectual Quotient (IQ) is given earlier in the book, but basically, IQ is the ability to concentrate and plan, organize material, to use words, and to understand, assimilate, and interpret facts. There are many measures that are used to determine one's effectiveness from an intellectual standpoint. However, the Stanford-Binet IQ test is the standard measure used across the world to determine from an intelligence standpoint how effective one is.

Emotional dimension

When I became a born-again Christian, my understanding was that I was not the same. I was a new creature. I was created anew and renewed in the image of God. My early Christian experience told me that once born again, I would do the things that Jesus did; behave the way Jesus behaved; like the things that Jesus liked, and hate the things that He hated. You see the Bible states in 2nd Corinthians 5:17, *"Therefore, if anyone is in Christ, he is a new creation; the old has gone, the new has come!"* Once we are saved, we become new creatures. The old man has perished and the eternal God enters us and lives in our life. Strangely enough, though, my behavior, my attitudes, my mannerisms, and other matters crucial to the life experience of Christ did not take place immediately. You see, as a spiritual being, I had begun a journey that would require me to examine every facet of my life to be able to allow the Holy Spirit to come in and engender change. This means that my spiritual, intellectual, and emotional dimensions needed to be regenerated for His purpose, for His use, and to His liking.

Emotion, according to the Merriam-Webster dictionary is: a) obsolete: disturbance, b) excitement or the affective aspect of consciousness, feeling; a state of feeling; a conscious mental reaction (as anger or fear) subjectively experienced as strong feeling usually directed toward a specific object and typically accompanied by physiological and behavioral changes in the body.

Emotions range from feelings of anger, sadness, hopelessness, love, joy, fear, shame, or the countless associated feelings that fall into a subcategory of the ones listed above. Each of us experiences a wide range of emotions and how we handle them at times determines our destiny and our future.

Daniel Goleman, in his book, *Emotional Intelligence: Why it Can Matter More Than IQ*,[2] states that there are categories of emotions which are arranged in families, but also there are members in the specific families. For example, love is a main family; however, it has members such as acceptance, friendliness, trust, kindness, affinity, devotion, adoration, infatuation, and *agape*. Goleman goes on to state that an emotion, by his definition, refers to the feelings and their distinctive thought's psychological and biological state, and a range of propensities to act.

The point I am making is the spectrum of emotions is wide and varied, and the number of emotions we can express, given a particular situation, has a one-to-many relationship. This means for any one activity, upset, or reaction, we could have many emotions that stem from that one basic action.

So how do we define this dimension? The key to understanding this dimension is no different than the intellectual or the spiritual. We all exist in each of these dimensions. Specifically, in chapter 5, I discussed Goleman's concept of *high road and low road functioning* where high road refers to actions in the intellectual, while low road refers to actions in the emotional. As human beings we operate almost as three different and distinctive entities all wrapped up into one, and we cannot choose one over the other. This is synonymous with God being God the Father, God the Son, and God the Holy Spirit. They are three different and distinct attributes of God, but we cannot separate one attribute and consider it separate from the totality of who God is.

Likewise, in each of the three dimensions, we cannot separate our emotional function from our spiritual functioning. We, as human beings, operate in a physical universe. I am sure you have heard the question posed, "Are you a spiritual being living in a natural, physical existence, or are you a physical being living a supernatural existence?" The concept here is we are physical beings; however, we operate in the spiritual dimension, but not without incorporating emotional actions into what we do. It is not strange that the Apostle Paul in his writings mentioned that the Fruit of the Spirit (see Galatians 5:22-23) is love, joy, peace, patience, kindness, goodness, faithfulness, gentleness, and self-control. All of these attributes of the Spirit, though taken in a spiritual context, are emotional characteristics that God, in His infinite wisdom, has asked us to demonstrate as key attributes of His character. We should, therefore, try to have the character and the characteristics of God that are outlined in Galatians 5.

So how can I be a spiritual being living a physical existence with demonstrated emotional capacity? Is it possible? Or better yet, is it possible to just ignore the emotional dimension and focus on the spiritual and intellectual dimensions? I do not believe it is possible; however, in my own journey and experience within the church, I have seen where the spiritual and intellectual are given, or in some cases required, for entry, but the emotional dimension is considered a second-class member of the triad-dimensions.

We have seen and experienced where individuals with serious psychological challenges ranging from obsessive-compulsive disorder, schizophrenia, bi-polar disorder, manic-depressive disorder, etc., have joined a church. These are all serious psychological disorders that have crippled or maimed the emotional dimensions of many people. At times the Church's response to the one suffering with these problems has been to "Pray about it and you will be fine." Additionally, individuals who suffer from these types of disorders are shunned, cast aside, or otherwise made to feel like second-class citizens. I do not for a moment advocate these individuals should be able to exercise leadership roles; however, there is a stigma associated with psychological and emotional issues that the Church must come to grips with.

The emotional dimension is as real as the spiritual and the intellectual. Do you wonder why some members of the church who have been there for years still deal with emotional control, but yet are individuals who have been serving God for a long time? Do you wonder how someone can be angry or fearful and still consider themselves lifelong servants of God? Do you ever wonder how you can suffer from some emotional shortcoming, but instead of dealing with the issue, you put it on the shelf to be dealt with another time? The key is the emotional dimension will not disappear. It will not separate itself from your spiritual or intellectual self; and it will continually manifest in your life until you have dealt with it.

Most recently, I had the wonderful opportunity of coaching someone in the area of emotional intelligence. This person has been serving God for almost twenty years. Having been through a number of emotional upheavals in my life, I can quickly discern what kind of emotional shortcomings someone suffers from. In this case, the woman suffered from always trying to please people. Needless to say, when confronted with the fact that she exemplified this kind of behavior, she was offended. I met with her and her husband, at which time he told me in no uncertain terms to, "Leave the emotional out of this. This is work. I do not want emotions to be brought into this."

The thoughts that immediately came to mind were 1) God bless him, Father, because he does not quite understand what he is asking for, and 2) this individual does not have a clue as to how a human being operates. To ask for a separation of dimensions is to ask me to come to work and leave my hands and feet and just bring my torso. It is beyond impossible to separate out the emotional from your physical existence. Again, this example occurred in the church environment and the individuals making this request had been Christians for over two decades.

I am not passing judgment on them; however, it became clear to me they did not understand who they are. The behavior and sentiment expressed by the woman and her husband is common in the church. Too often, our request is, "God bless me financially (give me the intellectual qualities to make my life better) and spiritually (help me to be the best person I can be for you, Lord)." The result is that we see the problems, address them in prayer, and move on, hoping and trusting God will remove the fear, the anger,

ONE PERSON -
SPIRITUAL, INTELLECTUAL
& EMOTIONAL

the lack of self-control. In my experience, it doesn't work that way. Often, God requires us to adjust things in our emotional lives, and by adjusting these things in our emotional lives, we are then sure to improve our spiritual meters. Coming to grips with the emotion is where God operates and changes us supernaturally. God requires us to embrace the complete us, change the complete us for His joy and the greater uplifting of His Kingdom. It is not strange He should tell us we are new creatures. We are new creatures in our living (spiritually), our thinking (intellectually), and our expression (emotionally).

Note To Reader: Chapters 12 through 17 are case studies. They contain actual cases of individuals who serve in church and social sectors, but have emotional challenges that affected their work in both positive and negative ways. You may pick or choose which case you read or you can go directly to chapter 18, which focuses on the things we should do, as individuals and groups, to incorporate emotions and emotional intelligence into our existence.

CHAPTER TWELVE

Sandra Karmen: Independence and Failure in Self-Discovery

. . . .

Sandra Karmen is a divinity school graduate, and with her family she immigrated to the United States from St. Kitts in the Caribbean in 1989. She is the founder of a non-profit group dedicated to helping women and youth develop leadership capabilities.

It was years after school and after ministering that she found her vocation. "I found out I was very passionate about…working primarily with young women, and about helping them to really focus their lives in finding their passion," she says.

A divorced woman without children, Sandra came to heightened awareness of the unexpressed feelings all around us, and the value of articulating them through life experience, which is fuel for her career. The path she has traveled has led to questioning God about His purpose, and what to make of the often difficult or hard-to-understand life experiences people pass through.

"What I've seen tells me," she says, "that my emotions are there for a purpose and I have a choice as to what I can do with them. Oftentimes we are not told what to do and we never learn how to deal with that. I think our emotions are related closely to our spirituality. Why doesn't somebody teach us?" she asks.

A woman of thoughtful observation, practiced remembrance, and shared emotion with family and friends, she feels like she is on the way to becoming more perceptive, and becoming a person living a fuller life. Part of that process involved realizing the impact of the missing men in her life: a father she never knew, a beloved grandfather who died before she became a teen, a disconnected brother, and a husband she lost through mutually misplaced priorities.

Moments in life that others might long forget remain vivid and meaningful for her. They provide a source of reference allowing her to understand behavior and feeling more fully, and to help those around her register a deeper sense of meaning where others might throw up their hands, ask "Why?" and fail to see even the hope of a flickering answer take shape.

Beginnings

Her formative memories began in the Caribbean. She cherishes thoughts of her days there with older twin sisters and a younger brother. Another brother came along years later. "That's where my foundation is—my family, my friends, my teachers—the people who had the most significant impact on me." Her father died when she was a toddler.

Still, she remembers a strong sense of family and community and the constant involvement of grandparents, who filled in while her mother and stepfather worked away in Guantanamo Bay, Cuba. "I grew up in a very community-oriented environment," she says. "So it was kind of a village-type atmosphere and I was very involved in the church…Everybody just cared about everybody. And we were all so connected as kids that it never gave me any chance to feel like I was missing something."

Although she rarely saw her stepfather, father-absence was no issue for her while she was little. Her grandfather filled the gap, staying close, telling stories, and playing marbles with her and her siblings.

It was only after she was in her teens, after the family moved to the United States and years after her grandfather had died, that she began to feel troubled about her father. "People who were close to my mom would say " 'Oh, she's just like her father.' " Relatives said he was apparently loud, assertive, and sociable, and they saw those things in her. Those observations lit a fire…"What was he like…how did he die… what happened?" But because her mother was reluctant to discuss him, answers came slowly. "You know, he loved you and we had a great relationship." She got comments like, "You know, he loved you and we had a great relationship," but little was mentioned about him in the family. It was also during her teens that the weight of the value of what she had had with her deceased grandfather began to take hold.

"I almost felt like his favorite. My family would joke and say that." As he lay on his deathbed, family members called her in. "I remember his last words to me… 'Just remember that I will always love you and no matter where you go I'm going to always be with you.' And those are my last memories of my grandfather."

For a long time the quality of her relationship with him eliminated any need to consider her own fatherlessness. The loss of her grandfather was hard, she says. "I think one of the things I always played over and over in my head was, 'Just remember that I'm always going to be with you.' " She recalls their special relationship and spending more time with him than any of her other family members. The depths of grief came later.

By age sixteen, she was in the United States, a new place with new schoolmates, and the close family connection she'd felt was less certain. It was then she felt the importance of that one central relationship in her life, her grandfather. "He was the one male figure I felt completely safe with… very affirming. So I grieved a lot."

Trust and respect, she realizes today, were critical internal issues for her. Her grandfather, a person she felt she could talk to about anything, was the one person she found she could rely on when as a young girl an otherwise trusted uncle began making sexually inappropriate comments to her in private.

"I can remember someone in my family saying to me about my uncle, 'Well, he's a very friendly guy.'" But her grandfather was different. "He understood me. He didn't try to justify, he didn't try to invalidate what it was I was saying. It was just the fact that if it made me uncomfortable, then that's it."

Trust had also been an issue with her stepfather. "There was something about him that always made me uncomfortable and I said that to my mom. 'I don't like the way he looks at me, I don't like the way he compliments me.' …'Don't talk to me that way. I don't feel it's appropriate for you to talk to me that way. I think you should talk to me more…like a dad.'" It was, she says, quite the opposite of the way her grandfather acted and treated her.

"I'm thinking maybe a part of me is looking for my grandfather's type, you know, authoritative—you can trust me, you can talk to me—but you also understood he was the voice in the family."

Her early experiences with males were easygoing. Mother allowed no one-on-one dating, and group fun was the only sanctioned way of getting to know boys. "It's like when we had a meal in our house and my girlfriends and all the guys who hung out with our group would all be at the house, with everybody eating and laughing and playing games."

Her teen rebel period hit when she was seventeen or eighteen. Now in the United States, her stern mother was confronted with the reality that Sandra was growing up and would do what she wanted to. In the end, "She was okay just as long you kept everything out in the open."

Assimilation into a new country was difficult, even though she calls herself a quick adapter. "I had no frame of reference…in St. Kitts I learned Caribbean history. I knew nothing about American history. I didn't know who the first president was and I didn't care." But she engaged and soon joined a debating team. "I got involved. In my first week of school I walked in the office and asked the guidance counselor, 'Do you have a debating team and…how do I join?' My first priority was to get involved. On the other hand, my sisters were completely and totally different; it took them a lot longer to get into any activities. My brothers followed my lead. Whatever I did, my brothers somehow felt like they had to live up to."

Responsibility

Over the next year, in one way or another, she acquired a leadership role among her siblings, particularly with her brothers. It was a telephone call between two and three in the morning from a brother that first brought the importance of that role into sharp relief.

Her youngest brother was wandering a street some distance away, not in trouble, but feeling lonely and lost. She remembers the alarm she felt. She says he wanted to talk about the pressure he was feeling to perform well in school. He said he felt he had no one else to open up to and it seemed no one else in the family had problems. And it seemed to help him when she assured him he was not alone, and that one way or another everyone hurts.

Another time she made an impact on her brothers without trying. They had come to take pictures of her at a conference. "I was speaking. It was a women's conference …and I began to open up about my divorce and as I started to open up I started crying. I was very vulnerable with my audience." She says her youngest brother said how much that did for him. She says it struck her when he said how he appreciated that for the first time in his life he realized I hurt and I was hurting."

Vulnerability was clearly a problem her brothers grappled with. The brother who had called Sandra had been a high school football player and had enjoyed some success. But he was now struggling after losing a football scholarship due to academic difficulties.

"He was talking to me and saying the pressure was so overwhelming. Then he said to me 'I'm tired of putting on a face like I'm okay, Sandra, when I'm not.' I remember him crying on the phone and saying, 'My friends come to me, everybody comes to me and tells me what's going on with them, their problems, and I'm always laughing. I'm always smiling but I just can't do it anymore. I feel like I can't do it anymore.'

"I remember those words, because it really sounded like someone on the verge of trying to check out of here. And I remember how eye-opening that was and, not doing it intentionally, but just being able to give him the freedom and saying, 'Mario, you can do what you need to do, you don't have to stay.' It was like giving him permission and saying it doesn't mean that you're failing. 'You're going through other things in your life and you're going through a major crisis with some things you have experienced at school with football, with the scholarship and everything being lost and taken away.' So he was breaking under the pressure and I remember him clearly telling me that."

The experience taught her to meet people on their emotional level. She agrees that often we tell people to "Move on; it's not all right to fail," when sometimes we ought to be able to *give permission* to let go of something.

In the end, "He felt like a big, a huge burden was lifted off his shoulders. And eventually he did come home and took the semester off, and went to the county college. In fact, he did very well and really came back.'

"I think that was a valuable lesson for all of us. And I think primarily for me and my other brother because we are the two driven ones…It made me look inward to understand the effect…my mask had on other people. I didn't realize the impact my actions or how I dealt with things had on someone who is looking to me for some kind of direction.

"It also allowed me to go inward and examine myself and ask whose dream did I want Mario to live? Since then I've had to pull back to allow him to navigate his own path…I had my dream for him, but I realized it really isn't about me; it's not about my development. It's about him. He will never fully grow, develop, learn, and blossom into the person we want if we're trying to dictate his every move. So I learned a lot from that."

She says she realizes she sounds and acts at times like her brother's mother. She says that learning and adapting to a new culture and language was difficult for her mother and stepfather so, "I kind of stepped up to the plate and took on that role.

"I would go to the parent-teacher meetings with him …if I saw him at school and he wasn't performing well, I would pull him from the school. I would say, 'Okay, Mom and Dad…Mario is not doing well here and we have to figure out something.' So for a long time I did play more of a mother than a sister in his life."

The weight of responsibility eventually gave way to a measure of resentment toward her mother and stepfather. "Because I felt like they weren't doing what they were supposed to be doing. And yet I felt like I couldn't drop the ball." She also felt guilt over wanting her own life.

"I had done it so long it…was difficult to pull away…I didn't want to abandon my family." But she says she nearly broke at times from the weight of unspoken expectations. The weight, she realizes now, may have been in large part self-imposed.

"Maybe I'm putting the pressure on myself," she says. Culturally, she feels that in her place in the family, she might have been seen as a failure if she had not done as she did when the need was there. She agrees the question exists and ought to be answered: What is driving me?

Breaking up

It was, in part, some of that responsibility that led to her divorce. Speaking of her former spouse she says, "I think he became a little bit overwhelmed with my family dynamic, especially where my brothers and I were concerned…I did feel like I needed to do for them what needed to be done. That became an issue in our marriage."

She says her husband had a good relationship with his family, but he came from a Haitian culture that did not require the kind of involvement she felt. She tells of one night when she found a note he'd written in a Bible, consisting of five words: *Family, God, Church, Friends, Me.* It wasn't until they entered counseling that she realized he had listed what he saw as her priorities, in order. "He said, 'I am last in everything that you do. Everything else is first.'

"He didn't feel like I wanted to be a wife to him… At times he would say, 'Sandra, you don't love me. It is very difficult.' And then upon closer examination, I could clearly see why he would come to that conclusion...I spent hours at a time with my family and I guess, at that time for someone who was newly wed, it didn't occur to me it was an issue.

"Over time he began to be resentful and came to a place where he was so angry that his anger was unbearable ...And at that moment what was probably a wake-up call for me was probably too late for him."

She says on the surface she believed that she'd followed the biblical concept of leaving father and mother, and cleaving to her husband, but "...in looking back I really hadn't. Because I didn't see my family as intrusive or taxing or demanding." She recalls a night her young brother called. She dressed in the early morning hours, left her husband, and drove to see him, not realizing it was a small matter that could have waited. And in that recollection she realizes that her internal pressure to respond was a more powerful force than any need articulated by her family.

After the divorce, Sandra decided to move. She gave herself permission to move away from her family. "And what it taught me was your family does pretty well without your having to be there after all...I recognized I had to go; it was okay for me to go."

Going also affected her church life. "Actually, I withdrew. I think I said I was going on a sabbatical." Her former husband felt her involvement with the church ran too deep. "He really felt I gave too much, but I didn't want to be guilty of not helping." Sandra had a lot of food for thought to work through, and admitted she did not have all the answers she might have earlier assumed she did.

For a while, she thought God had failed her. "I said to God, 'I don't understand this and it's doesn't make sense to me and it's not fair. I've given my life and I've done everything I think you've required of me...my theology is just not working for me.' "

But it was the combination of belief and emotion that was falling short. "They weren't congruent, they weren't working." She felt blocked, unable to fully express her emotions to most people, including friends and pastoral mentors in church. "They weren't working," she says.

She withdrew, finding solace with one trusted friend she felt she could open up to. "I knew there were people who would want to be there for me. But I didn't feel like people were necessarily available; I thought people were too busy and someone could say, yes, they wanted to listen to me, but they wouldn't necessarily want to hear it all again."

It was a year before she says she began talking to God again. And it was the death of her grandmother that opened a new set of doors for her.

She arrived at the hospital after a church service. Her cell phone had been off and by the time she turned it on outside church and received the call, she learned that her grandmother had died. Her entire family had been there for hours. And by the time she arrived, they were gone.

She walked past a nurses' station into the now quiet room. Alone with her, she recalled her grandmother had been at her wedding and it was the only granddaughter wedding she'd ever seen.

It occurred to her to sing to her grandma. "I sang one of her favorite songs for her, *Closer Than a Brother My Jesus is to Me*, and I said, 'Goodbye, Granny' and that was it." And in leaving she realized she was the last in her family with her grandmother on that day, an event in her life utterly symmetrical with her own history.

Resolution

Thinking of the events that led to her divorce, and of her grandparents, she felt a kind of comfort and wholeness. "I was going to be okay. And then I thought about their faith and their history.

"I kind of came to the end of myself. I thought 'Okay, God, you're still God, you're still sovereign. I still don't have it figured out, but I remember one of my favorite Bible verses...*I will never leave you nor forsake you.*' And ...that's kind of what got me back on my journey. It's a resolution for me and it shifted my thinking a little about spirituality and things I've learned."

She says she realizes that before an infinite God, "I can't always figure out or have all the answers to your next move or your plan for my life. But I do believe that as much as I think my grandmother and my grandfather loved me, I believe just as much that you love me even more."

She told her pastor once, she says, that people in her church were too friendly and there was too much love to cope with at the time. But now, she realizes she needed that display from God to help her connect emotionally, rather than pull away. People, she realizes, are both transparent and authentic at times. Understanding, she realizes, "is something with this love thing."

What was happening was an unexpected lesson from God in understanding oneself and others. She has come to understand emotions are like pain is to our bodies: telling us something is going on that we need to respond to, but we have a choice.

"I have a choice. I don't have to react; I can act upon it. For example, in Ephesians 4:26 it's so clear where Paul says, be angry but "*In your anger do not sin.*" That tells me my emotions, like those of everyone around me, are there for a purpose and I have a choice of what to do with them."

Questions to Ponder

• Have you captured the main theme in Sandra's story?
• What does the role of culture play in one's spiritual growth if pride is a prevalent dynamic in your upbringing?

- If you discovered a note, "Family, God, Church, Friends, Me" in your spouse's Bible, what action needs to be taken immediately?

- Is it possible to confuse consistent and optimal serving in the church, which is detrimental to actually serving oneself and family?

Takeaways

- Self-awareness affects self-regard and self-actualization. A shortage in self-awareness will lead to actions that become detrimental to those around you—and could affect your marriage, your relationships, and those you truly love.

- Pride affects impulse control, which affects stress management. Failure to address or acknowledge shortcomings can result in reactions based on low impulse control, which could result in highly stressful situations for the individuals and the environment.

- Culture is not destiny. Emotional shortcomings resulting from cultural lack do not predestine one to cultural behaviors. When one becomes a believer, all former behaviors are disowned—hence, cultural behavior should not be a deterrent or barrier to spiritual development and fulfillment.

CHAPTER THIRTEEN

HELEN MARTIN: PSYCHOLOGICAL DISORDER AND RECOVERY

· · · ·

Helen Martin is a forty-something native of the Bay Ridge section of Brooklyn, New York. She grapples with mental instability and unreality, deep-rooted since a childhood exposed to violence in her home and resulting in emotional self-protection. She has in recent years sought God, attempted suicide, undergone therapy, and has been treated with anti-psychotic medications as a result of her victimization all those decades ago.

A middle child with two brothers, she relishes the memory of her early creative ability, a gift that would become an important lifeline for her. "I used to speak into tape recorders and read stories," she says, "and I had a very strong love for drawing. In grammar school I was very much into reading and creating different things, even if it meant making things from multi-colored construction paper...I was also a writer at a very young age."

Her creative talents would serve her as a means to create a fantasy shell she could turn to as a buffer when life at home became difficult.

She loves aspects of her kindergarten memories. "I had a wonderful kindergarten teacher named Ms. Potts. We used to call her 'Pots and Pans.' She was a wonderful teacher because she actually empowered me as a young child to really create."

She describes a neighborhood tucked away near a busy highway overpass, a shuffled and rich variety of homes and mom-and-pop businesses reflecting an array of cultures. Her family lived in a double-block home. She remembers a Greek family across the street, an Irish florist nearby, Italian families and businesses, and people of Arabic descent. And lots of kids.

She remembers a "...candy store where we used to buy bubble gum for two cents. We had the deli down the street and a little pharmacy on the corner. It was a really quaint little place." And even with its barking dogs and the noise of occasional nighttime teen drag races nearby, it was safe.

"As little kids, we used to lay down blankets right there in the driveway where the cars would come from our backyard and...play with our Barbie dolls and our Ken dolls, and build little houses."

She and her brothers were close-knit. "We were close, intelligent, and we were all very well-spoken kids. We loved to play together, to joke around, and we liked to just do things that kids would do, but we had a certain deeper connection that was ingrained and developed from a very young age."

Struggles between their parents cemented their bond. Each parent, she recalls, was responsible for anger, argument, and physical confrontation stemming from what she calls bitterness and baggage each had brought to their marriage. To survive, she and her brothers played a continual game of emotional chess. "You had to figure out how you could get to a baseball game without letting them know you were going to the baseball game, because they, being absorbed in their problems, wouldn't take you."

Physical violence, verbal abuse, and depression—
along with the occasional visit from the police—were a
normal part of life and triggered continual plotting and
planning with her brothers. "Are we going to have to
walk to school or are we going to have to count on going
to our friend's down the road at the flower shop because
their own dad would drive them in the van?" Describing
why the help was needed was a problem; it was always a
question of what to say to hide the pain.

Because no one she knew at her age seemed to be
going through the kinds of trials her parents created, she
found no one she could relate to. Her creative instincts
kicked in, and she began to build what she today refers
to as onionskins around her—layers of alternative reality.

"Being extremely creative and living a sort of fairy tale
life in my mind, I would create stories. It became like a
mystical, fantasy thing." She says she described her home
life in glowing terms to friends, "…to create a false sense of
intimacy so that others would think I had a healthy life."

The reality was she was learning to deceive. "It was
a sad time," she says. As a child, she says, "…you were
supposed to love life, you were to love putting your Barbie
dolls out, you were to love sharing with the other kids,
you were to love cracking your bubble gum, you know, all
the things that childhood was supposed to mean. I knew
in my gut as a child there had to be a way I could get to
that place of just not fantasizing about it. But I also knew
it would take a long time."

In fact, even now that time has not yet come. "It's
the story of my life," she says, using the word *torment* to
describe her journey. "I no longer want to depict a fantasy
life to others." She has committed considerable energy to
finding peace through church and God.

"I don't know why I had to portray this fantasy thing all my life, but I do know that if I can just be me and not paint anything mystical, I am finding every day there is a great sense of the joy and contentment I was supposed to have as a child."

She needs, she says, "...to simply unpeel the onion skins of the pain that was around my body, my mind, and my soul. Everything needed to be unpeeled and He would be there all along. But the tormenting part was when this was going to end. Why am I still feeling this way? It's now two weeks, and now a year and I'm still peeling and peeling and peeling and peeling...but I always have the ray of hope that it's getting better."

But the layers of her onionskins are anything but thin or easy to get through.

Depths of Damage

That Helen's world is complicated might be a vast understatement. She recognizes people she meets sometimes have negative reactions to her. "I will admit I do things differently and I am very, very different. I could say so many things about myself that are sometimes odd or even unique."

A chaotic childhood fed her psychological problems. At the age of eight, she began pulling her hair out, a compulsive mental disorder that results in permanent damage. She says that reactions from other children were cruel. "Sometimes," she says, "the whispers were loud like thunder. They pierced my soul.

"I wear beautiful silk scarves now every day of my life," she says. She is always conscious of stares, and continually wonders at people's reactions. She has allowed some people to think she is undergoing chemotherapy, although in recent days she has been more transparent.

"I have found over the past year telling people the fact that I have a disorder that's not cancer—something I have not been able to understand and society has not been able to put its finger on. It's another disorder and it actually is a form of self-inflicting pain. Do I understand it? No. Did it hurt me? Yes. I'm sure it hurt the people who are close to me, like my family."

She says she believes that as they meet her, many people will see her as courageous. "I truly believe," she says, "people are drawn to my difference. I ask God, 'Why do I have to pull my hair sometimes?' I don't understand it, but as far as other people are concerned, it's their choice how they relate to me."

Between breaks in violence, her parents substituted things that children desire for affection. She, in turn, essentially bought friends with a bounty of playthings. "My parents used material things and possessions to convey their love to me. I always was the little girl on the block who not only had the rabbit fur coat, but I had every Barbie doll and every Ken doll and accessory that you could think of."

She says, "I didn't care if you took my Barbie doll home with you. I didn't care if you took two of them or three of them. Take the Barbie house because I knew I could get another one and I knew it didn't mean to me what it meant to you because I had an overabundance. So when they played with me they played, honestly, on my terms."

This sad bartering of things in exchange for company bred ugliness. "Children can be malicious, they can be jealous. Their families couldn't afford these things. I was the only girl like me. These kids had brothers and sisters and their parents couldn't afford buying them Barbie dolls every Christmas. So they began to take my things and I would let them, for lack of a better term, abuse me in that sense. I wanted them to accept me, and I saw my toys were just material goods. What I wanted to get from them, I think and normally so, was the sense of acceptance. Like I was a part of the kids on 69th Street."

But no amount of toys-for-affection bartering could make up for what was wrong at home. There, a normal love relationship between one's mother and father included violent sex. Close proximity to that, in a sense, crippled her.

"In my home," she says, "the intimacy between a man and a woman, a father and a mother, was always bathed in… violent intimacy." She says lustful intimacy was imposed on one partner or the other, but was generally initiated by her father. She does not say if she was ever abused.

"Oddly," she says, "children really don't understand at a young age, anyway, but I got to see both sides of it." As a young woman her relationships with men were clearly affected. She says as much as she wanted to see life clearly, to have known the "pure" enjoyment of being a child, she "…now has this picture of what mom and dad were doing and how violent it was." She found herself attracted to men who would, she says, "…display harsh behavior toward me instead of genuine affection." She says she came to associate harsh lovemaking with genuine satisfaction, something she admits to knowing is "crazy and distorted.

"In order to feel emotion, I needed to feel pain, so I equated what I saw from back in my childhood at a very young age with actual love."

Digging Out

Helen attempted to find therapy over the years, which took her to a psychotherapist in uptown Manhattan and through therapy groups elsewhere. "I had to have peace," she says. Finally, she sought out a counselor specializing in spiritual dynamics at a time she equates to a spiritual awakening.

"I knew I needed someone who had some... understanding of biblical principles. I just knew there was a need for me to have something that was not trendy." She brought along her current man-friend and, curiously, asked him to describe her problem. "I just asked him... 'Would you please tell so-and-so what I need from an intimacy standpoint?' And he was very clear with her about the details of how I needed to have some form of rough intimacy or even just unkind words or gestures.

"I had always needed some form of a savior. I don't like to be facetious, because although Jesus Christ is my Lord and Savior, I needed a savior whether it was a robot from Madison Avenue who's going to come and rewire me, or an actual therapist.

"I needed something in my life. I hadn't been to therapists throughout my childhood, but I saw a lot of them in my teen years. I would search them out; out of this hunger to just understand why I was the way I was—why I thought the way I did, why I pulled my hair out, what was driving me. I knew I needed someone to come and save me. I just knew it was time, and then I heard about this thing called 'having a relationship with Jesus Christ.'

"This is the Jesus I read about in the Bible as a little child, the children's Bible, the white children's Bible. I used to read it and read into the tape recorder because I loved the parables. Back then I didn't know what these things were all about, but I knew Jesus was a kind soul riding on His donkey.

"So I asked Him to be my Lord and Savior. When I came to Him I told Him, 'I'm coming to you because I need peace.' That was it; I needed peace from this world of torment…so that's why I started. I needed someone to save me. So I chose that route over a professional therapist."

Still, answers did not come. "Honestly, it just created another war in my mind. It just created another war and another level of torment," she says. "He was the King of Peace, I accepted Him into my heart, but the fact of the matter is the urge to pull hair did not stop, the view of myself as being a person who sometimes was anxious and full of guilt—false, true, healthy, or distorted—was still there."

What she did gain was a sense of hope. After a few months, she began to see her problems through a different lens. She began to believe "I was living in sin. I was sleeping with this man in an unhealthy way…because of my own needs, unhealthy needs," she says. "I began to see when I started unpeeling the onion skin, I didn't have to sleep with someone to really feel alive. I didn't have to be treated in a violent manner or a hurtful manner and feel pain to feel comforted."

She also seems to have acquired a sense of patience. "God makes all things beautiful in His time," she says. And in that awareness she believed she'd found the direction she could build on. "The development of my relationship with Father God was becoming more of something solid that I knew I needed to develop," she says.

Helen says she needed structure and advice she could trust, because her lack of emotional connectedness essentially robbed her of a dependable sense of reality and proportion. "I couldn't connect with Him fully so I took baby steps. I just grew in my desire to want to relate with Him." She thanks God for "the glimpse of hope that was in my heart as a child," because most people ultimately had let her down.

She says she could not talk to anyone about "why I felt I had to pull a hundred hairs out of my head the night before…they thought I was some crackpot who belonged in Belleview Hospital. I began to see I couldn't really count on anyone. I couldn't develop trust with anyone. There were very few people to have confidence in."

As a young person seeking solace among churchgoers, she found little help. "I would rather go to a bar at that time than to tell them I didn't know why I had such an urge to hurt myself. How could you reconcile that with another youth group member?"

Helen says they were incapable of understanding. "It's the story of my life," she says. Those she encountered kept her at a distance. " 'She's the one who had, you know, the bald spots,' " she says.

At another church, she found it impossible to connect with the upscale BMW and Bentley-driving, filet mignon crowd. "There was something inside of me that said this must be a cult or something." She left in favor of another church. "It was a very doctrine-based, multi-cultural church and I felt really good there." She found the support of elder women there "who necessarily didn't understand the actual details of the pain such as trichotillomania (the compulsion to pull out one's hair), but they knew the power of God." She says she found true acceptance. "They knew the Father God, so they would talk to me with such strength and…their spirits would bolster my spirit."

Still, because the church and her workplace were far apart, she eventually left. "I remember getting on the train and there was a very strong impression in my spirit, one I never felt before, that God was communicating to me inwardly that it was time for me to go. And this is exactly how He gave me the words: 'It's time to sever the umbilical cord.'

"It was time for me to get out of Brooklyn." And so she did, moving to New Jersey, aware that with her emotional problems, "you will always take them with you; you need to deal with them." But, she says, "I knew enough to pray and to ask God to guide me to an apartment complex that would not be far from a church that was doctrinally sound."

Sitting at the back of the church, she recalls an unsettling moment when a minister spotted her and called her to the front. "He said, 'I see a cloud...of darkness, a cloud of heaviness around you,' and he said God was going to '...give me an emotional and psychological transplant and He was bringing me into a place where I would meet people who would genuinely care for me and that in God's eye I was a rose.' I remember that day and how beautiful it was," she says.

But rather than find a new sense of happiness, she felt isolation. "Something psychologically transpired...it was very dark and I just bottomed out and I was not able to go to work. I stopped showering; I stopped putting on makeup. When I did go to work, I was totally oblivious to anything, unable to accomplish very much."

She asked for help at church. "I didn't realize how severe the depression had become. It was a chemical imbalance that was so intense I can't even recount it. It was in my eyes, it was piercing and dark. So they flew me out to California. I went to a clinic there for two weeks. I was on suicide watch and they had to put me on high levels of anti-depressants."

She recalls talking to other patients, encouraging them. "I didn't even realize that in the midst of it all that this was a gift...Part of the gift of who God has made me to be is to encourage and to bring hope to others, even while I was in the midst of my turmoil.

"When I left there I was chemically regulated. I was on a lot of medication, sometimes twenty pills a day. They had me on anti-psychotic medication and every drug you could think of. I was seeing a psycho-pharmacologist."

She says she realizes the drugs helped her to focus, but could not fix her problems. "God," she says, "knew I needed to feel my emotions. I didn't want to be medicated. I wanted to understand and I wanted to get better and get healed so that I could really bring hope to others."

Happily, a strong support group in her new church helped. "The support group was awesome. I remember for two years straight I would go there every Thursday night and slam my hand on the desk because they were so good."

Unfortunately, spiritual assistance was not enough. There was still a disconnect. "They must have thought I was insane," she says. "They threw more Scripture at me with their limited understanding of spiritual, emotional, and psychological connectivity," she says, careful to point out that compassion was never a problem.

"I couldn't divulge the damage and need for another kind of help in the intimate environment that was under the auspices of that church's support group. It disturbed me; but I needed that place." She also needed empathy, she says .

Failure of the Church?

She says she knows she was in a healthy place, but points out, "You have to remember the physical aspect too. They tried what they were capable of doing." She describes the emotion of receiving a card from her pastoral team for sharing the pain and the deliverance she'd come to see through the ministry. But, she says, "I sat and wept over the card."

"I can't give credit where credit is not due and I'm doing a disservice to you and your healing—you *are* bringing healing to the nations—if I continue to sit in this environment and say, 'Oh, praise the Lord, I don't suffer with depression anymore.' I could just put my wig back on my head and make you think I have a full head of hair. But I'm not putting the wig back on my head and I'm taking a stand for people like myself and others who sit in pews or are up on the pulpit and have so much pain. "

She says that ultimately she cannot blame others for the progress she has been unable to make. "I am the one who is responsible to my Creator. I take responsibility, I have been taking it, and I'm ready to come out of the closet. I would rather others see me for the broken person I am."

She agrees her heart hurts because of the lack of connectedness to the church. "His Spirit," she says, "can bring us through; we're the vessels...I will be the one to exit from the institution called the church if it means it's to follow wholeheartedly after God.

"I believe I'm a change agent and I've been commissioned by Christ just like He commissions all of us as His children...

"I'm going to learn to be the little girl who mom wanted to buy a piano for. At three years of age, my mother wanted to buy a piano for me and because I was very angry I told her I didn't want a piano. But you know," she says, "I want the piano at forty-four." She says she will "watch what God will do.

"I can do whatever God commissions me to do and I can bring these pieces of drama from my life to the forefront. It may not initially change or He will do what He needs to do with it, but I'm going out there with the raw deal—the truth of my life. God's Word doesn't go out without it bearing fruit. The rain falls on the just and the unjust and we move on."

Questions to Ponder

- Have you captured the main theme in Helen's story?

- Is serious psychological disorder an impediment or a significant foundation to spiritual success?

- How do anger, argument, and physical confrontation of parents affect the emotional and spiritual growth of a believer?

- How does emotional connectedness affect growth and progress in the service of God?

Takeaways

- Bi-polar disorder/manic depression, trichotillomania, and other psychological disorders are prevalent in the Church (as well as in society as a whole), but they are not an impediment to being used by God.

- A chaotic childhood can severely harm one psychologically and emotionally. Courageous leadership is to utilize your shortcomings for the growth and development of others.

- Emotional limitation is not destiny. The shortcomings that you were born with, from an emotional standpoint, do not determine your overall success or failure. Harnessing and admitting failure is the platform for success in the execution of ministry.

CHAPTER FOURTEEN

REED ORTENZ:
SELF (ESTEEM AND DISCOVERY)

. . . .

Reed Ortenz is forty-two years old, originally from northern Washington, married sixteen years, with three teenaged children, two girls and a boy. He and his family lived in the Northwest and Tennessee, then came to New York from Washington in 2001, when he took a job with Trinity Evangel Church.

"At the time I had spent nearly twenty-two years in television, on and off, working broadcast and non-broadcast jobs. Part of that time, I was working a management job which brought me here into another management position. But the church itself is the reason why I came out to New York," Reed says, "a place where cultural change still is an issue.

"It's high tension, fast-paced, and high volume... intense. Even when we go back—we regularly go back to Washington and Montana where my wife's parents live and visit during the summer for a week or two—we can feel the difference. And then when we come back east, we get within half an hour of New York, and we can literally feel, physically feel, a change from the Northwest. So it usually takes us a week or two to reacclimate back into this whole rat race. It's quite something else."

Reed says that he and his wife are still adjusting and are gaining the wisdom of perspective. "When I lived in Tennessee, they thought I was crazy. They could see I was intense and uptight, so it just depends on what part of the country you come from.

"Our children were young enough so it didn't really affect them that much at the time. Six years ago my youngest was just going into kindergarten. Now he's going into the sixth grade. So, they were young enough that they...pretty much went with the flow."

Today, he says, he and his wife have helped their children avoid being consumed by the negatives of a more aggressive cultural environment. "Our children are in most respects homebodies. They like being with family. My wife and I are young at heart, so we keep things interesting for them and they like being around us.

"They spend a significant amount of time back in the northwest. Really, since we've been out here in the east, they go back to Washington for two months and spend time with our parents. In a lot of ways, they are very well balanced and are exposed to a lot of things that other kids have not been exposed to. They can pretty much hang with anyone from the Amish community to New York City folks and everything in between. We have exposed them to a lot of things, even some things I was not exposed to. They love going into the city, but we had Amish neighbors for a period of time and they could relate to them or learned how to relate to them. For the most part, they are pretty well adjusted. They are your typical teenagers, but...it's tough."

Reed agreed that adolescents are growing up faster than ever and have little time for enough childhood experiences to develop. He reflected on that and how he grew up.

"I didn't accept Christ until I was eighteen years old. So I pretty much went through all those teenage years being a wild man and being exposed to a lot of things I thought were pretty normal, like drugs, sex, and rock-n-roll, for the most part.

"There were two things that rocked my world my children don't have to deal with at all. One, I was exposed to some sexual activity at a very young age, in kindergarten. Because of that for some reason, in fact even to this day I can't tell you why, but I had sexual contact with girls at that age. Never penetration, of course, just exploratory things, but it affects you. You don't know what you are doing, and that followed me. It opened up a whole sexual avenue I had to deal with—pornography. I also had to deal with being relatively promiscuous in high school. There were guys a lot more promiscuous than I was, by far, but I think I started with more baggage than a lot of guys my age did."

A second traumatic experience occurred in junior high. "I was in the school band and at the time that was, in the eyes of bullying classmates, a gay thing, a faggish thing to do. I was singled out and picked on and rejected right through high school. And that probably affected me more profoundly than anything and I spent more time working through it.

"That level of rejection really affected my confidence. It destroyed me emotionally…for a long, long period of time. And my parents didn't know how to deal with it. So they ignored the whole problem and they were not very lovey, touchy." He says he never heard his parents say they loved him, something he attributes to their upbringing. "No question, it took me years to work my way through." Reed says he eventually sought counseling and it helped.

"It hit me the hardest when I was in high school and college, where I was depressed a lot. I struggled with a lot of anxiety and lack of self-confidence. I was pretty destroyed from rejection. I would try to find fulfillment in sexual relations because of it. So I just fueled the fire.

"Then I got saved when I was eighteen and God did a lot in my life at that time. But at the same time, God touches your life and certain things are miraculous. You get saved; you quit smoking. You get saved; maybe you stop being depressed. But when you go through certain other things, I have learned God sometimes allows you to walk them out. It is a progression over a long period of time.

"One, I think you are able to speak into other people's lives when you experience something over a longer period of time. Sometimes you are forced to work through things on your own and other times the answers are just divine. You don't really understand why God would allow you to experience something or delay the healing for a long period of time. So I've been in and out of counseling. I started in college. I really struggled. I struggled with who I was, where I was going, what was my purpose in life, and where and how did I fit in. I didn't understand who I was."

Reed recalls that a feeling of aloneness and of secrets hidden from his parents haunted him.

"You're not really sure what you're doing. You just know something feels good and so you are driven by that motivation. But you have no clue as to how it affects you. It wasn't until many years after I got saved that I really understood the impact pornography and promiscuity had on my life. I needed counseling and talking through it to get healing in that area. As a child, you have no idea of the impact. No clue whatsoever.

"It affects you for a lifetime as far as I'm concerned. It's like being an alcoholic. For the rest of your life, taking another drink is a problem. I'm not tempted so much in my marriage, but I do have to control what I think, what I allow myself to see, what I allow myself to take in. I love my wife and I've never really had a problem in that area. When I'm in a relationship I'm very committed to the relationship. I've never struggled with having affairs, but it's always been a struggle not to allow certain thoughts to enter my mind. I don't dwell there very long. I try to remove myself.

"For the most part, I just either pray it through, or through time I've learned not to allow it to affect me. It's through many, many mistakes you learn these things. Eventually, it's like Moses—you can only go around the mountain so many times."

Reed says he had no emotional training at home. He remains sealed off in some respects. Tears don't come easily and he says he is not an overly emotional person, but does claim to be perceptive about acceptance by others.

"I'm more of an introvert than an extravert. Until I feel comfortable. Once I feel more comfortable and I get to know people, then some of the extravert in me comes out. But these are all things I've learned and they are things that are a part of me. I've learned to deal with it, but it still doesn't make going through rejection any easier." And rejection from the past continues to be a factor to be dealt with.

"When I was in my mid-twenties I was involved in a church. I helped out a lot with one of the guys who worked at the church. I volunteered a lot. I helped him and got to know him really well. I was over at his house one day and one of his kids, who was almost a teenager, was lying on his mother's lap totally relaxed and she was rubbing his head. I could not stay in the same room and watch. I was not comfortable with it. I was embarrassed. I didn't know how to handle a mother loving her child in that way. I wasn't hated as a child, but my parents' way of showing they loved me was to buy me things. They weren't rich, but I got things. They didn't know how to physically or emotionally convey their feelings. So I learned to exist in that kind of environment. When I was in an environment where there was more physical contact, between a parent and her child, it was uncomfortable for me. It's uncomfortable for me now sometimes. When my children want to give me a hug I reciprocate, but I'm very conscious of giving signals that I don't want to, because I do want to. But I still work through the fact this is not natural for me."

Expressing affection toward his children remains difficult. "I do find it challenging to relate to them emotionally sometimes. My wife is much better at it than I am. She probably deals with that weakness a little better than I do. I'm stronger in other areas and she's weaker in those areas." But opening up to his wife, explaining his *whys* was not easy.

"It took a period of time. I'm comfortable sharing it. I don't really feel embarrassed by it or ashamed of it. There has been a lot of healing in my life, and I feel God is still working on me in that respect." And weakness, he says, is becoming strength.

"It's a process. Just in the last couple of years I've seen more progress. I'm becoming more confident, because I had a rough fifteen years. And I'm just getting to the place where people are responding positively to me."

Turning Points

"Since 2001, God pretty much…unraveled my life… He really unraveled it to the point where it affected my job. From the mid-nineties up until 2001, for five or six years, I tasted failure for the most part. I came to New York and did okay for a little while, but the area, the church, the culture of the church, and some of the people at the church rocked my world and my life got really unraveled. It got to the point where they had to let me go. And so I was unemployed. My wife still worked and we still attended the church. I didn't have those kinds of issues with the church, but I was unemployed and I was going through grad school. I continued to go to grad school while I was unemployed. My wife continued to work and I couldn't find any employment. I eventually found a job in Iowa, of all places.

"In October of 2005, we moved. It was hard on my kids, which was hard on the family. God dropped us in a small town of about 326 people right next to Amish neighbors about a half a mile down the road. We had to drive about twelve miles into town to go to work. I worked for a factory in sales and marketing and it was during those nine months, with my being away from New York, God did some amazing things in me.

"One was being a neighbor with these Amish people who were so different from us. I never had been exposed to them. God opened up my heart to a group like I've never felt before. All of a sudden I had passion and compassion for people. I could sit for hours and talk with them. They would come to see us and show such interest in us and we, in turn, were interested in them. We just opened our hearts and our lives to them. I've never done that with anybody at all. I never had that experience.

"My wife commented she could not believe how compassionate I was to these people. Through our visits two or three of them actually got saved and left the Amish community. It was good for them, but bad for their family, if you know anything about the Amish. They are now ostracized.

"There was a former Amish family in the church we were attending. They had left the community two years before and through that relationship we learned a lot about the workings of the culture. It gave us insight on how to have a relationship with our new neighbors. It was phenomenal. The Amish in general don't really like the *English*. The English are people who are not Amish and, for the most part, the Amish don't want to spend any time with them.

"But they were different. We went to meals at their home. They would kill the chickens right there and that night you'd have them for dinner. They were really different and I had such good feelings for these people. Part of it was being away from New York and experiencing a different lifestyle, my wife getting a break from working, and just being somewhere new. God did something in my life.

"But I was still unsettled. I had always struggled with my career. Since I was seventeen I've always been behind a camera, and I felt like a fish out of water for a long, long time after I left television. Then when I came back east and worked in it, I still felt out of place. It was totally different. It was more management and administrative than it was production and fieldwork. They're two different things. I grew up in the Northwest. I grew up in a factory town, blue collar. I was never exposed to leadership, never exposed to management, even though my dad was a manager. It didn't matter; I didn't understand anything he did. To me he was a factory worker.

"Then you're placed in a position where you've got to exemplify leadership abilities and skills and you think *What am I doing here?* But going away gave me a break and God did some things in my life. I was still struggling but I felt compelled to call Pastor Paul back. I said, 'I have no idea why I am calling you but I just feel like I've got to talk to you.' And he said I'd been on his heart, too, and then we were chatting and within a half an hour he's offering to bring us back.

"It blew me away. Within four weeks of that conversation, I was back in New York. It was bizarre. But it was very, very important for me to come back because there were some things I had to face and deal with here. And so when I came back it was good for me. Over time there was a gentle, progressive healing taking place in my life, my heart, and my mind—emotionally and spiritually, and that has brought me to this point.

"I've been back almost two-and-a-half to three years now and it's been very, very good to be back. It's been good for me, good for my wife, good for my children, even though they love the Northwest and would go back in a second. They are calming down; they're relaxing. Everything is better now because I had been in an uproar for many, many years."

Reed agrees that the Iowa experience changed him because of the exposure to people in a non-threatening setting. Prior to going, he was a church media director, but ran into problems. Risk-taking, however, was not one of those challenges.

"I'm willing to take risks. I've taken a lot and failed a lot and I continue to take them. Why? Because I'm driven to understand what I'm supposed to be doing. And I will not stop until I do understand. I know God put me on this Earth for a reason. And I'm still working through some of that.

"For example, I've recently started a part-time photography business and I'm having the time of my life with it. I love it. Absolutely love it. It is, in fact, one of the first things—other than playing the guitar, which I've done on and off for many years—that I've actually had passion about again for a long, long time.

"I'm a lot more comfortable with myself and I'm learning. I'm slowly deciphering this without listening to someone else telling me what I'm supposed to do. It just takes me time because I have to weigh through a lot of different things. But when I land on it, I'm going to hit it hard and not let that deter me from where I'm going with it."

Dealing with People

Reed says a situation like cold-calling on the phone makes him anxious, an experience he had while in Iowa. "I had to feel good about myself to make the calls. Most of the time, I hardly made any calls. Even the guy who hired me for sales said he could tell this wasn't my calling and he was in the process of moving me into something more analytical.

"The funny thing is I am good at building relationships, but I am horrible at the initial contact. Once I get through the initial contact, I'm generally fine. For instance, if there were already an established relationship with a company I could go in and continue to build relationships with those people and be fine. I'd be very comfortable. The reason is because there is no fear of rejection."

Bringing it Home

"I look forward to going home. I can't wait to get home. My family means a lot to me. I'm not the perfect father, I'm not the perfect husband, but I'm a lot more comfortable in those situations than I am anywhere else.

"As I grew up my home was stable in a lot of ways and so I perceived my own home being the same way. I would try to provide a sound environment. It's been very difficult on us financially. My career choices and being unemployed a few times have really impacted us, even now. We are still reeling from that. If there is anything affecting our family life more than anything else right now it is money, which has a tendency to filter its way through everything.

"However, we've learned to deal with this. You learn to cope, you learn to adjust; you learn to get a plan. You know the magic pill isn't going to just drop on you; you've got to be proactive. That's why we started the photography business. We needed something outside of our day-to-day jobs to help bring in money.

"I love being married. I love my wife, I love my friendship with her, I love being around my children. I'm not always comfortable sharing certain emotions with them. I'm sure they are smart enough to pick up on that. But they're not saying to my wife, 'What's wrong with dad? How come he doesn't pay any attention to us?' That kind of thing is not happening because, for the most part, they talk to both of us. However, they talk to her just a little bit more.

"She is just that way. Everybody talks to my wife. Paulette just has that gift. She just has a personality that encourages people to come to her and talk. It's not different in my family; my kids go to her and talk. They will come and talk to me also. My oldest daughter is probably more like me than either of the other two. When we communicate I can totally understand her and so when she is struggling, I can pinpoint the problem almost immediately. And then walk her through it.

"Even in a free, stable home, kids are always trying to find who and what they are about and what they believe and how they should respond to their world. So it's interesting to watch them go through things, not at the level I went through, but to watch them experience areas I struggled in."

Reed says experience has taught him a lot at home.

"It's a struggle because I don't want to see them experience what I went through, because I knew how painful it was and still is. There is the father part of me who wants to protect them, and sometimes I find myself opening my mouth too much trying to talk them through. When I should just be quiet and let them talk and experience and figure it out. So I'm trying not to over-counsel, over-project, over-analyze, and over-preach.

"You've got to let them experience some things. It's good they have a place to come home to. It's good they have parents who love them. We explain to them sometimes we don't have all the answers, sometimes we don't know what to say, sometimes we might know what to say. But it's hard. It's hard for me not to say something because I don't want them to go through what I went through. I guess the protective part of me comes out and I want to shield them from everything and I have to remove myself. You know, back it up a little bit and let them be themselves.

Helping the Kids

"My relationship obviously has matured, I've gotten through things and it's different than it was when I grew up. I know when I'm at least able to deal with my children on some level. So if my teenage daughter, who is fifteen, is upset if I don't give her a hug and kiss, I can deal with it. I don't always feel comfortable doing it, but I'm getting more comfortable.

"I don't know why I'm not more comfortable. I wish I weren't that way. You have this picture in your head of an Italian father who is very emotional—almost to the opposite extreme. I'm nowhere near that, but I'm also not so dry that my children wonder, 'Does dad really love me?' But I'm not as expressive as I would like to be. And actually, I'm very conscious of it.

Tenderness and Physical Contact

"I can be tender with my wife and although it may not lead to sexual activity, I'm okay with it. But it's different with my daughter. I'm not afraid it will lead to that, that's not what I'm trying to protect myself from. I just don't know how to do the *tender* thing with her."

Reed says he has good relationships with his siblings: a brother who is almost two years younger and a sister who is about six years younger.

"My brother is more like my father, so I have a harder time relating to him. We get along fine, we communicate, and I actually led him to the Lord.

"With my sister, it's a whole different story. She is fine, but she is living a homosexual lifestyle. She has all kinds of problems. It's sort of a land mine. Not between us so much, but there is a lot going on that's complicated. We have a pretty good relationship, for the most part. I'm very loving toward her and I'm not judging her, but she also knows I disagree with her lifestyle. She knows that. I can give her a hug, we can talk, and we can hang out. But I could be on the phone longer with her.

"I don't really open up to anybody in my family. I never have. They are aware of things. I opened up to my father somewhat, a little bit, but not drastically. It was enough and it was very uncomfortable. He probably wouldn't like it very much if I totally opened up to him. Even if he were agreeable to it I don't know how much I would want to.

"Back in my college days—actually when I was really starting to figure it all out—I told him I was going to counseling. He's known I've struggled. I told him some of it was about him. We argued about it some, but not a lot, mainly because I didn't understand much at the time. He was gracious and he listened. I don't think he understood completely, because my parents don't know the Lord; they are not saved.

The Worship Relationship and the Vision

"It might take me a while to get into worship. After many years, I've viewed my relationship with God like my relationship with my father. It has taken me a while to distinguish between the two, realize there is a difference, and know that God actually loves me. It was nice to know He really cared about me and I wasn't just another person. I've been saved since I was eighteen, so it's been twenty-five years and I'm just now getting to the point where I feel comfortable in loving.

"When I worked in Iowa I went to a sales meeting in Chicago and I heard a teaching on the love of God. The preacher said God spoke to him about his whole message and it was one of the best things I've ever heard. It changed me as far as knowing how God sees me and how He loves me. And how important I am to Him. That was pivotal to me.

"It's taken me a long time to come to this point. It was three or four years ago when I started grasping this and gained traction. It really showed in my worship, meaning I can now be expressive. From a heart standpoint, it's gotten to a point where I can really feel like I'm worshiping. My relationship with God is like my relationship with everybody else. It probably wouldn't make any sense if I approached it any differently. It's a process; it actually takes work."

He says the work of that process is building satisfaction for him.

"Instead of it being for me, it's for God. So to me it's less selfish. In other words, I'm not worshiping so that I feel better, I'm worshiping because I feel better and I'm able to give that back. I'm getting more comfortable in my relationship with God.

"So in a sense everything reflects back to the emotional development you've had growing up and how it's affected everything in your life. I find that to be a travesty. We go to school to learn academically and intellectually; we train our bodies physically and we are encouraged to eat right and get a good night's sleep; and we go out socially, meet people, go to dances, and church. We are encouraged to worship God, but very seldom do parents train their children emotionally. We don't have schools for it. We don't have anyone to tell us about our emotions. It is very difficult and it really messes up our lives and our relationship with God. Even though God can overcome all of that, it's still a difficult process to go through.

"The most important thing is for me to train my children emotionally so they can navigate their teenage years and be confident and come out feeling good about who they are. I just don't want them to have to deal with what I had to deal with on many levels. I don't want them to have to deal with the emotional challenges and I don't want them to have to deal with financial challenges. I don't want them to have to deal with depression or self-confidence, or career issues. I don't want them to have to walk through the minefield I've had to walk through.

"God gave me a vision a few years ago. I was working out on the treadmill and the vision was so vivid I wept openly. I was walking in a charred, burnt forest and all the different trees were black because the fire had destroyed them. I'm walking through this scorched place and wearing a black coat and I'm covered in black soot.

"There is a demarcation line where the forest stops and just one step ahead was a green luscious field. A balmy breeze was blowing and it was a beautiful, sunny day, with blue skies and warm temperatures. There was a hill ahead and a gigantic tree was growing right at the top. As I stepped over into the green field, the black coat fell off me, I left all the darkness and soot behind, and I was free to dance in the open field where it was beautiful and sunny. That image still impacts me today.

"In my life, I feel like I'm close to to that lovely field and I'm starting to step out of the nasty, charred forest I have been in for so long and experience true freedom. Freedom at all levels—emotionally, spiritually, mentally, financially, everything. Just to be able to step over and be free. I want that for my children. I don't want them to have to walk through an emotionally burnt, devastating place.

"I don't know how to do this for my children because I'm not even there myself yet. It's something I pray about and ask God to help me raise these kids in a way that they do not have to walk through what I walked through.

"I hope their generation will be better. They are going to experience trials because I can't protect them from everything. I'm not even trying to do that. I'm not an over-protective parent, but at the same time, they have got to experience something better than I experienced because what I experienced was not good.

"These kids are living a dream compared to what I lived, and it is my prayer their kids will live an even better dream on all levels—emotionally, mentally, financially, and spiritually. They will have that because I chose to fight the fight. These kids are growing up feeling loved and cared for. They know we really love them and care for them and they are in a stable home. My wife and I love each other.

That in itself is so different from how I saw my parents act.

"I think about all of it. I think it will affect their freedom emotionally, mentally, and spiritually. For me, it seems to reflect a level of healing from all of this devestation. If I reflect on my vision a little bit, there are keys into my life. The black cloak and soot reflect the emotional and mental trauma I went through and the big tree at the top of the hill that stands very firm and solid represents God. With Him watching, I'm able to move around with a sense of freedom. But at the same time I can look back and see the charred area. It's not like I can forget it, I can still see it, but I also know I have stepped from one area to another.

"It affects you mentally, it affects you emotionally, it affects you spiritually, and it affects how you respond, how you react, how you interact on all kinds of levels. To me that's a process. That's something that didn't just happen; it's something that's been happening over a period of time. It's taken four years to even get to this, and I'm still working it out.

"Finally, I think there is a line in the sand. I used to always ask someone to tell me what to do, how should I think, how should I respond, what should I be doing here, what shall I be doing there. I realize now that I have to understand. Before I didn't know how to think, I didn't know how to feel. I didn't know who I was. Now I know and I am proceeding to build a healthy me."

Questions to Ponder

- Have you captured the main theme in Reed's story?

- Is it possible to have a self-esteem issue and address it only with spiritual directives? And if not, how would you address it?

- How does involvement in sexual activity affect one

emotionally? Can you live a spiritually fulfilling life and yet at the same time suffer from emotional shortcomings in the sexual arena?

- Is it possible to have been rejected both in ministry and the secular world and still live a successful spiritual life and, if so, how?

Takeaways

- Self-esteem and self-regard are intricately linked. How you feel about yourself affects how you perform, whether in ministry or in the secular world.

- It is possible to serve Christ for a long time and ignore a real emotional lack that exists in your life.

- Heredity is not destiny. Who your parents are and were does not define who you will be. Effective spiritual and emotional management can lead to overcoming generational shortfalls.

CHAPTER FIFTEEN

CEURGIN TARX:
LONELINESS AND DEFIANCE

. . . .

Ceurgin Tarx is an adult woman of Russian origin living in the United States, struggling to escape the trap of painful experiences far beyond problems rooted in place and language. She carries lingering issues of a childhood scarred by relentless physical abuse and abandonment, yet she seems trapped on a path in life that reinforces anger and mistrust of others.

Let down by shocking instances in her life of betrayal by her parents, by her former husband, and others, she is doubly afflicted by chronic illness that not only affects her, but also has handicapped her young daughters. Though far removed from places and persons who hurt her as a child, she has, even now, repeatedly encountered letdown, neglect, and disappointing treatment.

Painful memories remain fresh. "My mother was very… physically and verbally abusive. I don't think there was a day that went by when I wasn't beaten unmercifully, and not because I did something wrong. It could be something like my mother suddenly saying, 'You look just like your father,' and I'd be beaten with an extension cord in the tub full of water, naked. I was four years old."

Ceurgin has never known security or certainty. She was regularly abandoned by or taken away from a mother unable or unwilling to properly care for her while her father was away in the military. Shuttled from group home to group home, she acquired skills in survival through distrust. "I had to become extremely independent because I didn't know who to trust. I didn't know who I could rely on to take care of me."

When she was sent away by her mother to her first group home, she was physically abused by a mother figure there. "It was horrible. She put a pillow over my face, sat on the pillow, and beat me repeatedly. I still have a scar on my head where she beat me with the buckle of her belt."

She saw her mother each weekend. She says the woman who hurt her warned her that she should say that her bruises were from other children. "If I didn't she would beat me again." She only told her mother about it years later.

After being returned to her mother, every day brought renewed beatings. "I got a beating because she would be so emotional and angry and mad, and there was nobody else around but me. So she took it out on me."

Once when she was very little, her mother left her alone in a tenement stairway. "We were living with my aunt, and my mother left me on the stairs of her apartment building. My aunt kicked her out. They had gotten into an argument. My mother left me on the stairs in the apartment building and told me not to leave because some people were going to come and get me. I don't know how long I stayed on those stairs, but I know I was crying and crying." Soon two men appeared and took her to an orphanage. "I went in and out of orphan care for about a year and then my father sent for me and my mother."

Her father had sent for them to come live with him during his military assignment. There, life continued to unravel. "My father committed adultery," she says. "We were in one part of the country and he was stationed thousands of miles away. When he got settled, he sent for us. We got there and my mother found out that he had an affair and had fathered a child. They got a divorce, but my mother has not recovered.

"She talks about it today like it happened yesterday. She is still hurt by it and it's sad, but she's never had a decent relationship."

The air of mistrust toward people Ceurgin acquired in those years has never passed, and repeated experience has reinforced it. These days her refuge is God. "I think it makes me smarter because all the weight is off. You just feel it's Him doing most of the work. You're being led, doing what He says because it's easier. But emotionally, there is still a struggle."

She was a naturally quiet child. The effect of all the hurt made her more unwilling to express herself. "It silenced me, I know that. I wasn't much of a talker. I would never initiate relationships. Once a relationship was established I was always well-liked and got along with people, but initiating relationships was something I never did, ever."

She says that over and over adults were drawn to her at one time or another, and many offered to give her a home out of kindness. She realizes they may have been offering unconditional love, but it was a possibility she could not trust, although she wanted to. Moving from home became normal, and stability would have been a foreign concept.

Distrust and instability surrounded her life and caused her to retreat. Her friends were other children in dangerous situations who were also sent to group homes, and to her their predicaments were often far worse than her own.

EMOTIONAL INTELLIGENCE AND THE CHURCH

"When I looked at all the other girls and boys whose stories seemed more extreme than mine, I couldn't understand why I was there." This may indicate a level of denial or mental self-protection. She recounts the experience of a woman she's known since those days. "She had ten brothers and sisters. Her mother would have men come in and out of the house, and my friend would be raped by each and every last one of them from the time she was nine years old."

Beatings seemed normal to her and far less extreme than rape. The experiences she heard among her friends seemed worse than hers. "Their parents were either alcoholics or on serious drugs or prostitutes, and here I have two healthy parents. Why am I in a group home? I had a sister my father had with his second wife, and my mother has a son who is older than me who is living a prosperous life with his father. What happened to me?" she asks.

As a child experiecing daily beatings, her parents never exposed her to church or religion. When asked about her awareness of God, she recalls an episode when she was six.

Day after day that summer, her mother left her home alone while she went to work. She instructed Ceurgin to never open a door or answer the telephone. But no level of obedience alleviated daily punishments. One day, she says, "I was determined this was the day I was not getting a beating. So I cleaned up the house, made the bed, did all that so when my mother came home she would be happy. And I remember getting on my knees at six, praying to God and asking Him if I do X, Y and Z, can you promise not to allow my mother to beat me? And I was so confident in that prayer I just knew I wasn't going to get a beating that day because I did everything right.

"My mother came home. She acknowledged and praised me for my work. And then she snapped.

"I remember her finding a piece of paper on the floor I had kept walking back and forth over, without having seen it. She started screaming at me saying, 'You see that paper on the floor?' And she used that as an excuse to beat me. I got a really bad beating that day."

She routinely went to bed in tears. "I remember going into the closet in my room and crying. I know I didn't want her to hear me talk so I whispered through my tears and I said, 'God how could you do this to me? I did everything—cleaned the bathroom, made the bed and you still let her beat me.' And I remember saying, 'I hate you, I hate you, I hate you so much.' That was the first time I knew there was a higher being. After that I knew He existed but I didn't know who He was." And so for Ceurgin, the seeds of mistrust in others extended even to God.

Anger became a rising tide along the way. She remembers often fighting in the group homes, and rightly or not, finding justification in her behavior.

"I fought all the time. I wouldn't just fight people to fight them. I would fight them for justice and if I thought any injustice was done, I was so passionate about it I wanted to hurt you," she says.

"You didn't even have to hurt me, but if I saw you hurting somebody else I was going to hurt you and it didn't matter who you were. I think even now in my adult life I have that same passion. I'm not going to allow a wrong or injustice to be done and just sit down and be quiet. I'm going to confront. Now that I have an education and have had people mentor me, I know how to do it more appropriately than when I was immature."

Looking back, she recognizes fighting as a communications issue. "I didn't know how to communicate that I was angry or mad." Language failed her—and her family. "I didn't know how to communicate with words." She says her inability was deepened by the behavior of adult family members around her who resorted to physical contact when they were angry at one another.

And there was, and remains, the issue of control. "I have a problem with people trying to control me. When you try to control me I feel like I'm caged. You're not going to control me and I'll come out fighting."

Determination and a Life Rope

Ceurgin's anger in her youth resulted in her acquiring at least one positive characteristic. "I had the mentality that giving up was not an option; I had that drive." She saw how others, turning eighteen, left group home care, and ended up "on the street, hopping from one system to the next, or being thrown in jail," she says. "That's not going to happen to me. Giving up is not an option. I'm going to have to keep going." As a result, she was determined to succeed in school, and she did.

Around the time she was seventeen and in a group home, she gave in to a couple who had persistently asked her to visit their home and go to church with them. "Previously I would go to church with different friends and family members, but didn't really know what it was about," she says. She secured a weekend pass from her home and visited this couple.

That weekend, she says, "The pastor preached a message that really came home to me, and I didn't really know what it was all about." But he invited those gathered to accept Christ. She raised her hand and realized she was the only one to do so. "Everybody said congratulations, you just got saved and they were all excited. People were crying and people were hugging me and everywhere I went they would say congratulations.

"I didn't know what the big deal was about. Okay, I'm saved, now I'm a Christian, but why are people so excited?" She had felt rejection too often. What she had experienced took time to understand.

"I was seventeen," she says, "so I was going out to clubs, hanging out with my friends. I know a lot of people think they have to stop going to clubs, stop smoking, stop drinking, and stop doing all these other things before you can come to Christ. But Christ said to come as you are. Habits can be broken and replaced with God's habits." She says she felt touched in her heart. It was a new way, she says, "of living a new life...allowing myself to open up to God to fear Him." It was her route to survival. "I needed to survive."

Later, she says, "I got to know Him and to understand His Word," and how certain events in her life fit her growing knowledge. "He allowed me to reflect back and showed me how He was there the whole time; the whole time in each incident in my life."

Fast Forward

In becoming independent and a survivor, Ceurgin continues to weather personal storms. Her marriage was shattered by her husband's infidelity. Looking back, she and her husband argued often and, "I definitely thought it was me."

They met at a community gathering and she was impressed their initial conversation was, as she puts it, mature and without subterfuge. They communicated on and off for months. "We hit it off," she says; he was "humble." She opened up to him. "I gave him all the good and bad in me," she says. And she was surprised and pleased he still liked her and accepted her without criticism.

But not everything was perfect. She at first refused his offer of marriage because, "I couldn't put my finger on what it was, but there was something sneaky about him." But her friends pressed his case, telling her that he was a good man and good for her. "My gut was telling me 'I don't think so, something about him should not be trusted.' But she thought, 'It's just me,' so I gave in and we got married. And after we got married he had an affair and fathered a child."

She was amazed and utterly blindsided when it happened. "I was devastated. He actually told me over the telephone. He left that morning to go to work he said, 'I love you and will see you later.'" She stayed home that day and soon he called, chatted about household affairs, and then paused. "He said, 'I have something to tell you,' " and he did.

"You could not tell me this man would have ever had an affair. He could have done everything else, but that was something I never thought he was capable of doing," she says. "I remember falling to the floor. I put down the phone and I cried and cried. Then he came home and I was still on the floor and I just kept crying." She says she told her husband she forgave him. And somehow, she says, she felt the failure was her own. "Definitely. I know," she says.

Ceurgin says she tried to save the marriage, but he eventually told her, "The truth is I don't love you anymore. I just want my life back." But the reality was even worse.

Burdened by a chronic illness potentially transmissible to a child, she had been told by doctors she should not have children. And then she learned her husband not only had been unfaithful, but the other woman was pregnant with his child.

She says she was in the shower when she learned the truth. She recalls falling to her knees and screaming at God, "I don't understand!" She remembers expressing the injustice that she could not have children but, "You allow another woman to bear my husband's child and she's not even Christian."

Six days later, feeling unwell, she went to a doctor's office where she learned she was pregnant. "After the smoke cleared, I understood God's message. I knew my baby was a blessing—'This is how much I love you.'"

Her child was eventually born with the same illness she suffers from. Her husband has since had another affair and another child with another woman he is still with.

Remaking a Life

Years later, Ceurgin has remolded her life. Determined to succeed, she has earned a Master's degree from a university in the Northeast. She credits God for opening the door to that possibility.

"I sent references, plus my resume, and within two months I got an acceptance letter into the graduate school," she says. "I didn't have to take the GMAT test, I didn't have to take an SAT, and I didn't have to give them a work report." Other friends told her how difficult getting in often was. "It was so easy. I filled out the application and was accepted. I thought that was normal. When I realized it wasn't, I knew that God had a purpose. He got me in."

Even now, Ceurgin finds herself vulnerable to trust issues. In an interview, she sounds very much like a person who finds dealing with criticism extraordinarily difficult. Speaking of a mentor in her church, she recalls a recent difficult situation in which she felt particularly stung.

As a church employee, she relates the experience of being second-guessed in an employee-versus-employee controversy. "This woman lied to me and she lied to my mentor. And after that, everything went downhill for me. I became frustrated with my mentor and I felt like I was being set up. I'm a very truthful person. I like to confront."

Speaking of her mentor, she says, "He was more focused on my flaws, my faults, my past, and it impacted me." Ceurgin says she told the man her entire focus was on her job and nothing else, despite all the hurtful incidents in her past. "I've dealt with that. I'm past all that and I'm here now. He made me let down my guard with him and I did. I trusted him because I really thought he had my best interests at heart." Then, she says, this trusted church mentor "just threw me away."

She says it all connects—all of her experiences in life, including her soul-saving awareness of God. Despite repeated experiences with her inability to find people she can trust, she finds strength in dependence on God. "I think it makes me smarter," she says. "It doesn't affect my worship of God because it's not a struggle. I trust what I believe in."

Still, she cares about the people around her. She believes that community is essential, and, although she doesn't specifically say it, she indicates in her larger view that trust and the need to connect with others remains an important goal for everyone, as members of an interlinked community.

"We're the Body of Christ," she says. "If one person is missing or not functioning, it affects the whole body. We have to work together, you know. It's true my mentor still doesn't care. And not because he's heartless. He doesn't have the time to care and he doesn't want to make the time to care. There are a few million other things on his mind. And you have to take those things into consideration."

The need for palpable caring continues, she says.

"We reflect our leader and if he's not compassionate and if he doesn't take the time to come out and ask you how you are, it hurts." One woman she works with, who depends on the same church mentor, provides a clear example. "She said she went through a divorce, and not only did she go through a divorce, her husband left her for another woman. She was struggling; she had no food and then she lost her house. The church knew about it and then two years later her husband died. A year after that is the first time her mentor asked her how she was doing."

She says if a person in a leadership role feels the need to criticize and condemn, he also needs to take a moment to ask how the person he is supposed to be helping is doing. "If there's no connection, the one needing help walks in the shadows," she says.

Words her mentor said—"I can't trust you unless you trust me"— still ring strong and clear, and leave her with a sense of unease she has yet to resolve.

To this day, the shadow of trust given and broken lingers in Ceurgin's heart. It remains unresolved; a matter of introspection and communication with the one presence in her life she continues to rely on—God.

Questions to Ponder

- Have you captured the main theme in Ceurgin's story?

- Can we infer any shortage of emotional intelligence health on the part of Ceurgen and if so, based on previous material, what are the strategies to address her situation and circumstances?

- As a believer, does Ceurgen exhibit any characteristics that argue against her being a believer and, if so, what are they and how can we create structures that can help her be an emotionally and spiritually mature person?

- As a believer, what is the correct approach, from an emotional intelligence perspective, to interact and work with Ceurgin?

Takeaway

- Temperament is not destiny. Who you are and what you have experienced does not determine your destiny. One's emotional lack is not a deterrent to working through emotional and spiritual shortfalls.

- Impulse control, stress management, and the Fruit of the Spirit are significant control points for improved Christ-centered living.

- Your emotional dimension should not dictate your spiritual experience; instead, your spiritual and emotional dimensions are intertwined and need care and attention in order to grow.

CHAPTER SIXTEEN

KAITLIN SIMPSON:
TRAUMA AND EMOTIONAL DENIAL

. . . .

Kaitlin Simpson is a single woman living in New Jersey. At the time of our interview she was taking some time off after working in corporate America for twenty years and conducting full-time ministry for another four years.

The foundation of her early childhood was a solid, two-parent, stable family, at least for a time. Her parents moved their family to Newark from Maryland when she was small. Her early life as a middle child—she has one older and one younger brother—was pleasant. That life was eventually disrupted by two events: the separation of her parents before she was nine, and, at age ten, by social upheaval, the Newark riots in the summer of 1967.

The first, most fundamental change in what had seemed a steady childhood came from out of the blue. "There was never any arguing or anything in the home, so my parents' separation was very, very surprising to me because we seemed to be the perfect American home— two kids, a dog, a cat, everything was perfect. So when my parents first separated they didn't actually talk to us about it." She recalls it was an era in which separation carried a stigma, something that never would have been discussed with the children. "I remember asking mom, 'Mom, when

191

is dad coming home?' I was very close to my dad. And I don't think she ever answered me. But it wasn't too long before I figured out he wasn't coming home."

Eighteen months later, another tectonic shift took place.

"I'd been in New Jersey just about all my life. It was quite nice prior to the riots. What a difference they made. I remember two or three days when my mom wouldn't let us out of the house. She said, 'I need you all to stay close to home; there's a lot going on.' We had heard about it but we really didn't understand what a riot was.

"I remember going out to the main streets about three days later and I was so amazed how everything was destroyed. It was literally destroyed, and no longer was there the Newark we had moved to and grown to love. We stayed there a few more years and then moved to East Orange, which was much nicer than it is now. Watching that transition really was devastating because we had never seen anything go from being so beautiful to being just totally gone to ruins almost overnight. That was very, very difficult to witness as a child.

"Before the riots safety was not a concern. You didn't have to worry about where your children were going, about them being outside, or walking to the stores. I remember supermarkets and little family stores that were on Bergen Street, Clinton Avenue, and those areas. There was no fear in being out and about. I think what it really did was take away a sense of security about walking around as we got older. Going from knowing something is very, very safe to something dramatically less so was difficult."

It may have been the combination of these experiences at such a formative time in her life that led to her characteristic need as an adult to focus on the need for control in most aspects of her life. Control is an idea she has grappled with for a very long time, something that came to a head in an episode involving a close friend in recent times.

She recalls being shocked. "I think it probably took her ten years to tell me I was a controlling person. I couldn't tell by the way she acted that I was a controlling person. I don't think I wanted to control. I think I wanted her to have the structure and organization in her life to the degree that it helped her make better decisions, be better organized, and be in control of things that were out of control. You can lose control very quickly."

Whether she was aware of control as an issue or not, the lack of certainty when she was young vividly paints her memories and fuels her needs today. Her instinctive reaction to her parents' separation was not that a bombshell had dropped, but was tempered by something innate.

"I don't ever remember something being so shocking that it interrupted my ability to think, function, or prevent the normalcy in my life. I just said okay. But then I noticed in my neighborhood there were families that were single-parent homes. The neighborhood seemed to have more than when we moved in, which was only one."

For a time, she took responsibility for her little brother while her mother tried to make ends meet. "I remember my brother coming home from the hospital. I said, 'Mom can I hold him?' I was really surprised she let me. I think I learned to change a diaper in a day or two because this is my baby brother and he is better than a doll."

In spite of the difficulties of raising children alone, her mother maintained a meticulously orderly home. For Kaitlin, the takeaway was, "I just knew things had to be a certain way and needed to be in order; everybody needs to be in order, everybody needs to look a certain way, and I guess it was an assumed behavior because that's all I knew."

Her father was a postal worker who, she says, "always provided for the family. Whenever I asked dad for something, the need was met. I never felt the sense of abandonment.

"I don't know if it was my mother's choice to move on. Sometimes I think it was her choice, but I don't know. I don't know if I hold either of them responsible or I wished they had remained together, but I think my life would have been very different had I remained in a two-parent home. There were a lot of good things instilled in my brother and me as a result in being reared in a two-parent home and we learned a lot of responsibility. I don't struggle with emotions when I think back," she says. She indicates she has not lost faith in the possibility of a long-term relationship resulting in a traditional family. "Even now I have a desire to be married; I've had a desire to be married almost all my adult life."

She struggles with disappointment and finds it hard to admit she has to deal with it. She maintains a sense of peace and, perhaps, humor, saying there were only two things she wanted as a child and was never able to do: take piano lessons and join the Girl Scouts. "But as much as I hated the outdoors and bugs, it probably was not for me."

Her words of assurance are belied by the recollection and recognition of other life experiences that segmented her childhood, and perhaps increased her eventual search for control.

Life with mom and without father did not go well. She refrains from going into great detail, but says that after having a middle-class lifestyle, there was for a time no car and no telephone in their home. But, she says, "I don't believe for one minute that my dad didn't want to help or wasn't willing." She postulates that her mother might have decided she wasn't going to ask for anything, which may suggest a not unreasonable struggle for control on her mother's part.

Control became an issue in other respects. Kaitlin had been a natural student, something that, after her parents' split, was suddenly no longer automatic. "I was always an honor student. I did very, very well in school. My grades plummeted and I was surprised because I couldn't imagine why." Her behavior became a problem in school as she lost her bearings.

It was a problem for about a year and a half, she says. "My mom was very upset because I was always an excellent student. I never remember having to study or do homework because I always knew all the answers. I think subconsciously it might have been a cry for help. It might have been a cry for attention."

Eventually, she says, "I think my grades began to pick up and things began to get back on target."

All of that, she says, "was actually rather short-lived because then I went to live with my dad. I was with my mom for almost four years and then my brothers and I went to live with our dad—another transition. There were four stages in my life from childhood to teenager, not to mention the fact I attended seven schools from kindergarten to twelfth grade."

The scars from all of this turmoil reveal themselves as Kaitlin continues.

"I didn't keep friends. I'm jealous when people say, 'We went to kindergarten together' and they are fifty years old, and I think 'I am so sorry I missed that.' I wished I could say I have a friend I've had all my life. That's probably one of the things I really enjoyed seeing in other people's lives I wished I had."

She recognizes the price of that history in her younger brother's wiring, and a seeming tendency, based on her cautious description of him, to display a lack of self-discipline. It becomes obvious to her that he never experienced the kind of family foundation she enjoyed in her youngest years.

"There were times I felt bad for him because he didn't have the privilege of having a two-parent home and I see his behavior is totally different than my other brother and mine, totally different, scarily different sometimes. I feel bad because he didn't have the presence of a dad when he was very young. He did later on, but not from infancy up until age four. I think that had a lot to do with shaping some things in his life."

She describes in hazy terms the events that led, after four years, to her moving away from her mother to live with her father. "Some things happened," she says, "with the apartment we were living in and it was not fit any longer for us to live there. An urgent decision was made, and my mom said okay."

She describes a life with her father and her role as caregiver to her younger brother that strengthened the bond with her father. "My dad worked nights. When my brother was about five he was just starting in kindergarten. He was in school during the day and my dad picked him up after school. Then I took care of him and fed him and put him to bed because my dad was sleeping since he went to work in the evening. So we still spent a significant amount of time together and we were very, very close."

She often thinks back to those times. "I've never felt the sense of abandonment. I've become more and more independent. I've always felt I could take care of myself, even as a kid. My dad would call me the little mom in the house."

She says as segmented as her life was, it made her into a stronger person. "I've had to learn how to adapt very quickly and adjust to different situations," she says. Even after all she'd been through, those tests would continue to come.

Two and a half years after moving in with her father, he remarried, "This is now phase four of my life, prior to being eighteen," she says. "Now we've gone from a family of three children to a family of eight children," counting her stepmother's five teenagers in the house.

"Here I am halfway through high school and things were completely different because my role now changed. I've never had to share anything and now I'm sharing a room. That was a big adjustment, because now we're combining families, moving, and changing schools. It was a lot of adapting in my life at that time."

The finality of the news of her father's remarriage didn't go over well with her. She'd hoped her own parents would resolve their differences and remarry. "I said I'm not going to the wedding. They got married in the house and I said I wasn't going to be at home, that way nobody could make me be a part of the wedding. As a matter of fact, I was with my mom."

Afterward, "I didn't want to share my room, but that was out of the question. My stepsister and I were very different in the way we did things. I wasn't used to anybody invading my space, so I didn't like that."

But she developed a good relationship with her stepmother. She was, she says, a very kind, very patient, very strong woman who had lost her previous husband and did a good job of bringing up her children alone. "Spiritually and otherwise she had a great influence on my life. She was very easy to talk to. She encouraged my relationship with my mom. She was never threatened by it and I consider that to be very rare."

Pushing on

After high school, her father and stepmother separated. She worked for two years, and then attended college for one semester in Florida. She found she could not relate to those around her, judging them comparatively immature, a feeling she attributes to growing up faster than others her age. She returned to the Northeast where she went to work.

"I went to work because, at that time, I couldn't trust what was going to happen. I had to really start taking care of myself. It became clear to me I needed to know what to do, because I was an adult now and nobody was really obligated to take care of me except me. And so, that's when I decided I wanted to work."

Her background set the stage for what so far had been the terrain of continued uncertainty. The concept of control—emotionally—of life experiences and of others around her remains an ideal that continually expresses itself. As a young adult, she says, life had to be perfect, and there was no room for laughter, no place for fun. "Boy," she says, "it was a hard life." During her first year back at work she set a high bar for what she calls her need for *ultimate* customer service. "I appreciate that," she says.

An obsessive focus on quality and behavior came at a cost. "I'm naturally a task-oriented person, but I think some things in my life, as an escape, made me more task-oriented." For her it was, and may remain, a place to mentally escape reality and to "kind of camp out because it's safe there. I had to learn, if you will, to be vulnerable, to cry, and to be okay with what's not my strength, with where I'm weak."

Nowadays, she says, she gives herself permission and space to not "hold it together." She says she remembers one time coming before the Lord simply to cry. She suspects that for many years, at least since she was a pre-teen, she hadn't ever cried. She says over the years her heart was hardened, she had shut down emotionally, "shut down from being vulnerable, and shut down from being weak. I hated weak people. I knew people around me who were weak, who couldn't make a decision, who couldn't think, and who fell apart over everything.

"I remember sitting next to a woman on an airplane one day and she was having a bad day. Everything was so dramatic. She spilled her coffee when she put the sugar in it, she got mad, she cursed, and I'm sitting there thinking 'It's coffee; get over it, for goodness sake.'"

After many years, life led to Bible college and community college experiences. Her love of learning had led her to being hooked on schooling. "My dad calls me the 'lifetime student' because I'm always in school," she says. In a sense, she remains fundamentally searching in many ways, perhaps affected by indecision related to control.

For example, she wants to be married. But, "I don't believe that's going to happen for me. I've waited a long time and I would love to be married if I feel the person is right. I have absolutely no problem getting married, none whatsoever. I've had proposals but I did not feel the person was right for me or I was right for him. I don't struggle with it and, not to sound super-spiritual, but I really trust God so strongly in that area of my life and I believe it's going to be the right person and it's going to be done once. I've had to totally surrender that area of my life to the Lord. I could very easily make a decision on my own, but I don't want to do that."

She says she has been "a typical reckless young adult, making bad decisions, in bad relationships, engaging in bad behavior—drinking and drugs." Her relationships dissolved for many of those reasons.

"I was looking for a steady relationship and did have a few over the years. Some that would be considered lengthy for my age—two and a half years and about a year. One guy wanted to get married, but I said I think I'm too young. I probably wanted more companionship than I did security."

Her interest and involvement in church and with God, in a sense, snuck up on her.

Salvation Experience

"One of my brothers had gotten saved. I wasn't used to that terminology; I didn't know what it meant. He was going to church and I knew he was dating the pastor's daughter. He said, 'I read the Bible, and I'm so excited I can't even sleep at night.' I said to myself, that proves it's not for me because I already can't sleep at night."

But a seed was planted that day; something about what he said "gripped my heart," she says. Sometime later she called her mother and asked if she'd take her to church. Her family life had not been religion-based, and she had no idea if her mother was a regular churchgoer or even if she went to church. "I had not lived with her since I was twelve," she says. "I had no idea.

"We went to the church that Sunday and the pastor preached about a sense of control. That screamed at me because I never had thought about it before. At the end of the message, he gave a call for salvation and he said there is a woman here God is speaking to. He said 'You know God is talking to you and I dare you to come up.' "

But she didn't. "*Nobody* dares me. I didn't move and I crossed the arms of my heart. I remember leaving the church and getting into the car and my mother saying to me, 'You know he was talking about you.' I remember being so annoyed with her and I was thinking, *You're not even where you need to be; how are you going to tell me somebody is talking to me?* But out of the three hundred people there, she was absolutely right.

"When the pastor gave the altar call the following Sunday, I had no idea what was going on. I had no real exposure in the way of salvation or Scripture, nothing. I think my ignorance was the best thing for me because I didn't have to unlearn anything. Sometimes I look at people and I almost pity them because they have all these traditions they have to work through.

"And so I was baptized and that was it. I started going to church regularly. I knew I needed to, and inside I knew there was something more. I just knew there was something more but I continued to live the life I was living; nothing was different. But I knew the Holy Spirit was wooing me into the love of God. I think subtly God sent people to come across my path."

She realizes she had a fear of a Godless death. "I think subconsciously I knew I would go to hell. God gives us an innate ability to know things about Him and somehow I made that connection.

"I believe I was saved that Sunday, but until we actually respond we don't know. We do it more for ourselves; God already knows. I don't believe you get saved when you go to the altar. Something has already happened in your heart before you go up. The truth is, I may have gotten saved that Sunday when I didn't cross my arms outwardly, but by responding openly you give yourself the tangible satisfaction of knowing. I think that's the thing that really helps us to begin our walk."

The Switch and the Hitch

Her life has never been the same since. She began realizing the lifestyle she was living was no longer meaningful. "I used to love to dance and hang out and go to clubs. And even though I would try to make myself do some of the things I was accustomed to, it was uncomfortable; it was extremely uncomfortable. Relationships became tense," she says, because the absence of purpose was evident.

She found purpose and satisfaction in Bible study, and revamped her life over the next three years. "It was like I was on a fast track. I was teaching a young children's Sunday school class. I knew I was growing… but I knew there were a lot of things that still weren't right, that were a struggle to me. I was very vocal and would share things with people. Sometimes they would get really uncomfortable and say things like 'Why don't you understand this?' and 'You don't get it.' I was really opinionated, so some things hadn't changed."

Her tendency to speak out—perhaps too quickly— strongly and self-assuredly is nothing new. She recalls saying things to her mother that upset her. "She would be really bothered and she would tell my dad, and he would say. 'If nobody is going to die let's not lose any sleep over it,' and that made her more upset. But I always remember, even at a very young age, saying what I felt and how I felt." She says her emotions often caused problems. "When I was little I would bite people on the shoulder if they picked on me and I didn't like them."

Curiously, she doesn't see herself as strong-willed, although she admits to the connection between that quality and control. "I see strong-willed kids now and think 'I wasn't like that,' and I'm not like that now, comparatively speaking. I have to admit, though, I always was that way but I think I suppressed it a little bit when I was with my mom because it bothered her so much."

She struggles even now. She recounts being with women in a prayer group and the subject of marriage came up. Frustration set in because she couldn't connect with them. "In my mind, nobody was getting it; *nobody* was getting it. I needed somebody who understood what I was saying and apparently that group didn't. I felt like I was going to choke somebody because they just weren't listening."

Her feelings, she believes, are the outgrowth of long-term stress. "It's related," she says, "to wanting to do things, having goals, and having really challenging times, difficult times, and sometimes an almost impossible time of getting some of those things accomplished. I have to take responsibility for a portion of it because as a controlling person I want to control everything. Sometimes I don't ask for help until the last bubble has gone up out of the straw. "

Road to Resolution

For any flaws she might have, Kaitlin exhibits an extraordinary level of awareness. She listens, thinks, and considers the balance between life as it is, and life—with God's help—as it might be.

Physical challenges played a role in her recent resignation from full-time ministry as a church-life director at her church, although she continued academic work in organizational management.

Full physical health is her priority. "I think we have a responsibility to physically take care of ourselves; our bodies can break down. Sometimes this is due to our own choices, and sometimes things just pass down from past generations. There are a number of ways things can transpire in our lives."

Part of getting back on track physically, she says, involves coming to clarity about where we honestly fit in God's plan; it's a tug-of-war between life and role. She says, "I enjoyed by far more of what I was doing before I was on staff than I did when I was on staff. I became a staff member because we all think it's noble for us to do full-time ministry because we want to honor God. But I never had a peace about it from day one, nor did I have peace the entire time I was there. And that just made it that much harder to be there.

"I went against my own instinct; so trying to live peacefully when it never was peaceful was difficult. I even attempted to manufacture peace. I try to make everything a learning opportunity, I don't care how good or bad it is. I think it's only bad if you don't learn. Still, it was just a constant, constant struggle and it was really frustrating, absolutely frustrating. I can't say it any clearer, it was absolute frustration."

Her struggle in finding her place comes back to the matter of control and the reactions of people around her to her efforts at control. Change—things and people that change—keep her off-balance.

"I can organize and put things together and know how it's supposed to run—the mechanics of it, the electronics of it—and it will do that every time for you. I probably should have been an accountant because that's how I need things to be, like clockwork. When you do something that wasn't a part of the plan, that wasn't what the rule was, and that's not the law, you're changing it. Then I have to rewrite it and I don't have time to rewrite the laws. Wait! And now it's all out of whack because there is no structure and no control."

She recognizes she has pushed people away by imposing her own order on people. "In personal relationships, I think my bar for expectations is pretty high. As I've gotten older, I recognize we are all flawed and I think I'm pretty good at accepting that. There are many people in my life I love dearly. There may be some things in their lives I might not care for—the way they perform or conduct their business, but it doesn't stop me from loving them or accepting them. I don't consider myself controlling in my relationships. I enjoy having them in my life and contributing to and receiving from them."

One weakness in her life is she sometimes seems to minimize other people's views. She recalls the friend's assertion that Kaitlin is too controlling. "The big missing piece here is, and again, she said that based on what *she* felt was controlling. It was that I have a strong personality. That's what she meant by it and I don't deny it at all."

She sees her mortal life and her life with God as an intellectual puzzle. "God is the one person in my life who can be disruptive and I give Him the lead to do that," she says. "There are many times He does things that totally go against the grain of comfort for me. But I always know I'm never going to be hurt and I'm never going to be disappointed, so I'll take the risk; it's okay. With people, obviously, it's different because they are not God."

She reflects back on the decision to leave her church ministry and says it drastically changed her life. "I don't believe in not being committed. I believe the Bible teaches that and I think it's important to be committed. I think I needed that time to work through the process, and I'm satisfied this is where I'm supposed to remain until God says to move. No matter what I'm feeling, I'm not going to run ahead of God."

Questions to Ponder

- Have you captured the main theme in Kaitlin's story?
- How important is it to deal with emotional trauma during ministry service and how does and should one address it?

- Can past experiences blind you to the need for emotional and spiritual transformation? Can you have spiritual transformation and still experience lack in the emotion that affects spiritual growth?

- Is it possible and how can the Church reject those who are emotionally scarred? Is this an example of spiritual pride?

Takeaway

- Emotional denial is a symptom of spiritual deficit. Denial of the existence of emotional lack can undermine spiritual progress, which inhibits spiritual development and growth.

- The need to control correlates with the emotional intelligence component of adaptability and the sub-component of flexibility. Experiencing low tolerance for flexibility has severe impact on those we serve, and could undermine the very Fruit of the Spirit of patience and love.

- Failure is not destiny. Emotional, academic, spiritual, or physical failure is an ingredient of ultimate success. What one does with failure is indicative of the potential for success. Absolution of pride is the acceptance of failure and the realization and launching pad for success.

CHAPTER SEVENTEEN

HAROLD MINOR: PHYSICAL ILLNESS AND LIFE DIFFICULTIES

. . . .

Harold Minor is a complicated man. A cancer survivor, recently relapsed, he is the product of a good, but challenged family. He grew up with one sister and three brothers, and he describes growing up in a tough South Bronx neighborhood in a family dependent on public assistance. Today, he is married with three sons, a man with creative talents as a painter and artist, formerly a museum employee, and more recently employed in ministry and in subsequent creative production for a major church.

One way or another, he has become a man dealing with discontent, conflict, anger, purpose, and control issues. He is a man who has for years turned to God for answers and direction. For many years he has dealt with resentment toward those who seem unwilling to allow him the space to do what God wants him to do.

Harold paints a picture of a conflicted life, simultaneously describing himself at a good place in his life, yet admitting family disconnects. "Discontent is not a bad thing, as long as it does not consume you," he says. "Our needs are being met...we are in a place where God is transitioning us and so I'm pretty happy with where I am relationally with God. My relationship with the Lord, with my wife, and my relationship with my children are all very strong, so personally I think I'm in a good place."

His internal conflicts spill over into his view of his primary relationships, as they have even from a young age. He speaks of being the only "born-again" member in his family growing up, minimizing and relegating his mother's devout Catholicism to "religious talk." He sounds judgmental in speaking of his parents and siblings, perhaps suggesting a lack of compassion despite his obvious expressions of love of God.

He has constructed a life-framework for himself that sets him apart from the people around him. "Every person needs to make a decision as to what they need to do for themselves regardless of their loved ones," he says. "You know, if I had a choice to serve God and pursue His purposes in place of having a relationship with anyone, I would choose God, over all, hands down."

Harold's perspective, conflicts, and search for control are in part a reflection of a volatile relationship with his alcoholic father. "I can't change him. God needs to change him. There was a lot of pain there at one time and now it's just the disappointment and fear," he says.

"The volatility of that experience, coming home and not being sure whether or not you were going to get hit or screamed at was frightening. You had no control over it. It created a lot of anger and I was a very angry child. And even into my teenage years I got into a lot of fights because I had a lot of anger inside."

"What is interesting is that my father's alcoholism caused me to become self-righteous," he says. He describes drifting away from his siblings, with the exception of a sister, because of lifestyle differences related to his being born-again. "It causes a certain distance to be there naturally because I'm living a certain way and it doesn't line up to the choices they make."

He says the situation would ordinarily be a prescription for failure. "I set out to change that. I wanted to become something despite the odds. And so I never drank and I never smoked, and I never did drugs," he says.

But, he says, "I was very angry and a lot of that self-righteousness in me was wrapped in this cloak of anger and it was not until I was in my early years in college that God really dealt with me. I was probably nineteen years old when He finally started to touch those areas and really made me realize I wasn't in control. I started asking bigger questions like 'Why on earth am I here? What's the purpose of this whole life? If I'm not in control, then who is?'

"I lowered my expectations on everybody. The person who was supposed to be my biggest advocate, embodying the most intense love, was my biggest enemy—my dad. He is supposed to love and care for me and he's coming home and telling me I'm a loser." He says he proved his father wrong. He was the only member of his family to graduate from high school and college.

He expresses shock that his father took credit for making his success possible. "It's unbelievable what a person can do in their own imagination and their own corrupt mind," he says. His father had bombarded him with assertions of worthlessness. Then, "he rationalized the reason he condemned me was because he knew I was going to do the opposite."

Considering the emotional storm he lived in at the time, it comes as small surprise that his realization of God's place in his life was dramatic. The anger was suddenly washed away, replaced by a self-possessed certainty and intensity. "I think it went along with my character at the time that when I put my mind to something, I wasn't going to waste time doing it. It was that kind of intensity," he says.

The intensity of his newly acquired persona produced a pushiness that characterized his interaction with women. "I had everything in control and everything was going as I planned and it got to a point where I was looking for somebody to share my love with in an intimate way," he says. "I don't know if that was a fault or if it was just a benefit to me, but it was just who I was. Whenever I dated, I scared most of the girls away because I became too committed. I spoke of commitment too quickly, which is kind of odd because women want to see commitment and I was very committed. So whenever I got involved in a relationship, it was very intense for me."

The issue was, in large part, a concerted effort to assert control in his life. "This was part of the self-righteousness that was building up over those years. I was going to be in control. I was looking for the one I was going to be able to commit to. And so I wasn't really looking for love; I wanted to look for the person I knew was made for me.

"I wasn't going to give away something I valued so highly myself, and I wasn't even a Christian. I was just a kid in the South Bronx growing up where everybody was sleeping around and getting pregnant. Premarital sex was rampant with children being born out of wedlock all over the place, people doing drugs, and here's this kid not doing any of that. I looked like an oddball in my community because I just I wasn't doing the things everyone else was.

"I was a virgin," he says, "until I got married. I never slept around and that was part of my control. This was part of my self-righteousness that was building over those years. I was going to be in control."

He says his focus wasn't so much about finding the love he never felt; rather, it was about developing the ability to share love in a way he never had before. "I had this plan and the plan was I was going to be successful,

I was going to be married and be happy...something I didn't have growing up."

He met his wife in college—she was a middle-class graphic design student from a New York suburb—and slowly developed a relationship before they began dating. "She was looking for somebody that would be committed, someone to love her, and take care of her and be her knight in shining armor. I fit the bill and I told her that," he says.

Despite his assertion of certainty and control over his direction, he admits to straying early on. Confusingly, he minimizes his error. He admits its potential magnitude, but rather than focus on its impact on her, seems only to see its meaning for him, as if the experience was something done to him.

"I cheated and, as minuscule as it might seem in the big picture, it was enough to rock me. I had built a house of cards that I called my life and I was in control of, and all of a sudden this one card got pulled."

The experience led him to intense self-questioning. He stopped seeing his wife-to-be for a year. He says he befriended a born-again Christian who helped him get back on track. "He recognized something that was happening in me and immediately started to nurture it." Harold says he developed and fed a hunger that grew inside, and which came to a head in a church service with a pastor who delivered just the right message at the right time.

"It felt like nobody else was in the congregation at that moment. I gave my life to the Lord that day and I went back to my girlfriend," he says. "She didn't know I had cheated. I was carrying around a lie for a year and I couldn't keep on carrying the lie."

Harold doesn't dwell on her feelings, admitting he picked a bad time to drop the news—the night before college graduation, a time of celebration. He talks about the effect of the admission on him. Tellingly, he uses the pronoun "I" a lot in describing the moment—"I picked the worst time," "I could hold off," " I needed," etc.

"I didn't have to do anything else because He forgave me of my sins. I was a new creature; I was a new believer. God was telling me 'Harold, you need to tell her. Before you can go on you need to let this go. It's going to affect the rest of your life if you don't tell the truth, if you don't say what brought you here. And if you are ashamed of your testimony, as the Scripture says, if you are ashamed to say what brought you to Christ, then you don't really love Me.' I just said 'God, I can't carry this any more, and if this ends my relationship then so be it.'"

Naturally, his girlfriend felt betrayed. "She cried; I mean I caused a lot of pain for her that night." But, he says, she knew he was changing, radically, "and she was curious to know what was happening and so she stuck around." And, he points out, they stayed together.

"I came to the understanding," he says, "I wasn't in control and I needed somebody to take control of my life. And that somebody was God."

The Change

Harold says suddenly even his language changed. Profanity, formerly a constant in his vocabulary, suddenly vanished. He credits God for, as he puts it, getting his attention. "It was so dramatic people around me noticed. They would look at me and say something is different and it wasn't just physical. That was the one thing I recall having changed immediately that really gave me a sense of 'This is real.' I could not have done that."

He says he found God speaking directly to him, giving him direction. "I would hear His prodding in my spirit telling me, 'You need to ask forgiveness from your friends, the people you cut off.' Because I had cut everyone off when I came to the Lord." And he was an eager listener due, to some degree he says, to his continuing need for control. "I knew when I made a commitment to Christ it was going to be full throttle; there wasn't going to be any gray area between me and God. I'm very stubborn that way."

Harold says he believes God can change a person's character and inclinations, to "make us better than what we were." He says God forced his change and enabled a change in his wife-to-be. "So her curiosity to find out what was causing me to change made her realize that she was missing the same thing."

Over the next several years they built their relationship with God in a way some might find odd. Rather than two people who become one, he says counter-intuitively, "We made a conscious decision to try to stay as distant from each other as possible. We needed to grow independently in the Lord rather than depending on each other to grow. We didn't want to use each other as a crutch in our relationship with the Lord. I think that was a healthy decision on our part, not to have this co-dependent relationship where we would be relying on each other. She would sit on one side of the sanctuary, I would sit on the other side…because we knew we needed to grow spiritually on our own."

Hard Transitions

His developing relationships with his spouse-to-be and with God drew the enmity of his father. He recounts his father pointedly saying, "You're a sinner and you're always going to be a sinner, and this relationship with this woman you have is hypocritical because I know what you used to be like."

Harold says it was a continuation of the hate —his word—his father always seemed to have for him. "From a very early age I remember him having a very intense anger toward me. He just didn't like something about me. But," he says, "I knew in order for me to heal I needed to forgive him."

Before their wedding, at God's urging he says, he returned to his father to try to move beyond the past. Other people might have begun by offering an olive branch of deference, but, "I called him into my room and I said, 'Dad, I want to speak to you about something.' "

He began by telling his father that he wanted to apologize and ask for forgiveness for "'holding contempt and anger in my heart for you and not respecting you'...When God asked me to do this, I had certain expectations. I thought something miraculous was going to happen and somehow there was going to be some fruit or healing...

"It was very emotional...very hard for me to ask for forgiveness from this man." Then he mentioned his imminent wedding. "And he looked me," Harold says, "dead in the face, sober as a stone, and said, 'I told you I'm not going to your wedding.' He turned around and walked out. I felt like I had just been kicked in the stomach. I felt like I bowed to this man and he kicked me in the face while I was down. And I wept and I wept and I wept. Not so much out of anger, but from complete confusion. When he left, I cried out to God and said, 'God why did you ask me to do this?' "

But he felt rejection—and healing. "I remember it so clearly. He said to me 'Now you know how my Son felt when He came to His own and His own didn't accept Him and didn't His accept forgiveness.' " He placed the experience entirely in God's purview. "I would have never,

never put myself in a position to get hurt like that. I don't think anybody in their right mind would." It was, he says, an *aha* moment in his life.

Sometimes when you have a fracture and it doesn't heal properly, he says, you have to break it again to set it right. That is what God had done, hurting him to heal him. And he says, "That is my desire, to be broken for God."

His wedding day was wonderful and his father did not come. "I've had to look outside of my experience on how to be a father," he says. "I'm giving my kids something I never had and a relationship with God I never had. I want to be an example of a God-fearing man who wants to live right for God and make a difference in society because of the God he serves."

He admits the possibility his boys may not turn out as he hopes, but, "I'm sure God will give me the grace to handle whatever comes my way."

His marriage is challenged because of financial troubles and by his health problems. He was diagnosed with leukemia in 2001, a cancer that brought him down quickly in a short period of time. Suddenly, he says, his survival was in question and he conceded control to God.

"I went into it very clear-minded and very opened-minded saying, 'God, whatever happens in this, let your glory and your will be done.' When I was in the hospital I was very intentional about witnessing my faith to those who were in a similar situation." He made it through, but his finances were wrecked, and the young family went on public assistance.

"It was a very strange period of time because I was very confident and I felt I heard from God that the cancer wasn't going to kill me. It was there to produce something in me. Am I going to look at it in despair and futility or am I going to look at it as giving praise to God in every situation?" He says he gave God an ultimatum: "If you take me, you are in charge of them. You are going to have to take care of them."

He says through the worst of it, his wife stayed positive and full of faith. And the situation brought out something like a religious limelight. God, he says, was using him. "So many people who came to visit me at the hospital," he says, "left more encouraged because of my disposition. Because of my attitude they were blessed. Sometimes when people would come, whether they were family members or church members, I would lay hands on them and pray for them. They were coming there to see me and God was using that situation to really bless them. I was in the bondage of my own illness and God was able to touch people and heal people.

Deepening Struggles

"It was very humbling for my wife to have to go on public assistance. She had to do it on her own," he says. "My focus...was on trying to get healthy." He credits God with providing food for his family. "All kinds of people and our neighbors would come and knock on our door and drop off groceries, or would make dinner for us. People we didn't know, unnamed people would send thousand-dollar checks to us in the mail. We just saw God's grace being poured out on us," he says. His cancer in check, he says, "God was allowing us to succeed and to continue growing."

His words overlook the deep money woes. Because he was working only a short time in a new church-related position, he was not entitled to disability benefits, and so for his family public assistance became a continuing need. "We were eating humble pie at that point."

He says it all intensified his focus on and relationship

to God. Reminded of Psalm 23 and *the shadow of death*, he realizes that shadows can't hurt. "If," he says, "you're in the valley and you're passing through, this means you're not dwelling there, you're going through it. This is a period of time when you are passing through; it's an important journey you just have go through."

After a time, the cancer returned. For seven months he underwent autologous—self-generated—stem cell transplantation and chemotherapy. Again, help through a food pantry and assistance from friends and community helped the family get by. "It just really brought us back to that place of humility and dependence," he says. His wife was getting worn down from the stress of financial trouble. "Without having money come from Heaven and drop on our laps," he says.

Self-assured to a fault, and confident in his relationship with God, he does not express empathy for his wife. "We've accomplished more and we're in a much better place now than we were when my wife was working," he says. "My kids are being home-schooled, my wife is staying home, and when we were both working she prayed for this situation. When God answers prayer it doesn't mean the answer doesn't come without consequences and sometimes those consequences aren't exactly what you had in mind. But it doesn't mean God didn't answer your prayer.

"I have," he says, "no regrets for things that happened. I wouldn't change them because they have deepened my relationship with God. They've rooted my faith even deeper.

Overcoming, Doing, Becoming
"Looking back, and I often say this to people, the last six or seven years have been the hardest to walk with

217

God because of the challenges I have faced. It has been the hardest. And I use a caveat by saying they have been the best experiences that I've had," he says.

Harold's creative talents led him to follow high school with further schooling in illustration. He became a freelance illustrator, had a hard go of it financially, and went to work at a major museum in New York, where he worked for six years fabricating exhibits. He moved on to direct exhibits at a small children's museum and from there, he says, God called him into the ministry, starting with a position overseeing a children's ministry.

"I always had a passion for kids and a passion for education. Not so much formalized education, although I pursued that at some point." He doesn't say when, but, "I went back to try to get my certification to become a teacher of education, and God very quickly put the stops to that and said, 'This is not the kind of teacher I want you to be; not a formal teacher in the classroom. I want you to teach children spiritual things.' And you can't do that in a classroom so I stopped going to school.

"I loved…designing and building exhibits and it was really hard to leave, but I wanted to do God's will. I wanted to pursue God and I said, 'God, I leave that behind and count it lost.'"

He postulates that God used him as His instrument in his various stops. "That has always been my prayer. I have no doubt…I had to let certain desires die so God could resurrect them the way He saw they were going to be useful to Him." He says he's dreamed of running a spiritual museum. "I do," he says, "see God being able to use some of the skills and some of the creative aspects of who I am to bless the Body of Christ or to bless people in general."

Creative to the end, today he runs a new media ministry in a large church, to facilitate spiritual understanding. "I'm fabricating or designing props or designing object lessons using drama, using video, using multimedia to assist or to come alongside of the sermon to drive it home further. We've seen a huge impact on people's lives by creating that *aha* moment for them in the message in the sermon. When Jesus taught, He taught in parables, stories, and illustrations of that day so people could understood that which was common to everyone."

He admits frustration in having bounced from endeavor to endeavor in search of the role God wants him to play in life. He says he enjoyed the children's ministry, but felt he'd done all he could do there. He says he told colleagues and superiors that the "fire had gone out" and he needed a change; he was no longer happy. "I feel God impressing me to go in this direction. Can we work toward that?"

He became sick again in the midst of this internal flux. "I saw that as God putting a stop to my plan and I said, 'You know what? I can't do this. I know I've got to change the way I'm doing things.'" After his last episode with illness, he talked with his pastor about tailoring a position for him. The pastor promised he'd work on it. Shortly afterward, he says, he had a vivid dream that rocked him.

"I dreamed I was in a waiting room. I had a gun stuffed in the back of my pants like in a classic movie," he says. He shuddered with anxiety and the fear of being discovered. Then, he says, "I rose, walked into a restroom, and threw the gun in the trash. I woke up in the morning with the feeling of anxiety and fear," and asking God what the dream might possibly have meant.

The morning became even more remarkable in his office at work just before a chapel service. "I'm reading the

Bible and I hear an audible voice. It made me turn around because I thought there was somebody in the room," he recalls. "And the voice said, 'Are you all right, are you okay?' I turned around and I knew I was hearing from God. I started to laugh because it was such a silly question and I audibly said, 'God, what a stupid question—am I all right? If anybody would know, it's you, so why would you be asking me this? Obviously, if you're asking me the question, it's because I'm not all right and you want me to see something. So what is it? What is it that you want me to see?'" I felt like Adam in the Garden. You know, when God said, 'Adam, where are you?' What do you mean where are you? God, you're God, you're all over the place. You know where he is so what are you asking him for? It was that kind of moment."

That afternoon, a pastor came to visit and asked him how he was. "He used the same words verbatim, the same words I heard that morning," Harold says. Harold told him about the dream and asked about its meaning. He says the pastor explained the waiting room might represent the desire to change the place in his life, and possibly the gun represented power and the yearning for control. "And he said the fact that you got up and went into the restroom and threw it away means you're going to make the right decision. I was completely blown away at that point.

"From early in my childhood," Harold says, "it was a matter of God taking control. He wants control. He wants to be in control and it's all been about giving up that control and letting Him have His way. And that's been an incredible journey. You know, I wouldn't change anything about it because it's been such a deep rearranging of my own life.

"And I can see God preserving, weaving himself in and around and through every aspect, every fiber of who

I am and that's all been based on my decision, my choice. When I speak to people and I share my testimony or in counseling to encourage them, I say our choices make all the difference of whether it's going to work or not."

Earlier, it's worth noting, he said, "Financially, I'm not happy as to where we are as a family, particularly for my wife and my children." But he adds, perhaps contradictorily, yet consistent with his take on God's involvement in his life's direction, "I think the most important things are healthy. And for that I'm thankful."

Questions to Ponder

- Have you captured the main theme in Harold's story?

- Can we correlate the emotional dimension of a near-death experience with the potential for spiritual growth?

- Of all the major scales of emotional intelligence—self-perception, self-expression, interpersonal, decision-making and stress management—which one is affected by anger? Can we correlate that with the Fruit of the Spirit?

- Love, joy, peace, patience—how do these interact with the component of anger experienced by Harold?

Takeaways

- A lack of forgiveness leads to an emotional constipation, which leads to potential health issues that can affect us permanently.

- Anger affects almost all major sub-scale categories of emotional intelligence—self-awareness, self-regard, empathy, interpersonal relationship, reality testing, flexibility, stress tolerance, impulse control, and optimism.

- Illness is not destiny. Our illness strengthens us and draws us close to God. Illness doesn't define us, but activates us to another level of service for God.

PART V

The Power of the Next Step

O ver the next five chapters, we will go into detail as to what it means to really and truly change and transition. This is transition that involves pouring out to God, our Father, our deepest fears, our deepest hurts, our deepest pain, and trusting Him that He will be with us and help us through the change process.

In the previous chapters, it is clear we have discussed emotional intelligence at length. We have gone through the definition. We have reviewed the historical context in which EI came to be. We have discussed the biblical examples and implications of emotional intelligence in previous times. The big question that remains is "Now what? What do I do now that I know about emotional intelligence?" After reading these many pages, I am sure God has been dealing with you about some changes you need to make to more effectively be what He has called you to be. If you, in fact, have wondered, I have the information. I know EI is important for me in my progression—in life, at work, at church.

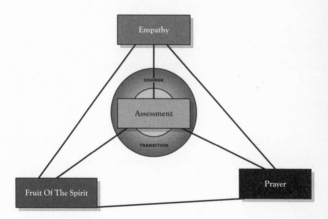

I have concluded, based on my own research, there are five steps that are required in order to maneuver through the journey I have been on for many years. These five steps I will call *Power Steps*. They are: 1) the Power of Empathy, 2) the Power of Assessment, 3) the Power of the Fruit of the Spirit, 4) the Power of Prayer, and 5) the Power of Change and Transition.

In general terms, before we can focus on making changes in our hearts, we will need to ensure we understand other people whom God has allowed to cross our paths. Understanding them, knowing what they are feeling, and showing we care is the crux of empathy. Assessment is an activity we should be practicing at all times. If we are called to be like Christ, we should be endeavoring to change every day. We should be endeavoring to be more like our Savior, Jesus Christ. It is with this constant searching of our spirits and souls we will be able to capture things in our very beings that do not embody Christ and so be able to cast off these behaviors that are not representative of Him who calls us.

In order to have lasting enduring change, we need prayer. Prayer is conversation with the Father. It is conversation with the One who has saved us and challenged us to live a life holy unto Him. Without prayer, we cannot incorporate change in ourselves. The Fruit of the Spirit represents for us the embodiment of who Christ is. The Fruit reflects our very likeness in Christ. So we pray to ensure the Fruit is demonstrated in our lives. Finally, if we are challenged to be more like Christ, to demonstrate the Fruit, then we should change. Change is instantaneous while transition is a continuous process. The Scriptures state in Luke 2:52, *"Jesus grew in wisdom and stature and in favor with God and man."* We continue to grow and, as such, we continue on this cycle to be more like Christ. The power triad will help us to be more like Him. In the next five chapters, we will go in depth into the power triad.

CHAPTER EIGHTEEN

THE POWER OF EMPATHY

• • • •

I n order to demonstrate the specifics of the Power Steps, I will cite passages from the Bible in 2 Samuel 11 and 12. This is the popular and well-known story of King David's fall into sin with Bathsheba and how David utilized all the power principles to get up and move forward even though he had stumbled. The story is not reflective of any one person's story, but as we examine it, my hope is that each of us will be able to identify with the story and how we at times have fallen. As we all know, the journey of the Christian is laden with times of falling and getting up again.

The synopsis of the story is King David had sent his army into battle and while his men were away, the Bible tells us that the king was on his rooftop and looked over and saw the beautiful Bathesheba bathing. David sent for her and she came to the king at his request. He slept with her and, in short order, she conceived a son.

When the king discovered he had fathered a child of the wife of one of his warriors, Uriah, he sent word to his captain, Joab, to send Uriah home. Upon his arrival, Uriah went straight to the king's palace instead of going home. While at the palace, King David instructed Uriah to go home. The king's intent was for Uriah to sleep with Bathesheba and, by doing so no one would know the child was the king's. Instead of going home, however, Uriah decided to sleep at the entrance to the palace. On finding this out, King David asked Uriah to stay for another night. Uriah told the king he couldn't go home and enjoy himself while all his comrades were staying in tents. David then attempted to get Uriah drunk so he could go home. That attempt also failed because Uriah slept on a mat among his master's servants.

Failing to get Uriah to go home and sleep with his wife, David sent word to Joab in a note that instructed him to put Uriah at the front of the battle where it was the fiercest and as the battle raged, to pull back so Uriah would be killed. The king's order was carried out and Uriah was killed.

After the time of Bathesheba's mourning for her husband was over, the king sent for her and she became his wife. This whole situation was contemptible. God was displeased. The king had schemed to have one of his very best warriors killed in order to cover up his sin.

The Lord sent the prophet Nathan to speak to King David. The prophet was instructed to bring to light the sin David had committed. Instead of speaking to the king directly about what had occurred, the prophet told the king a story wherein a rich man who had many lambs took one ewe lamb from a poor man who had only the one. The one lamb was precious to the poor man because it was the only thing he had. Nathan asked David what he thought of this.

King David burned with anger at the very thought that a rich man had taken from the poor. David's word was *"As surely as the Lord lives, the man who did this deserves to die"* (2 Samuel 12:5). This is a perfect example of empathy in action. David had expressed sincere sorrow at the fact the poor man in the story had been so wronged. He wanted justice. He wanted to see someone pay for such a crime. The example Nathan used in his story was likened to that of the king who had taken from Uriah the one wife he had, and then also had taken his life.

Empathy, by definition, is the ability to be aware of, to understand and to appreciate the feelings and thoughts of others.[1] It is the ability to take the place of another. It is the ability to see the hurt, pain, and discomfort another feels. Empathy does not mean that you agree with the other person. It simply means we adjust the way in which we are feeling to reflect what others might feel. In the psychological realm, it is exemplified by the process of *mirroring*, wherein one who delivers hurt is asked to mirror the exact feeling another might be feeling.

King David's first act in the Power Steps was empathy. He had recognized the sincere hurt caused by the rich man taking the one ewe lamb of the poor man. In this case, King David agreed it was important to be empathetic to the plight of the poor man, but he did not recognize the person in the story was actually a reflection of what he had done to Uriah.

The first part in Power Steps is empathy. It requires us to be empathetic to all we come in contact with. It requires us to show the feeling of another based on what we have seen and observed. In most cases it doesn't mean we agree, although we could. But it does mean we truly understand the anguish and hurt of another.

There is a young man, whom we shall call Charles, who was recently employed at a church. He was so excited at the prospect of working for the chancellor. The vice president who told me the story said he, himself, was actually excited about having a new face in the office. Within a few weeks, this young man was depressed. He had thought when he began working everything would be going well since he was working for the chancellor. One encounter changed all that. On day six of his employment, Charles was summoned to the chancellor's office. The chancellor told him he needed to complete an entire manual explaining all the activities of the staff and how they proceed in their jobs. He was told not to interview anyone, but to create the manual based on what he thought was the best thing to do.

Charles came to the vice president seeking advice because: 1) he was shocked that he would be given such an assignment, and 2) didn't the chancellor know he was new and he needed to get to know the other employees and to understand the current processes before he could enact changes. Actually, the chancellor knew because he interviewed and made the final decision to hire him. The vice president spoke to the chancellor, whose response was "He should know how to do this. He has a Ph.D. from one of the best schools in the country."

There are two things at play in the above example. They are 1) a lack of empathy and 2) emotional tone-deafness. The chancellor demonstrated both of these. The chancellor was right in his expectations of Charles, however, as research has shown, it is not only intellect that makes a person succeed, but also sincere operation of the emotions that will ultimately lead to success. Emotional tone-deafness is the inability to understand or interpret others' emotions. Whether conscious or not, a person who is emotionally tone-deaf makes the decision to eliminate emotion in the execution of processes and procedures. In this case, the chancellor, with the hope of getting to the end result, had consciously or unconsciously eliminated any thought as to how Charles might have felt. Charles was new. He was suffering through the first few days of getting acquainted with the new environment. He was trying to figure out the political landscape.

Though those are all valid and they focus on the emotion dimension, the chancellor was not interested in any information related to that. He was tone-deaf. He did not understand how Charles felt, nor did he care to understand. Had he taken a step back and looked at what someone feels when they are starting a new job, he might have been able to apply some empathy in the form of: 1) giving Charles time to assimilate into his new environment, 2) showing care and love for the new employee, and 3) understanding the emotional upset Charles might have been experienced when told he needed to complete the project and he needed to have it done in short order without any information from other colleagues. Empathy, if utilized, would have caused Charles and the chancellor to connect on a deeper level so they could have actually understood the work that needed to be done and how it could have been done.

We, at times, can become totally tone-deaf when dealing with others because we just want to get the work done. We are interested in performance to the detriment of emotions and relationship. This story took place in a church, but it could have been in corporate America as well. It doesn't matter. It means we need to apply empathy to be able to understand what other people are experiencing and how they are feeling. We need to be attuned to someone's emotional upsets and state of mind.

In 2006, I went on a mission trip for two weeks to the Dominican Republic. We had approximately fifty people with us on the trip. I was having a good time preparing for a leadership conference we would be having later during the week. I was sitting at a table with a group of five people during dinner one evening. We had all gathered for the evening's debrief and a particularly mature woman (I'll call her Laura) started to talk to me. The conversation was as follows: "Rupert, our pastor has lost a lot of weight hasn't he?" My response was, "Yes, Laura, he sure has. God has blessed him in getting rid of those pounds and I am glad he's running frequently now." Laura's response was "I don't know, but it appears the weight he's lost, you've gained."

I still remember this story and, actually, I will probably remember the story and this lady for the rest of my life. Whenever I feel that I am eating a bit too much, her face comes to me. Whenever I see others overeating, her retort comes to me. Was she being honest? Of course. I had gained five pounds over the past few weeks and I weighed 169 pounds and was 5 feet 7 inches tall. I felt slender and I didn't feel like I was overweight. My pastor had lost seventy pounds. How could she say that…especially with other people around?

Let's examine this for a moment. 1) Was she telling the truth? Yes, but I had gained five pounds, not seventy. 2) Did she mean well? Yes, I do believe she meant well. 3) Was she a Christian? Yes, she has been serving the Lord probably for as long as I had been alive, which was over forty years. 4) Then how could she say such a thing?

This had nothing to do with her service to the Lord. Actually, I am more empathetic toward her now because I know she didn't know any better. Did that eliminate the hurt? No, it didn't. She was completely un-empathetic. She lacked the basic ability to connect with me on a deeper level and to understand her words were going to create a hurt in me that would probably last a lifetime. I still see Laura today at church and I hug her like I never have before. She has helped me to understand just how dangerous our words are and to be more empathetic toward others. This might be an extreme case because Laura, at her age, really didn't care what people thought and felt.

Even in the service of God, empathy is required. It doesn't mean we check our emotions at the door and move forward without caring how others feel or express themselves. Empathy means we take the place of another to understand what they might be feeling, how they might respond, and what they might conclude based on our actions. It requires us to be sensitive to others and how they seem.

Empathy is tied to emotional self-awareness. If we are not aware of our emotions and what our emotions communicate, we run the risk of hurting our closest friends and family. Emotional self-awareness is one of the hallmarks or cornerstones of emotional intelligence. Emotional self-awareness is the ability to recognize my feelings, to differentiate between them, to know why I am feeling these feelings and to recognize the impact my feelings have on others around me.[2] To be emotionally self-aware and to be empathetic is the first step in the emotional intelligence sphere.

A final thought on empathy. The most empathetic person in the Bible was Jesus Christ. I still remember the words my pastor said to me as I began this journey of experiencing emotion in its true form. My pastor said to me, "Jesus never let anyone feel less than themselves." He understood how others felt—the shame from a divorce, the condemnation for sinning, and the hurt from abandonment. Jesus understood it and in His interaction with men, no matter who they were, He never let them feel less than who they were.

Can you imagine if you shared the hurt others have given out to you? How would you feel if you were the one who was receiving all the hurt you had endured? You wouldn't feel good. You wouldn't feel you deserved it. Jesus took our place on Calvary. He didn't agree with nor did He condone the sins we committed. One thing for sure is that He went to the Cross to take our place. That is empathy in action.

Jesus is God and He came to Earth to become man so He could take our place. As I close this section, I wonder if we consider how our words and actions might have impacted others with whom we have come in contact. If we could pause for a moment and take the place of those whom we might be sharing our anguish, upsets, and thoughts with, I wonder how we would receive it? That is empathy in action. It is to stop time, think about what I am about to say, how I am about to say it, to whom I am about to say it, and rehearse it before delivering it.

As we continue the story of King David, we recognize he was empathetic when he thought of what was happening to someone else. Is there anything we are doing that, if we were to separate ourselves from the situation regarding others, we would pause and be as outraged as King David?

Closing the Section

1. Pause for moment. Can you think of a time when you could have been more empathetic with someone because of what they said or did?

2. Ask God to give you insight.

3. Close your eyes and meditate for a minute; then open your eyes.

4. Pray the following: "Dear Lord, I know I need to be more like you. Whenever I am with anyone, I pray that my actions and my words will not cause them to feel less than themselves. God, give me the power of empathy to be able to understand others better and treat with consideration the very ones that you have put in my midst. Thank you. I ask this in Jesus' name. Amen."

5. Write down what God has revealed to you.

CHAPTER NINETEEN

THE POWER OF ASSESSMENT

· · · ·

Assessment by definition is the action or an instance of assessing. It is to make an evaluation or an estimate of a thing, an activity, or a person. Assessment in certain situations can be painful, especially if there are significant differences between what is perceived versus what someone thinks or believes. In chapter 18, we began the story of David's sin when he slept with Bathsheba. We left the story shortly after David had committed adultery with Bathsheba, she had conceived a child, and David had her husband Uriah killed. The Lord sent the prophet Nathan to confront David about his terrible sin.

Nathan told the king a story about a rich man who had taken possession of the only lamb a poor man had. David was incensed by what the rich man had done and immediately ordered that he be put to death. This is an example of empathy.

Nathan's response to him is told in 2 Samuel 12:7-13:

> Then Nathan said to David, "You are the man! This is what the LORD, the God of Israel, says: 'I anointed you king over Israel, and I delivered you from the hand of Saul. I gave your master's house to you, and your master's wives into your arms. I gave you the house of Israel and Judah. And if all this had been too little, I would have given you even more.
>
> 'Why did you despise the word of the LORD by doing what is evil in His eyes? You struck down Uriah the Hittite

with the sword and took his wife to be your own. You killed him with the sword of the Ammonites.

'Now, therefore, the sword will never depart from your house, because you despised Me and took the wife of Uriah the Hittite to be your own.'

This is what the LORD says: 'Out of your own household I am going to bring calamity upon you. Before your very eyes I will take your wives and give them to one who is close to you, and he will lie with your wives in broad daylight.

'You did it in secret, but I will do this thing in broad daylight before all Israel.'"

Then David said to Nathan, "I have sinned against the LORD." Nathan replied, "The LORD has taken away your sin. You are not going to die."

There are two evidentiary assessments in the passage: the first is a self-assessment and the second is a direct-assessment. The direct assessment came from God through His prophet Nathan to David. It is obvious from the passage David had committed adultery with Bathsheba. It is evident from the passage he had not seen the sin in the light God had seen it. He had a view that normalized, or toned-down, the drastic effect of his actions—not just the adultery, but the plot to kill Uriah, Bathsheba's husband.

Too often, we do not see ourselves. We do not see ourselves the way others see us. We go along blindly thinking everything is okay and all is well when there is critical evidence we have done something wrong, not from a moral perspective, but something that is not received well by others. The adage goes that, "We are the last to know we have bad breath." We are the last to know how others perceive us, and the effect our actions are having on others around us. Needless to say in David's case, he had committed a tremendous sin and through Nathan, God gave him a direct assessment by letting him know, through the story, that he had committed a terrible sin against God.

There are two possible outcomes to our actions. There is a penalty and there are consequences to our actions. In this case, David's penalty was surely to be death, but Nathan quickly let him know he would not die. However, there were consequences of the sin he had committed. These consequences ranged from the death of the unborn child to upheaval in his family line.

Direct Assessment

Direct assessments can be painful. They can be confrontational. They can cause us to pause and take stock of what we have done and what has occurred in our lives. How we react to the assessment is more powerful than the actual acts that led us to the assessment. God wants us to recognize who we are and what we are. He wants us to understand we are not perfect. But the attempt should be made, as Matthew 5:48 tells us, to be perfect as our heavenly Father is perfect. We should strive to be more like Him. However, at times, others will confront us about our behavior and our actions.

In chapter 1 of this book, the story is told of my initial, direct assessment by my senior pastor dealing with the fact I was causing hurt to people and I was not aware of it. My first reaction was denial because I could not believe I had been a Christian for so long—over twenty years—and could be exhibiting behaviors contrary to the very teachings of Christ. It is possible for each of us to do that. The Bible states in Romans 3:23, *"all have sinned and have fall short of the glory of God."* It doesn't matter in which dimension we have done things that are not reflective of God, whether it is in the spiritual, emotional, or intellectual. The important thing is we will be assessed either by those around us or even by God himself, through His Word or a prophet.

By definition I am a pacesetting leader.[1] A leader who is a pacesetter has a high standard; has a high level of energy and stamina; ensures things are done on time, on budget, and meeting all requirements; demands excellence from others, and if they don't

237

deliver, the pacesetter jumps in and takes over the situation to get the desired results (*see Appendix for chart depicting the leadership styles characteristics*). I was that person. But in doing so, I was demanding too much from the folks I worked with at the church. A crucial and almost critical requirement for all pacesetting leaders is they have other pacesetters around them, and if not, the result could be disastrous. I am driven, and by being that way, I wasn't aware I was hurting people.

After denial, we then address the fact we are at fault and have done something not reflective of true Christianity. In 2 Samuel 12:13, David said, *"I have sinned against the Lord."* Once he had a direct assessment, he complied and agreed based on his self-assessment that he certainly had done something wrong.

Agreeing something is wrong is the first step in having the Holy Spirit lead you toward addressing the challenges you have. My performance was wrapped up in ensuring things were done right at this mega church. I cared less about people and who they were and what they were doing. Instead, I was focused on getting things done to the detriment of those around me.

Self-assessment

Once my senior pastor confronted me, it was just the beginning. By admitting the fact something was not right, I knew I needed to understand what was going on in my life that caused me to want to focus only on performance. This led me to seek out those who could help identify the specific issues, from an emotional perspective, that were driving me toward the place where I ignored others for the sake of achieving success. This led to a self-assessment using the Bar-On Emotional Intelligence Test.[2]

The Bar-On Emotional Intelligence Test assesses an individual on the various emotional intelligence key components of intrapersonal, interpersonal, adaptability, stress management, and general mood skill scales.[3] Chapter 7 details the various components with the associated definitions. The Self-perception component is knowing oneself and addressing the inner self. It is understanding the key actions it takes to be successful, such as self-regard, self-actualization, and emotional self-awareness. The Self-expression component addresses outward expression based on internal perception. It consists of emotional expression, assertiveness, and independence.

Interpersonal skill understands our relationships and how we interact with the environment in the area of empathy, social responsibility, and interpersonal relationships. Decision-making addresses the way we use emotional information to make decisions. It is done through problem solving, reality testing, and impulse control. Stress management is the ability to withstand stress in the environment while keeping control of our circumstances, which is evident through our flexibility, stress tolerance, and optimism.

The EI test presents the individual with 133 questions and from there, through technical analytics, is able to tell the individual where he or she stands from an emotional intelligence standpoint. After completing the test, from a personal perspective, it identified areas such as interpersonal relationships, impulse control, and emotional self-awareness as areas in which I was not fully developed. I struggled with this because I thought I had mastered these areas. The assessment, however, indicated I had not. I accepted, like David, there was a shortcoming in my life. As a pacesetting leader, I was moving in an expeditious manner without due care for those who were around me. The result was there were hurt people. From the assessment, I knew I needed to improve these areas and fortunately, I was able to garner information as to what I needed to do in order to improve.

360° Assessment

Interestingly enough, the self-assessment test tells the individual who they are and what they are supposed to do to improve. The important word here is *self*, which means it is an assessment based on my responses as to what I feel and what I think. The most telling evaluation, however, is to have others give you input on your assessment. The 360° assessment takes into consideration ratings of others and what they think of us.

I was fortunate to be able to have the 360° assessment done on my behalf. I thought since I had done the self-assessment and I was working on myself, the evaluation of others relative to my emotional quotient would be completely in line with what I thought of myself. I was eager to get the feedback from others so I solicited thirteen individuals to provide input into my assessment. I asked supervisors, peers, friends, family, pastors, etc., to provide their honest, anonymous feedback as to what they thought of me in various situations as I performed my job or lived my daily life.

I received the results and it was like having an out-of-body experience. The individuals who gave me feedback about my assessment were correct in what they thought of me in areas of deficiency and excellence. The stark difference was that I thought of myself as being more developed in certain areas, but those who provided the assessment concluded I was not. The result of this assessment was shocking and numbing. My best friends and compatriots rated me disastrously on some areas I thought I was well developed in. They indicated from an impulse control perspective I did not and was not able to control myself during situations that were highly stressed. They were not comfortable with me from an interpersonal perspective. The anger I exhibited at times, when things were not done according to how I liked them, was not well received.

This is assessment at its highest level. It is to have others who are close to you and distant from you tell you exactly what they think of you. Denial, anger, hurt, and all other emotional reactions are inherent in this process, but accepting the information and making a decision to improve is key to our development. The assessment indicated that even though I had been a Christian for over twenty years, I still had shortcomings. I still needed to deal with them and the assessment pointed them out in raw detail.

King David was assessed by God and Nathan. He even did a self-assessment. He knew he had done wrong. After we have an assessment, the question is what should we do? What do individuals do after an assessment? In order to grow in Christ, it requires us all to humble ourselves, accept our shortcomings, and begin the work on them. As Jesus said, said, *"Be perfect therefore, as your heavenly Father is perfect."*

Closing the Section

1. Pause for moment. Please see endnote 2 of this chapter, related to assessment. Plan to take the assessment.

2. Ask God to prepare your heart for what will come from the assessment. Are you someone who receives feedback well, or do you tend to deny assessment responses?

3. Close your eyes and meditate for a minute; then open your eyes.

4. Pray the following: "Dear Lord, as I prepare for this assessment, I ask you to search my heart. I ask you to bring to fruition all the areas you want me to improve. Lord, I long to be like you. Though the results might be painful, I ask that you give me wisdom through the information that will be provided through the self-assessment or the 360° assessment. Lord, use these instruments to allow me to be more like you. I pray this in Jesus name. Amen."

5. Write down what God has revealed to you.

CHAPTER TWENTY

THE POWER OF PRAYER

. . . .

In chapter 18, we began our focus on 2 Samuel 11 and 12. The backdrop is King David's adultery with Bathsheba. In chapter 19, we discussed assessment and how important it was for the king to assess himself as to the sin he had committed with Bathsheba. God's confrontation with the king was to send His prophet Nathan to tell David a story of a rich man who had taken possession of the only lamb a poor man had. Unbeknownst to David, the story Nathan told was the story of David's own life and indiscretion.

Once confronted with the fact he was the one about whom Nathan was speaking, David swiftly made an assessment of himself and confessed with the following words, *"I have sinned against the Lord."* Once he had admitted his sins, the Lord through Nathan pronounced judgment upon him and 2 Samuel 12:14 tells us, *"But because by doing this you have made the enemies of the Lord show utter contempt, the son born to you will die."* Shortly thereafter, the Lord struck the child born to Bathsheba and he became extremely ill. The next statement leads us to the power principle of the next step—prayer. In 2 Samuel 12:16, *"David pleaded with God for the child. He fasted and spent the nights lying in sackcloth on the ground."*

It is interesting to note David prayed to God when he recognized he had done something terribly wrong. He responded to God before God passed judgment on him. He prayed to God even before the child died. David knew instinctively that God was a God of mercy and if he prayed, he hoped that forgiveness would come. He would later worship God even after the child actually died.

So why did David pray and what does this passage tell us as it relates to our journey and the power of the next step? Prayer by definition is to have a conversation with God. But it is not just to have a conversation. It is to have a conversation in order to connect with God. Dick Eastman, in his book *The Hour That Changes the World,* writes, "Prayer is the divine enigma—that marvelous mystery hidden behind the cloud of God's omnipotence. Nothing is beyond the reach of prayer because God himself is the focus of prayer."[1] E. M. Bounds agreed in *The Necessity of Prayer*, when he wrote, "Prayer is the contact of a living soul with God. In prayer, God stoops to kiss man, to bless man and to aid in everything that God can devise or man can need."[2]

The power principles speak first about empathy, understanding others, and putting oneself in the other person's shoes. The next step in the principle is the power of assessment, which is to understand where we are currently relative to where God wants us to be. The third of the principles is to pray. We pray because knowing and understanding who you are, knowing where you are, and what needs to be changed, does not guarantee change. It is possible for us to focus on the things that need to be changed and to rely upon our very own strength to accomplish change in our lives. As we've stated before, Matthew 5:48, says, *"Be perfect, therefore, as your heavenly Father is perfect."* At no point did God expect us to be like Him all on our own. As one reflects on this power step, there are some things to consider.

Answered Prayer

Recently, I was driving in my car with my lovely wife Maryann, and I asked her a question that had been troubling me. "Maryann, do you think there are some questions that God answers quicker than..." Before I could finish the sentence with "others," she quickly interrupted and said unequivocally, "Yes!" This brings me to the purpose of why you pray from an emotional intelligence standpoint. You pray so God can change you. Not just change you, but change you into His very being. We know we can never be perfect, and we will not receive perfection until we get to Heaven. One thing for sure, though, is while we are on Earth, God wants us to be more like Him (the Fruit of the Spirit) in our everyday life. So we pray to be more like Him. But praying to be more like Him is not just a verbal request and—*abra ka dabra!*—we become what we pray for.

Getting back to my wife as we drove that day, the reason she was so quick to say yes is because God is waiting for us to ask to be like Him. I have found a key that causes us to be more like Him, but it is not something that is well received by most Christians of our generation. That prayer is "Lord, break me today, so I can be more like you." Prior to His death on the Cross, Jesus said some interesting words to Simon Peter in Luke 22:31-32. It reads, *"Simon, Simon, Satan has asked to sift you as wheat. But I have prayed for you, Simon, that your faith may not fail. And when you have turned back, strengthen your brothers."* You see, the enemy is just waiting to sift us. He asks Jesus' permission to sift us, to tempt us, to break us. The secret is that lasting change is a result of breaking. Change in the emotional dimension is from breaking.

So when I asked my wife if there are prayers God answers more quickly than others, it is not that Jesus answers the prayers quicker, but that the enemy is forever tempting us to see who we really are in Christ. The key is Jesus has already prayed for us and interceded with the Father on our behalf. So by praying to God to break us, it is without any thought these prayers will be answered more quickly than we really want; it is in the answering of this prayer God will be glorified.

When I began this journey in the emotional, I thought I knew everything I needed to know about emotional intelligence. I had read all the books. I read a total of twenty-five books in three months. My yearning to understand this dimension was all I lived for. Once I did the assessment, I recognized that the reading of books was not what leads to transformation and change. It was the experiencing of God changing us to be like Him that really delivered the change. In this lies the great challenge. What do I do to be more like Christ? It means to be broken in order to be more like Him.

Types of Prayer

For those who are not aware, there are many types of prayers we can pray. There is the prayer of praise wherein we praise our Father and just exalt His name. It is an act of divine magnification. There is the payer of confession wherein we confess our shortcomings to the Lord. There is the prayer of intercession wherein we intercede on behalf of someone or some community, state, country, or region. There is the prayer of petition wherein we seek God for our personal needs and desires. There is the prayer of thanksgiving wherein we give the Lord thanks for what He has done. These prayers will be needed as you journey for change in the emotional dimension.

Prayer of Praise – Definition: Praising God for the journey we are about to go on. It is important to praise God for what He is about to do in our lives. The fact that one is confronted about an emotional shortfall should not be reason to become resentful of those who have given us such news. Consider God put someone in your life to give you feedback and you're in receipt of this feedback. Consider the feedback a gift. How can it be a gift? How can critique be a gift? Is anything lost with God? No. Then it is a gift because with this gift, God will change you for His glory. He will change you so you can reach to the height He has created each of us to attain. So praise Him when you receive feedback that will lead to change. There is an old saying: "Nothing goes to waste with God." So begin praising Him now for what He is about to do.

Prayer of Confession – Definition: Pray about the wrong we have done. Pray that the emotional upheaval caused by our lack might lead to sound change. To confess means first recognizing we are off track and then making the ultimate decision to correct the wrong. It was extremely difficult for me to accept the information I received in my assessment many years ago. Some of the feedback was hurtful. One statement said, "Rupert does not know how to build relationship." I consider myself a happy guy. How could someone say such a thing? The assessment stated my emotional self-awareness was low. How dare they conclude that about me?

Obviously, I was in denial. After I thought about the findings, I recognized it wasn't so much about me, but about what God was telling me through these assessors. Once I recognized that, I began to think through things I might have done in the past relative to how I behaved and responded to others. Soon I had memories coming back of the wrong I have done to others. I quickly and immediately, like King David, said, "Lord, I have sinned." Confession is good for the soul. As we discover things in the emotional, we should constantly pray to God for His hands to reach in and change our circumstances and for us to be more like Him.

Prayer of Petition – Definition: Prayer of brokenness. Petition in the emotional realm can only be captured in one word— brokenness. Whatever you find as a result of your assessment, it is important to bring to God. As I stated, every time you receive feedback, take it to God. Ask God if it is true. Be prepared that the answer, nine out of ten times, is going to be "Yes, it's true," and be prepared to go through the excruciating pain to change. The prayer I fear the most is "God, break me today." I know He will answer it. The result is sometime during the day, God is going to bring something to my attention through others. I can immediately deny. The time periods between denial, praise, confession, and petition have become shorter and shorter as I have been on this journey. Lately, I do not deny. I accept what others say, take it directly to God, and in short order, I am praising Him for the change that is about to come. I am confessing all I have done and petitioning Him to change me so I can be more like Him.

Prayer of Thanksgiving – Definition: Prayer of thankfulness. Thank God for the breaking. It is the antithesis of what we are taught to be joyful during times of trouble. The Bible states in 2 Corinthians 7:4, *"I have spoken to you with great frankness; I take great pride in you. I am greatly encouraged; in all our troubles my joy knows no bounds."* James 1:2 says, *"My brethren, count it all joy when ye fall into divers temptations"* (KJV) and in the NIV, *"Consider it pure joy, my brothers and sisters, whenever you face trials of many kinds."* Why would I be joyful when I am assessed and I receive feedback I am not who I thought I was? How could I be joyful when I have done all I can and others around me are telling me I need to do more? How can I keep changing when I have changed all I can? These questions will permeate your very being as you go on this journey. The most interesting thing is that as you go on this journey, you will not be who you were when you started out, but instead you will be someone who has been dramatically and drastically changed for His glory. Again, Matthew 5:48: *"Be perfect therefore, as your heavenly Father is perfect."* God calls each of us to be like Him.

A story is told of a religious sage who was approached by a young student who asked him where success was. He said to the sage, "O great one, please point me to success." The sage lifted his head up and pointed to the left that led to a dark tunnel. The young student took off and as he went there was a loud noise as the student ran into many fixed objects. It sounded like a car wreck. The student came out hurt and upset. He said to the sage, "I asked you to point me to success, so please do that. See what you have done?" The sage lifted up his head and pointed left into the dark tunnel. The student took off and again the same thing occurred—noise, objects hitting objects, pain, hurt, turmoil. The student came out of the tunnel irate and upset. He said to the sage,

"See what you have done. I am hurt, I am in pain, and all I asked you was to point me to success." The sage lifted up his head and spoke. This time he said, "My son, success is right down the road, right after pain, hurt, and turmoil." We cannot get to where we need to be without going through pain. It is for that reason we rejoice and are thankful for what is happening to us because our Father knows that right after pain and hurt, comes success in Him.

Emotions in the Midst of Prayer

Emotions do not move God. Neither crying, weeping, anger, wrath, nor any of the other countless emotions actually affect God. It is prayer that moves God to action. My intention is not to be uncaring about the feelings you might experience throughout the Power Steps—Empathy, Assessment, Prayer, Fruit of the Spirit, and Change and Transition. The feelings, the hurt, and, at times, the unreasonable judgment you will feel from others are ingredients in the process to make anyone emotionally fresh and adjusted. By no means do I intend to conclude these do not matter. They do, and as humans we have to learn how to process them while praying and going through the many feelings. The birth of Samuel, in 1 Samuel 1:1-20, is an example of this:

> There was a certain man from Ramathaim, a Zuphite from the hill country of Ephraim, whose name was Elkanah son of Jeroham, the son of Elihu, the son of Tohu, the son of Zuph, an Ephraimite. He had two wives; one was called Hannah and the other Peninnah. Peninnah had children, but Hannah had none. Year after year this man went up from his town to worship and sacrifice to the LORD Almighty at Shiloh, where Hophni and Phinehas, the two sons of Eli, were priests of the LORD. Whenever the day came for Elkanah to sacrifice, he would give portions of the meat to his wife Peninnah and to all her sons and daughters. But to Hannah he gave a double portion because he loved her, and the LORD had closed her womb.

And because the LORD had closed her womb, her rival kept provoking her in order to irritate her. This went on year after year. Whenever Hannah went up to the house of the LORD, her rival provoked her till she wept and would not eat. Elkanah her husband would say to her, "Hannah, why are you weeping? Why don't you eat? Why are you downhearted? Don't I mean more to you than ten sons?" Once when they had finished eating and drinking in Shiloh, Hannah stood up. Now Eli the priest was sitting on a chair by the doorpost of the LORD's temple. In bitterness of soul Hannah wept much and prayed to the LORD.

And she made a vow, saying, "O LORD Almighty, if you will only look upon your servant's misery and remember me, and not forget your servant but give her a son, then I will give him to the LORD for all the days of his life, and no razor will ever be used on his head." As she kept on praying to the LORD, Eli observed her mouth. Hannah was praying in her heart, and her lips were moving but her voice was not heard. Eli thought she was drunk and said to her, "How long will you keep on getting drunk? Get rid of your wine." "Not so, my lord," Hannah replied, "I am a woman who is deeply troubled. I have not been drinking wine or beer; I was pouring out my soul to the LORD.

Do not take your servant for a wicked woman; I have been praying here out of my great anguish and grief." Eli answered, "Go in peace, and may the God of Israel grant you what you have asked of Him." She said, "May your servant find favor in your eyes." Then she went her way and ate something, and her face was no longer downcast.

Early the next morning they arose and worshiped before the LORD and then went back to their home at Ramah. Elkanah lay with Hannah his wife, and the LORD remembered her. So in the course of time Hannah

conceived and gave birth to a son. She named him Samuel,
saying, "Because I asked the LORD for him."

The story is told of Elkanah, Hannah, and Peninnah. Both Hannah and Peninnah were married to Elkanah. Based on technical theology there is a phrase, "The Law of First Mention" and since in verse 2, Hannah was mentioned first, it can be concluded she was the first wife that Elkanah had married. I must state that although there are practices of polygamy numerous times in the Bible, it is, however, not the norm in present day society. One of the wives, Hannah, was barren, but Peninnah had children. The lack that Hannah experienced coupled with the fact that Elkanah loved her more led to rivalry and hurt in the home.

The evidence that Elkanah loved Hannah more is observed when they go to celebrate the yearly feast. Each time, Hannah would get a double portion of the peace offering from Elkanah. The result was Peninnah would taunt Hannah about the fact that she was barren and did not have a child. The irritation went on year after year. Peninnah would abuse Hannah with her taunts. There was a lack in Hannah's life and she was reminded of it by Peninnah. It wasn't a friendly reminder, but one that seared Hannah's soul because in those days not to have a child was a type of shame. The taunts caused Hannah to weep.

She was weeping at one of the feasts when Elkanah asked her, *"Hannah, why are you weeping? Why don't you eat? Why are you downhearted? Don't I mean more to you than ten sons?"* In this case, it is clear Elkanah had completely missed the point. Hannah was emotionally hurt, and Elkanah, instead of dealing with the emotional issues at hand, made the issue about himself and tried to solve the problem instead of listening. Hannah was hurting. She was ashamed. She was downtrodden because she didn't feel worthy, yet Elkanah was wondering why she would not eat.

At times while going through emotional trauma and change, you will not feel like eating. At times you will not feel there is anything you can physically do to stop the pain and hurt. At times it feels as if the world does not care about the change you're processing and going through. This was evident in what Hannah was feeling. In verse 10, it speaks of the anguish Hannah felt, which she could not take anymore. *"In bitterness of soul, Hannah wept much and prayed to the Lord."* Then Eli, suspecting that Hannah was drunk as she prayed, asked her how long would she keep on being drunk. Hannah responded by saying, *"Not so, my lord. I am a woman who is deeply troubled. I have not been drinking wine or beer; I was pouring out my soul to the Lord."*

The important thing is Hannah saw something in her life that needed to be changed and adjusted. She hurt from the taunts Peninnah made toward her. She had feelings. She was a human being. She hurt. It does not dismiss the fact that she hurt. It does not dismiss the fact she showed the very emotion that is in the makeup of most of us. God could have had mercy on her before she poured out her soul in anguish for not having a son. He didn't. It wasn't until she prayed. It wasn't until she brought the matter to the foot of the Cross that God began to move. It wasn't until she brought the matter to God and made the request that if He gave her a son she would give the boy back to Him. It was Hannah's prayer that shaped God's reponse. It was Hannah's prayer that moved God. It was Hannah reaching out to God and asking Him to rectify the situation. God responded by giving her a son. His name was Samuel.

In James 4:2-3, the Bible states: *"You want something but don't get it. You kill and covet, but you cannot have what you want. You quarrel and fight. You do not have, because you do not ask God. When you ask, you do not receive, because you ask with wrong motives, that you may spend what you get on your pleasures."* It is clear Hannah's motives were right. She wanted a child so she could give that child back to God.

As we bring this section to a close, I return to the beginning with King David recognizing he had sinned. He knew there would be a penalty and a consequence for his sin. The penalty was death, but the prophet told him God would not kill him. However there were other consequences: the baby would die; Amnon, King David's first-born, would be murdered; Absalom, David's third son, would be slain; and Adonijah, his fourth son, would be executed. King David decided to fast and pray to ask God to change the consequences of his actions. Unfortunately in the end, the baby died and all the tragedies in his family ensued.

In both of these stories—the sin of David and the birth of Samuel—prayer resulted in different outcomes. King David's son who was born, as a result of adultery, died. Hannah had a child, Samuel, who became the greatest prophet in Israel's history. Both individuals prayed. Both sought God to change their circumstances and both had a different result. We will discuss the different results in chapter 22, but suffice it to say, God does not move or act except as an answer to believing prayer.

As you continue on this journey of change and enter in to the Power Step of Prayer, it is important to note it is essential if we are to experience any emotional change or transformation, God needs to be involved. We can read all the psychology books we can get our hands on. We can speak to all the psychiatrists in the entire country. We can seek out leaders, elders, or ministers to help straighten us out and get us on the right path; however, without God and prayer, it will not happen. God wants us to engage Him for change. He is the One who designed us and made us. If we deal with impulse control; if we are unable to manage stress; if others look at us and find we are emotionally unaware; if we have challenges managing interpersonal relationships; if we desire to be more empathetic; we will not change until we have met with God about what we want to change. We must be careful of our motives, as mentioned in James 4:2-3. If we genuinely want to change because in the end God will get the glory, then I am sure He will meet us and the power of prayer will be a living evidence in our lives of the transformation in the emotional realm that comes from God.

Closing the Section

1. Pause for moment. Please consider the results of your assessment. God has arranged such a time as this for you to be transformed.

2. Ask God to prepare your heart for change. Ask Him to prepare you for the pain that will come from this. Ask Him to put thanksgiving and joy in your heart for the journey you're about to embark on.

3. Close your eyes and meditate for a minute; then open your eyes.

4. Pray the following: "Dear Lord, I have seen the result of the assessment. God, I know I am not perfect, but you call us to be more like you. Lord, I surrender to what you want to do in my life and I commit to making the changes that will be reflective of a true follower of yours. Lord, ease the pain, but keep me in the fire until I become more like you. I pray this in Jesus' name. Amen."

5. Write down what God has revealed to you.

CHAPTER TWENTY-ONE

THE POWER OF THE FRUIT OF THE SPIRIT

. . . .

From our story in 2 Samuel 11-12, King David was told through the prophet Nathan that the child Bathsheba was to deliver was going to die. King David, upon hearing that pronouncement, decided the best action he could take would be to pray to God and hope the Lord would have mercy on him and not take the child's life. The king fasted and prayed and sought God's forgiveness. The pronouncement, however, was irrevocable and the child died. In chapter 12, verses 20-25, King David illustrated some of the characteristics of the Fruit of the Spirit, though love, joy, peace, gentleness, and goodness. Upon receiving forgiveness from God, he decided to clean himself up, go to his palace and change his clothes. He had compassion on Bathsheba. He showed love to her. From this love came the wisest king of Israel—Solomon.

In Galatians 5:22-23, Paul wrote the Fruit of the Spirit is love, joy, peace, patience, kindness, goodness, faithfulness, gentleness, and self control. The interesting thing is none of the Fruit implies intelligence or demonstrates itself in the intellectual dimension. The fact of the matter is the Fruit of the Spirit gives us guidelines on how to operate in the spiritual and emotional dimensions. Below, I have listed the Fruit of the Spirit in order and the basic definition from Webster's dictionary for reflection on the expectation Jesus has for those who His. As you read, you will see that built into the very foundation of each word is the emotional character of our Creator, God.

Love – strong affection for another arising out of kinship or personal ties; attraction based on sexual desire; affection based on admiration, benevolence, or common interests; warm attachment, enthusiasm.

Joy – the emotion evoked by well-being, success, or good fortune or by the prospect of possessing what one desires; the expression or exhibition of such emotion; a state of happiness or felicity; a source or cause of delight.

Peace – a state of tranquility or quiet; freedom from civil disturbance; a state of security or order within a community provided for by law or custom; freedom from disquieting or oppressive thoughts or emotions; harmony in personal relations.

Patience – the capacity, habit, or fact of bearing pains or trials calmly or without complaint; manifesting forbearance under provocation or strain; not hasty or impetuous; steadfast despite opposition, difficulty, or adversity.

Kindness – a deed; effort on one's behalf or interest; of a sympathetic or helpful nature; of a forbearing nature; arising from or characterized by sympathy or forbearance.

Goodness - the quality or state of being of a favorable character or tendency; that can be relied on; legally valid or effectual.

Faithfulness – steadfast in affection or allegiance; firm in adherence to promises or in observance of duty; given with strong assurance; true to the facts, to a standard, or to an original.

Gentleness – the quality or state of being free from harshness, sternness, or violence; mildness of manners or disposition.

Self-control – restraint exercised over one's own impulses, emotions or desires.

The most interesting conclusion I drew as I researched the meanings of all the different descriptions of the Fruit of the Spirit was, "How could God expect this much from us? How is this possible? Does He expect me to demonstrate all that is mentioned in the Scriptures in Galatians 5:22-23?" The fact of the matter is, after reviewing the definitions it could cause anyone to cringe because of the high expectation that is placed on those who desire to be called a Christ-follower. How could anyone demonstrate such and remain a normal human being? To achieve this would require supernatural powers. How could one actually live a life within our current society and have all of this? My first view was that this is impossible. The Scripture that immediately comes to mind is Zechariah 4:6, *"So he said to me, 'This is the word of the Lord to Zerubbabel: Not by might nor by power, but by my Spirit,' says the Lord Almighty."* We cannot do anything of ourselves, but we can depend on God to show us how to demonstrate these characteristics as a follower of Christ.

In my earlier days as a Christian, I thought there were many fruits related to the Fruit of the Spirit. How could there be many items listed as Fruit of the Spirit? My intellect, which can be one of the most significant detriments to my spiritual growth, questioned the meaning of the Scripture: Galatians 5:22, *"But the fruit of the Spirit is…"* How could there be one fruit? If there are nine associated descriptors, then obviously there must be nine fruits. Not so. The verse suggests that we are to be like Christ—one being—with many characteristics—nine descriptors—representative of the one being. It is not surprising that Matthew 5:48 calls for us to be like Christ: *"Be perfect, therefore, as your heavenly Father is perfect."*

The Scripture instructs us to be more like Christ. In order to be like Christ, therefore, we must incorporate the Fruit of the Spirit in our lives. It is not that we have many fruits, but we have the one character of God, which carries with it nine characteristics—love, joy, peace, patience, gentleness, kindness, goodness, faithfulness, and self-control. These are characteristics of Christ.

If we are to be like Christ, however, we need to have the character of Him who we represent. Dr. Win Green, a pastor in Princeton, New Jersey, a graduate of Yale and Asbury, and author of the book *All You Ever Wanted*, which is a study on the Fruit of the Spirit, explains the nine fruits in this way, "that when the Spirit of God plants itself in your heart, it will yield NINE different kinds of spiritual fruit."[1] This is something for us on Earth who find this so incredibly hard to understand; however, it is something that is possible with and through Christ. In order to experience and demonstrate all the Fruit of the Spirit, it is important for us to have our lives fixated on being more like Christ.

Now what does this have to do with emotion? It has a lot to do with it. The most interesting analysis in reviewing the Fruit of the Spirit is that most, if not all, of the definitions are derived from the emotional dimension. As mentioned in prior chapters, we operate in many dimensions, namely: the emotional, spiritual, intellectual, and physical. Most of the attributes of the Fruit of the Spirit exemplify themselves in the spiritual dimension, and are rooted in the emotional character of any person. Love, joy, peace, patience, and the other five characteristics require us to have a grounded and sound emotional underpinning to our very being before trying to experience growth in the spiritual realm.

My journey in chapter 1 began with me apologizing to my staff for the manner in which I had dealt with them over the years. Even though I was a solid Christian for over two decades, I had shortcomings in the emotional dimension. It was not until I adjusted my thinking as to what God was asking of me in Matthew 5:48, that I recognized I needed to change to be more like Him.

To be more like Him meant I must have the characteristics of Him who is my Lord and Savior. To be more like Him means I must have the Fruit of the Spirit alive and flowing out of my life. Even though I know the definition of the Fruit according to Webster, it is not until I parlay the general meaning into experiential meaning that I truly understand what the actual Fruit of the Spirit means. A great philosopher once said, "A man with an argument has nothing over a man with experience." I could give you all the definitions you need to truly intellectualize the Fruit of the Spirit, but until you have lived it out...until you have understood it...until you have experienced it in your life, you cannot really understand it. I will share a paragraph or two on each of the Fruit.

But first, an important new term to understand prior to delving into each Fruit is *emotional conversion.* Emotional conversion means I understand where I am emotionally. I accept where I am emotionally. I am committed to make adjustments in my live to improve my current emotional state. Since most of the Fruit of the Spirit is grounded in emotional matters then, by default, an emotional conversion will mean I am going to instill all the emotional character in my spiritual life through the Fruit of the Spirit. At the time of conversion, you need to learn what it means to change who you are and what you are. This is one of the most difficult things to grasp because to admit I do not show love, to admit I am impatient with others, to admit there is limited or no joy in my life are significant admissions. It means even though I thought I was at a certain level, I am not there yet.

Now for the Fruit:

Love for all intents and purposes carries with it many definitions. There is a love specific to friendship. There is a love specific to a deep intimate relationship. There is love that is erotic. It is not by accident that God stated in Deuteronomy 6:5, *"Love the Lord your God with all your heart and with all your soul and with all your strength,"* which Jesus later said was the first and greatest commandment. In Matthew 22: 37-39, He follows these words by *"…and the second is like it: 'Love your neighbor as yourself.'"* In the first commandment, God says we should be connected with Him; however, the second greatest commandment is for us to be connected to those around us. If you were to go though an emotional intelligence assessment, you would recognize the characteristic of love becomes all-important to you. Before my emotional conversion, I thought I was the most loving individual in the world. I loved my wife, I loved my staff, I loved my pastor, and I loved everyone because God called me to do this.

It is, however, possible to intellectualize a behavior, but not to demonstrate that behavior. Being impatient with my wife does not show love. Being impatient with those who are supposed to be supporters around me does not show love. Making sarcastic and hurtful statements to others does not show love. You can demonstrate all the negative characteristics above and yet have been serving Christ for a long time. Time with Christ does not equate to experience with Christ. Love requires us to be introspective. It requires us to analyze our behavior and to assess whether the way in which we are treating others around us demonstrates the quality and character of God. After my Emotional Intelligence 360° assessment, I recognized the idea I had of myself was quite different from the thoughts that others, who loved me, had of me. There were blind spots—big blind spots I did not recognize. The assessment caused me to focus more on the very meaning of love that Christ was conveying in the greatest commandment, and also that which is portrayed in 1 Corinthians 13, appropriately called the Love Chapter.

Love requires an external focus. It is not about me. It is more about others. How I treat them. How they feel when I am in their presence. How they feel about who I am. How they feel about how I might react to them if they do something I don't like. Love requires us to abandon ourselves and focus on those who we are in contact with. As a follower of Christ, I would never want to be in a place where someone said, "You're not like Christ because you do not demonstrate love." Consider the implication of being in Christ, but yet at the same time treating others without the love Christ embodies.

Joy is a feeling of well-being according to Webster's dictionary. The Bible, on the other hand, gives a completely different account of what joy is. In James 1:2, the Scripture tells us to *"Consider it pure joy…whenever you face trials of many kinds."* I did not quite understand that passage. God is asking me to consider chaos, pain, suffering, and hurt as joy when they come upon me. My thought was that somehow the writer of the Scripture got it wrong because I can't consider pain and suffering as joy.

A friend of mine, Joy Payne, a fervent intercessor and head of the Refuge Deliverance Center, has what one might call a unique name. Consider *Payne* – Pain. Her name could easily be Joy Pain. Her name, when aligned with James 1:2, made it clear to me that when we consider these two phases, though oxymoronic, what the Apostle Paul was saying makes sense. Her name crystallizes for me what is meant by the Scripture, *"Consider it pure joy."* Dr. Win Green speaks about joy having a crazy cousin and that crazy cousin is suffering. Think about the crazy cousin in the context of the story of the sage and the young disciple of the last chapter. There is no joy without pain.

As Christians we expect everything to work smoothly. We do not expect things to go awry. We do not expect things to go wrong. We would prefer if everything goes well. The story above highlights it clearly that in order to achieve success, joy, and happiness, we have to endure some things we do not consider to be ideal. In order to gain the eternal prize, we must experience a degree of suffering. The suffering causes us to rely more closely on God who, in turn, works in our circumstances to increase our likeness to Him. Who would imagine that to be successful, you would have to go through heartaches and pain?

Lately, I have begun to look around at the people I come in contact with and assess who really demonstrate the joy of the

Lord. As I do this, it is becoming clearer and clearer to me that those who have profound joy are the very people that have been through deep anguish. They have a story because God has taken them through unimaginable things. I must temper this by stating I am not suggesting you should go out and look for ways to suffer in order to experience joy. What I am suggesting, however, is to get to a level in God where you are satisfied and joyful, you must experience things in your life that will not appear ideal. I ask you to look around at the folks you know. Look at the folks who are joyful and then check into their backgrounds and, I will guarantee you, they have been through some suffering and pain.

So contextually, what does pain and suffering have to do with emotional intelligence? It has a lot to do with it. The most painful time of my journey was after my assessment. It was after I recognized I needed to grow in certain areas. It was at this point I found that in order to be like Christ (see Matthew 5:48) I must endure things that do not live up to the aspiration of having a quiet and contented life. Looking back over my experience, I would not ask anyone to go through what I did. The anger, the hurt, the feeling of failure that comes from hearing what those who were close to me, who considered me a Christian, really thought of me was devastating. When they discovered I needed to grow and that I took ownership of that need, they seemed, for a time, to *disown* me. I thank God for their disowning me because I had no one to run to but the Lord. He embraces you and walks you through the deep changes you're about to encounter.

No one wants to change. To change requires us to endure pain and suffering. The Scripture tells us in the Book of James to consider it all joy, so as one goes through emotional adjustments— growing in love, getting rid of anger, getting rid of narcissistic behaviors, managing stress, controlling impulses—there is going to be pain and suffering. But all the pain and suffering is for Him, who wants you to have His characteristics and His Fruit. Galatians 5:22-23 *"But the fruit of the spirit is love, joy, peace, patience, kindness, goodness, faithfulness, gentleness, and self-control"* is therefore tied to Matthew 5:48, *"Be perfect, therefore, as your heavenly Father is perfect,"* which is tied to James 1:2, *"Consider it pure joy...whenever you face trials of many kinds."*

Peace means to be completely settled in God. This means nothing can cause you concern or fear. Fear causes disruption in our lives. Fear causes us not to rely on God, but instead to rely on our own circumstances and our own strength. Peace means it is not our battle to fight. One of the best examples of peace was when the Apostle Paul was in jail, bound in chains, and an angel woke him up. I want you to imagine being in jail and sleeping so soundly it takes an angel to wake you up. You must have peace while experiencing hurt and change.

From an emotional intelligence perspective, peace is correlated with self-control. You cannot have peace if you do not bring your body under the subjection of Christ. Peace means that no matter what is going on around you, you accept that it is not your battle. God does not want us to be moved to and fro by our circumstances and what we experience. I learned this when I was at an off-site meeting about five years ago. I was in the meeting with my senior pastor and our radio agents in Dallas, Texas. I received an urgent call that one of our key staff persons had submitted their resignation at our corporate office in Montclair, New Jersey. I immediately left the meeting and called home to deal with the situation. Moments later, my senior pastor came out of the meeting and asked me what I was doing. He said, "You don't need to deal with that. Don't be moved and be thrown back and forth by things. Be like a lion. The quietest place in the jungle is where the lion is and nothing moves him until he is ready to move." At that moment, I understood what peace meant. It means I am not controlling the ship. God is, and I didn't need to be moved by situations and circumstances that are out of my control.

Emotional intelligence requires the same. It means we are to master our thoughts, feelings, and ideas and to manage them in such a way they do not cause disruption to us or the people around us. Peace means we remain calm when others are losing their heads. Peace means we are not emotionally moved back and forth by circumstances that do not clearly reflect how Jesus would handle a particular situation. Peace means to control our *low road* functioning and not to have our amygdala (the emotional trigger in the brain) overpower our rational mind and be driven by our emotions. Jesus said in John 14:27, *"Peace I leave with you, my peace I give you."* This means we already have the peace, but at times our emotions take over and this leads to a complete lack of control on our part. Embracing peace means we have emotional control over our circumstances and we are not driven by fear or other emotional dysfunction.

Patience is something I struggled with earlier in my walk with Christ. It was not until I got an emotional intelligence assessment that I recognized I do not have what it takes to be patient. In the book *Primal Leadership: Realizing the Power of Emotional Intelligence*,[2] the authors outline the type of leadership styles that exist: Command and control, pacesetting, democratic, affiliative, visionary, coaching, and finally, narcissistic (see appendix for more detail). I am a pacesetting leader. By definition, a pacesetting leader is one who is a high-capacity person and completes tasks at a rapid pace. This person is characterized by little patience as he or she is on a mission to complete what needs to be done. This definition works well for me and I accept that is who I am. It becomes contrary in a certain respect as it relates to those to whom God has sent my way to either direct or manage. A pacesetting leader is needed when an organization is in need of a rapid change of direction as well as when an organization is in constant drive and needs to attain stretch goals.

In order for a pacesetting leader to function well, he must have the right support cast. He must have others who are highly energetic, passionate, and highly motivated. What happens if you put a pacesetting leader into an environment where others around him do not exemplify the characteristics he thinks are needed? That was the situation I found myself in. In my leadership position in corporate America, I managed people in the United States, Amsterdam, and Singapore. I was a mover and a shaker. When I got to Christ Church and took on the role of chief operating officer, I felt I could do the same. The two things I needed to be aware of, however, were 1) this was not corporate America, and 2) in everything God will get the glory. This brings me back to the Scripture passage from James 1:2, *"Consider it pure joy... "*

When I arrived at Christ Church, my senior pastor asked me to do a staff analysis and give him a recommendation of who to keep and who to lay off. I did the analysis and told him we needed to "get rid of 50 percent of the staff." He asked me if I was crazy. I remember the exact words he used: "Rupert, God gave us these people. He sent them our way. We are to use them in the manner in which He wants." I did not quite understand that years ago, but I do now.

God used my personality, which at the time seemed the complete opposite of who He is, to change my very character to be more like Him. The harsh reality of getting an assessment as outlined in chapter 1 was because I had been harsh and rigid with others. Even though I was a Christian for so many years, I still had emotional inadequacies in my life that caused me to hurt the very people God had given me to lead. I am not the only one, and I am sure there are many leaders who are spiritual stars, intellectual geniuses, but lack the basic emotional intelligence underpinning it takes to have an effective and long lasting relationship in the ministry.

Once my assessment was over, the Lord took me on a long journey to a place of fulfillment where I examined everything I did wrong. My temperament, my personality, and who I am were at the foundation of all of this. Who we are right now does not determine who we will become. As stated in his book *Emotional Intelligence,* Daniel Goleman states, "Temperament is not destiny." What it requires, however, is for us, as individuals to be completely up front and honest about our shortcomings and to work on them. As a pacesetting leader, I lacked the necessary patience to effectively serve others. How could I lack patience when it is a characteristic of those who call themselves children of God? What that requires, therefore, is an honest assessment and the need to further develop that part of your personality to better serve those who are placed under your leadership.

One thing that will become clear to anyone who needs to work on the charactersitic of patience is you cannot lack patience and experience love as described in 1 Corinthians 13:4. It became clear to me through this Scripture that change is required in anyone's life who lacks patience. The Scripture clearly states, *"Love is patient."* Therefore, for me to be patient with someone I must love them, and vice versa. I must be able to utilize restraint, self-control, impulse control, and other personal characteristics that go against the grain of showing love. This caused me to be conscious every time I lost my patience that I must be falling short on the very being of Christ, which is love.

Kindness is expressed in the emotional dimension with care and feeling for those that have been entrusted to your care. The derivation of the word *kind* in the original Greek brings to clarity the meaning as it relates to the Fruit of the Spirit. It means to show demonstrated usefulness. It means to go out of your way to serve others. It means to recognize the need to show zeal in helping others.

To be kind means giving of oneself. It conjures up the image of a parent who would do anything to ensure their children are taken care of. From an emotional intelligence perspective, it is impossible to be kind and have EQ and EI characteristics that are in stark contrast to the behavior of being Christ-like. Kindness is demonstrated in Reuven Bar-On's emotional intelligence assessment category of interpersonal skills (refer to chapter 7). The subscales of interpersonal skills are empathy, social responsibility, and interpersonal relationship.

To be kind means you are high in the area of empathy—to be aware of, to appreciate, and understand the feelings of others; social responsibility—acting in a responsible manner toward others even though there is no benefit to you; and interpersonal relationship—the ability to establish and maintain mutually satisfying relationships. As we review the definition of the subscales, it is clear from a theological and Christ-centered perspective, it is impossible to be low in this area and to have the character of Christ evident in one's life.

Clearly, to be kind is to put oneself out to be useful to others. To be useful to others, when correlated with the EI subscales of interpersonal relationship, it is clear one cannot exist without natural and emotional growth in the area of interpersonal skills development. It means to go out of my way, and not just consider my wants and my desires, and look to the needs of others who are in my sphere.

Goodness, according to Dr. Win Green, is to constantly seek to raise the bar on what we ourselves consider to be good. To be good means we are reliable individuals others can trust to accomplish what we have said we would do either individually or which we would accomplish for others. Goodness means to embrace who we are, but constantly to be striving to be greater than we are. We must constantly seek to serve others and to become better than who we currently are. In Philippians 3:12, the Apostle Paul stated, *"Not that I have already obtained all this, or have already been made perfect, but I press on to take hold of that for which Christ Jesus took hold of me."* It is clear Paul's general thought was that he had not arrived, but he constantly seeks to be more like Christ in everything that he does.

The process of being good came clearly to me just two years ago. At times people around me would remind me I was somewhat smart. They would say things like, "Yes, Rupert is the brains. Rupert has got that all down pat. Rupert is so good at what he does." The fact of the matter is I never took to heart what others said. It wasn't until I was forty years old that I finally began to accept, "Yes, I do know a few things. I have been to good schools, written a book…" But to accept that fact is very dangerous. It quickly could have gone to my head. I could start believing the very words I said.

With goodness, however, comes humility. It is to accept the fact that one can be good. One can be at a certain stage in their life where they have mastered one challenging thing or another. This, however, does not mean we have a handle on what it takes to stay at that level. The most interesting thing is the moment we think we have arrived and are good, there will always be someone or something that comes into our environment to disrupt that thought. You see, goodness is only temporary. Goodness is a state of being within the circumstance of the moment. The instant we move to another moment, it requires enlisting a greater level of goodness than that which was previously experienced. The moment I start to believe the hype of who I am, what I have done, and what I have accomplished, God will gently bring things into my life that will cause me to take a good dose of humility.

The same is true for all of us. The level of goodness we have in our lives will constantly require us to give more of ourselves. Isn't God interesting in that He asks us to have the characteristics of goodness in our lives, not for a season, but for all seasons? Consider the Scripture, *"No one is good…except God alone"* (Mark 10:18). We are challenged that even though we think of ourselves as being good, God's goodness alone is the one that is a constant. God never changes. He was good. He is good. And He will be good. He is in a state of being God at all times. He is in a state of being good at all times. To be good means we have arrived. We should dare not say we have arrived, because based on the Scripture, to have arrived means we are, therefore, God himself.

Goodness correlates with the emotional intelligence component of self-perception, self-expression, and interpersonal subscales. For us to be considered good means we show empathy to others; we genuinely care about the well-being of those around us. It means we have abandoned ourselves and continue to raise the bar in terms of service to those around us and those that God has put in our path.

How can we be good, and show contempt for those around us? How can we be good and not care about the decisions we make and the impact they have on others? How can we be good and not show deference and preference to the very people God has in our lives? It is impossible to be good and show emotional intelligence characteristic deficiencies in our lives. If there is a lack in the area of goodness, therefore, it is incumbent upon us to assess where we are and to eliminate the flaws we have. Like Paul said, *"...but I press on to take hold of that for which Christ Jesus took hold of me"* (Philippians 3:12). We are called to goodness, not instantaneous or static goodness, but goodness that evolves over time, space, and influence.

Faithfulness is not a feeling. It is a principle. It is a conviction. To be faithful conjures up images of one who stays with someone in spite of who they are and what they do. Many of us live compartmentalized lives. We live lives borne out of separation. Recently I had an interesting conversation with a friend. I was speaking to her about the need for individuals to be more emotionally sensitive, to be more cognizant of those who are in our sphere so we can serve them better. I was confused when she responded that "the emotional stuff is best left outside of the workplace." I understood this to mean we should be one way in certain situations and another way in others. The most interesting idea to come out of the emotional intelligence and subsequent work and growth in my spiritual life in this dimension is I should be who I am whether I am standing in front of a huge crowd or sitting with two people. Being the same, no matter where we are, is the pinnacle of authenticity and integrity. Jesus was who He was at all times. He did not behave one way with certain groups and another way with others. He did not compartmentalize His life.

Compartmentalization leads to compromise. It means I could be faithful to someone in one instance and then be unfaithful to them in another. To be faithful or to demonstrate faithfulness means I will stay committed to you in spite of how I might be feeling. My feelings do not matter if I am driven by a belief, principle, or conviction of why I am with you and why I continue to serve you.

Faithfulness also means we are committed to act upon the faith which we have. The Bible states in James 2:26, *"As the body without the spirit is dead, so faith without deeds is dead."* One can say, "I am faithful." One can say, "I have faith." That's fine, but Scripture exhorts us to put action to our faith in order to demonstrate the very faithfulness of which God speaks. If I say I love my wife, I need to demonstrate that I do. If I say I love my employees, I need to demonstrate that I do. If I say I have faith to write this book, I must put action to my faith to ensure the book gets completed, my employees are cherished, and my wife is loved. Faith and works go together. Works alone don't yield faith; neither does faith alone yield works.

The most faithful person who ever existed was God himself. In spite of who we are and despite what we have done to Him, He remains faithful to us. The Bible states in Psalm 57:9-10, *"I will praise you, O Lord, among the nations; I will sing of you among the peoples. For great is your love, reaching to the heavens; your faithfulness reaches to the skies."* In this Scripture, David says the Lord's love is beyond all, and His faithfulness reaches to the highest of heights. Love and faithfulness go together. It is impossible to serve others if you're unable to love them. It is impossible to serve others if you're unfaithful to them.

Before He left this world, Jesus clearly challenged Peter by what He asked him in John 21:15-20. In this passage, Jesus asked Peter three times if he really loved Him. Each time Peter told Jesus he loved Him. Instead of Jesus taking Peter's first answer, He challenged him over and over again. Do you love me?—Feed my lambs; Do you love me?—Take care of my sheep; and, Do you love me?—Feed my sheep. What Jesus was saying was if you really hold true to what you believe, then remain faithful to it. Jesus was communicating to Peter, and to us, that no matter how we feel, we should remain faithful to our principles and convictions. The second greatest commandment is to love our neighbor as ourselves. This commandment is firmly grounded in a principle. It is grounded in the principle to serve others, and to remain faithful to them no matter what they have done. Jesus did the same for us and He calls us to do the same for those we come in contact with.

Gentleness is often threatened during times of distress. Gentleness, in its use in Galatians 5:23, is to be meek and humble. Of all the characteristics of the Fruit, the one that has the most impact from an emotional intelligence perspective is gentleness. Gentleness requires a certain degree of self-control. It requires us to assess where we are, what we are doing, and what actions we are taking despite the circumstances we are in.

As mentioned before, I am a pacesetting leader. It is characteristic of a leader who is out front, taking the charge, and leading the team. Patience, self-control, and gentleness are required traits, but all too often those traits and characteristics are compromised for the sake of getting the work done. I know I was very impatient. I would almost always try to fix things. I would always try to figure out what was happening immediately and address it. Though this is an exemplary trait, it is also dangerous because it focuses on high road (intellectual) rather than low road (emotional) functioning. It causes me to be reactive and quick to act regardless of the consequences of my actions.

The fact of the matter is whether I was a pacesetting leader who focused on high-level functioning or not, I needed to be broken in the presence and by the Spirit of God. This was needed in order to demonstrate His love in my heart for the people with whom God has entrusted me. How did God break me? That is what this book is all about. It is about the path I took from being solely an intellectual to being broken, to learning who I am, what I am, and what I should not be. It is the bringing together of the intellectual and the emotional to serve the spiritual dimension of life.

God breaks us in so many ways. I was a Christian who had been serving the Lord for decades; however, I did not have the tender, gentle character Christ had. It took confrontation. It took crying out to God. It took a yearning to be more like Him. It took a complete understanding and grasping of the concept of being like Christ. It took a complete change in the area of spiritual adjustment to not only see the error of my way even after many decades, but to admit it whether it was to one person or to thousands, and then to set out on a path to learn exactly what it means to be like Christ.

Anyone who goes through genuine emotional intelligence training can experience a significant transformation. If you are impulsive and if you truly experience emotional intelligence and spiritual change, then you will be less impulsive and more patient. You will experience a softness of heart. You will see others the way Christ sees them. If you lack empathy, knowing who you are and where you're deficient will lead you to grasp fully what being empathetic means, not just to you but to others around you. If you're unable to keep or develop personal relationships, then through training and experience you will be able to embrace the emotional change necessary for you to be more like Christ.

Just recently, there was a story on a national news network about a two dogs— Sparrow, a young dog, and Rose, his mother. They were walking together early one spring day when Rose turned and dashed across a major thoroughfare in New York

City. As she crossed the street, Rose was hit by a car. Instead of running away, Sparrow rushed to his mother, who was lying in the middle of the freeway. Sparrow's heroism was captured on national television. Many networks carried the drama as Sparrow kept guard over his mother—refusing to move from the spot where his mother was lying. Helicopters came overhead to cover the story; the fire department arrived, as well as the police and the EMTs. In the midst of all of this, Sparrow remained vigilant. He would not leave his mother, who was on the ground groaning in pain. Sparrow was not distracted during the crisis. He kept circling his mother, even though the onlookers, including the police, were there to rescue his mother. It took quite some time for the police to get close and to convince Sparrow they were there to save his mother and not hurt her. When they unrolled a blanket and placed Rose on it, Sparrow quickly calmed down. He became submissive. He humbled himself for the betterment of his mother. Once they took her away, he quietly left the scene and went home. Rose suffered only a broken leg and lived through the ordeal.

It makes me wonder if we can even be like that dog. It is during crises and times of stress that we truly are not seeing ourselves and what we are doing. Sometimes there is a bigger picture to be painted. Sometimes there are greater things to be done. Sometimes God is trying to get our attention with something that could have an even greater impact on what we are currently experiencing. But if we are not humbled and gentled, we will not receive it and miss the opportunity. When God gets our attention He will require us to change and adjust. He will cause us to change who we really are.

Character change and transition will lead to your being a more gentle soul. It will mean you're broken. It will mean you're bruised. It will mean you have been adjusted by the Creator himself and for His purpose.

Self-control is to control who you are. The interesting question is, "Which self am I controlling?" In earlier chapters, it was noted that we process and react to information in two forms. We either process information from an analytical perspective or we process information immediately based on history. The processing of information based on history, without input from the rational mind, is what we call low road functioning. To process information, taking into consideration our history and also rationally calculating the response, is called high road functioning. The question, therefore, is when we control ourselves are we distinguishing between our rational or our emotional response? Further, does our spiritual being play a role in our rational or emotional response?

Margaret Wheatley in her book, *Leadership and the New Science*, answers that question with the following: "No matter the distance, at the moment one electron is measured for its spin—say that a vertical axis is chosen—the second electron will instantaneously display a vertical, but opposite, spin. How does this second electron, so far away, know which axis was chosen to measure?"[3] Simply put, the atom is the smallest part of matter, which is comprised of electrons, neutrons, and protons. Separate out an electron and put one in San Francisco and the other in New York and they will spin in a counter-clockwise direction. Her research reflects the very possibility that things happening in one sphere of the world have an adverse effect on other areas of the world.

God is the ruler of the universe and He designed it. He therefore understands science and its impact on us. He also understands the supernatural. God is calling us to be self-controlled in both high road and low road functioning. It does not matter where we are, what we are doing, what dimension we are addressing—spiritual, emotional, intellectual, or physical—God is calling us to have control over our natural reactions and He is calling us to be the master of our own bodies. How is it possible to control everything in these dimensions? The next important step is to remember we, as humans, do not function solely in the natural.

We exist in the spiritual and God does things in the supernatural. In Ephesians 6:12, the Bible states, *"For our struggle is not against flesh and blood, but against the rulers, against the authorities, against the powers of this dark world and against the spiritual forces of evil in the heavenly realms."* This, therefore, means we cannot do this by ourselves. Without God in the mix, we are not able to have control over each of the dimensions. We are not able to have success over each dimension.

So we need to generate self-control over all that we do. Without self-control, it is virtually impossible to demonstrate love, joy, peace, patience, kindness, goodness, faithfulness, and gentleness. Self-control means to control our reactions, our impulses, and our desires to do and say things not considered exemplary of Christ. Self-control is about being steadfast. It invokes feelings of standing firm in spite of what might be happening around you. It means being strong on the inside in order to withstand all the forces you encounter on the outside.

When I went through the emotional intelligence assessment, the report indicated I tend to be impulsive. It is character-based since my leadership style is that of a pacesetter; I react quickly, and I also demonstrated anger. So how do I stop being impulsive and quit being angry? How do I shut down my emotional reaction to situations that are critical, but at the same time require high road— rational—functioning as opposed to just reacting off the cuff? I have learned I cannot do it by myself. No one can do this alone. It is for this reason we cite Ephesians 6:12. If it were up to you and me, once told we are impulsive, we would quit immediately. If told we tend to be angry, we would put an immediate halt to that quality. We would stop immediately and adjust who we are to what the reality needs to be.

Inner control or self-control requires help from the one who made us. It calls for us to rely more on Christ than we ever did before. It requires us to give up who we are and constantly seek God for His direction. It does not mean God will not adjust and change us without our asking. It does not mean He will sit idly by and let us generate the solution to our problems. He will, however, use circumstances to alert us to who and where we are in Him and wait for us to seek Him to help us. And even though we might already have self-control—indicated by the world *self*—we are dependent on Him because He is the one who will fine-tune us and make us more like Him. Self-control, therefore, means a reliance on God himself in order for us to control ourselves to deal with all that exists in our environment.

In order to rely on God, there are things that need to be done. First, you need to surrender all things. This means if you once thought you had all the characteristics of the Fruit and have arrived, then you need to make a mental note—you have not. A pastor once told his wife, "Honey, I don't feel like I am married." Her pointed response was, "Dear, adjust your feeling to the reality." Sometimes that is what is required of us to rely on God. We have to recognize that in order to change, we cannot do it by ourselves. We cannot get up one day and say, "God, I am going to change and I am going to have control over myself." It is impossible without His input, direction, and wisdom.

Second, your reliance on Him is a form of humility. What you're saying is you're not able to do this; you're incapable of doing it on your own. It is impossible to make the changes you need in order to be like Christ without the manifest presence of the Lord.

Third, your perceptions are not always God's—and vice versa. God made the heavens and the Earth. He shaped the world before anything existed. He created form and substance out of His very words. He created the waters, the seas, the sky, and the heavens. He feeds the trees, the animals, the birds, and the fish of the sea. He created us and gave us breath. With only that to indicate His greatness, who am I to think I have the same discernment as He? It is impossible. Getting God's perspective on controlling ourselves will help us in understanding His will and direction for our lives.

Fourth, self-control will lead to greater love. So how do I get there? Self-control leads to patience, which ultimately leads to love. If I love others, I will have patience with them no matter what they do or how contentious they are in their interactions with me. If I show patience toward them, I am showing the love of God to them.

Closing the Section

1. Pause for moment. Please turn to Galatians 5:22-23. Ponder each characteristic in the verses.

2. Are you prepared to receive all those characteristics and are you prepared to work through all that is necessary to embody those attributes?

3. Close your eyes and meditate for a minute; then open your eyes.

4. Pray the following: "Dear Lord, I know you're the true and only God. I ask you today for the Fruit of the Spirit. Lord, I know I am not able to do this by myself, but with your help and the knowledge I have gained regarding emotions, I can be what you said I should be. Lord, direct my path going forward and help me to embrace all, not some, of the characteristics of what it takes to be a follower of Christ. I thank you in Jesus' name. Amen."

5. Write down what God has revealed to you.

CHAPTER TWENTY-TWO

THE POWER OF CHANGE AND TRANSITION

. . . .

In 2 Samuel 12:18-20, the outcome of David's sin with Bathsheba was demonstrated based on God's mercy and judgment.

> On the seventh day the child died. David's servants were afraid to tell him that the child was dead, for they thought, "While the child was still living, we spoke to David but he would not listen to us. How can we tell him the child is dead? He may do something desperate."
>
> David noticed that his servants were whispering among themselves and he realized the child was dead. "Is the child dead?" he asked.
>
> "Yes," they replied, "he is dead."
>
> Then David got up from the ground. After he had washed, put on lotions and changed his clothes, he went into the house of the LORD and worshiped. Then he went to his own house, and at his request they served him food, and he ate.

The interesting thing is once the judgment was pronounced and executed on the king, he got up, brushed himself off, and proceeded to move on with his life. He forgot what was behind him, he forgot what had happened to him, he accepted his current state, and moved ahead to the future. Such is the impact of change.

Change, by definition, is 1) to make different in some particular, 2) to make radically different, 3) to undergo transformation, transition, or substitution, and 4) to become different. Transition, by definition, is *Passage from one state, stage, subject, or place to another; a movement, development, or evolution from one form, stage, or style to another.* Emotional adjustment requires change and transition. It requires more transition. Change is instanteous, however, transition is emotional and psychological. In order to be what God has called us to be, we must make some immediate changes. However, we must consistently transition from bad character to godly character over time. It requires us to forget about where we are and to press on. God calls us to be radically different. He calls us to be different, to think differently, and to undergo transformation. That transformation or transition, however, does not come without a price.

No Change, No Transition, Keep Plowing

Three years after I started this journey of change, I still had remnants of the very things I was trying to change. I received a phone call from one of the very people who was a catalyst for my being on this journey of change and transition. Seconds into the phone call, I realized I was getting agitated and upset by what the person was saying. Agitation led to upset, which led to anger. I was angry because the person to whom I was speaking did not seem to understand nor appreciate what I was saying. The angrier I got, the more my tone changed.

Knowledge of emotional self-awareness should have informed me I was getting upset. Further, I should have terminated the conversation. My amygdala, the key area of the brain responsible for all emotional decisions and functioning, sensed I was having a highjacking session. However, instead of containing myself, anger escalated to wrath. During the conversation, however, I did recognize I was going into full-scale highjacking and made an immediate decision to hold back. A pastor and close friend of

THE POWER OF CHANGE AND TRANSITION

mine would say to me, "Dial down" when I normally got upset in his presence. I recognized in an instant I had gone way too far and I needed to dial down.

The character of the conversation changed from one of confrontation to one wherein we were both seeking a middle ground so we could understand each other. However, by then the damage had been done. I had gone from upset to agitation to anger to rage. After the phone call, I hung up. I got in my car and headed to Route 280, one of the main thoroughfares in New Jersey. As cars passed me by, I just zoned out, feeling like a failure. I was disgusted with myself. Here I was, the one writing a book on emotional intelligence, discussing how God had done a great work in me, how He had taken me to a place where I have changed and I can even tell others about it, and still this thing, this growth, this remnant was still in me. Anger still existed in me. How could it?

I pulled over on the side of the road and began to weep. I could not understand. How could this be happening? Why is this happening? I have confronted the fact I have a problem. I have assessed where I am. I know, based on my assessment, I need not be impulsive and I need to be calm when dealing with stressful situations, but it didn't happen. I have prayed. I have surrendered it to God. He is my Creator. He knows everything. He said if we ask anything in His name He is faithful and just to forgive us. His Word states we if we ask with the right motive He would hear our prayers and answer them.

I had prayed to Him. I had turned this over to Him, but still I was suffering from it. The pain in my stomach was so deep. I have let Him down again. I owed the person I was speaking to an apology. How could this be? In the depth of my soul, the enemy told me, "See, you will never change. If you gave it to God and He still hasn't answered, you are destined for failure." I bought it. I accepted it. I started to cry even more because this thing that had been in me was *still* in me. It would not leave. It is a part of me and will never leave.

My attention turned to God. I remember specifically saying, "The devil is right, I cannot change." With anger, guilt, and anguish I started to speak to God about the injustice of it all. How could you let me down like this? I remember crying out to God as tears flowed down my face, "Are you not God? Can you not do this for me? Why must I suffer with this? You have brought me to shame. You have caused me to deny myself. You have brought me lower than the ground, but yet you have allowed this to continue. Are you not God? *Are you not God?*"

I quickly realized I was angrier with God than I had ever been in my entire life. I just started sobbing. I know I needed to apologize to God. I know I needed to tell Him I was sorry for accusing Him of not delivering. I know I could not speak to my Savior that way. I felt so hurt. I felt so let down by Him. I felt alone. I felt that nothing I could do would ever change who I was.

Then the Lord gently spoke to me. He said, "Paul and Job." As I sat there on the side of the road, I recognized God was teaching me two lessons: 1) Sometimes we will have things in our life we struggle with, but their resolution will be according to His timing, and 2) we can never challenge God as to who He is and what He is capable of doing.

His Timing

The Bible makes it clear the Apostle Paul struggled with a certain *thorn* in his flesh. Nowhere in Scripture does it specify what the thorn was. He died and went to be with the Lord, and God never delivered him from it. I am suffering with something that has come through the lineage of my ancestors. This anger has been controlled, but not cleansed. I have prayed about it and I have not been delivered. The question is not so much that I have not been delivered, but what to do now that I know God has not granted the outcome I would like. I really and truly believe in Matthew 5:48. I want to serve God fully and be more like Him. The Scriptures state I should be like Him. The way I reacted on the phone was in no way, shape, or form reflective of who God is.

What do I do now that God has not responded to my prayer? Even as I write this, tears are coming down my cheeks because God, in His infinite wisdom, has used the thing I struggle with to draw me closer to Him and to be more dependent on Him. I have been humbled again by Almighty God. He has caused me to see just who I am. I am nothing before Him. I am there to serve Him and to serve Him fully. It is not about me, but it is about my honoring Him, no matter what His timing is. It is for me to be responsive to Him and to draw closer to Him as I offer up my shortcomings to Him.

It is for me to put aside pride. It is for me to put aside the things that make me bigger in Him. It is for me to put aside the things that would cause me to increase in His eyes. He has caused me to see who I am. I am a sinner, far removed from God, but because of His grace, I can come to Him and say, "Father, forgive me because for a moment, I thought this was about me and it is not." It is about Him.

If He is God, Then . . .

During this change and transition effort, I thought if I asked God for deliverance and for change He would immediately do it. In the car on Route 280 that day, I realized I serve a sovereign God. One that is infinite. One that is never-changing. When I got home, I opened my Bible to Job, chapters 38-40. As I read those Scriptures, I felt all the pride I had, all the things that made me feel important, all the things that made me feel I have progressed meant nothing. I was dealing with the supernatural God.

Job, after losing everything, after his friends castigated him for his supposed hidden sin, dealing with the way in which he was suffering, he questions God. In Job 38-40, God responds to Job. His response gave resounding proof that He is the God of the universe, the Almighty, the Everlasting. Job was foolishly questioning the way God was dealing with him and his circumstances. The most interesting thing is God never did tell Job why he suffered. He didn't tell him the reasons for his suffering. Instead, God's focus was on the fact that He was being questioned at all.

I was wondering why God had not answered my prayers and removed this propensity to be angry. I dared to ask if He was God. If He was God then surely He could remove all these things and make me free. He could make me be who I wanted to become, which was perfection in Him. I was so naïve. I was so unknowing. I was such a neophyte in the manner in which I questioned God and His ways regarding me. As I read these chapters in Job, it gave me such clarity as to who He is. God focused on His glory in the universe, His majesty, His wisdom, and His power. The summary of chapters 38-40 is: "Do not question who I am. Take a look at what I do and ask yourself the question, 'Can you do this?'" The result is that I am powerless, ignorant, insignificant, inadequate, unwise, and foolish for even asking God why He had not done what I had asked.

The Lord's response to Job:

Then the LORD answered Job out of the storm. He said:

"Who is this that darkens my counsel with words without knowledge? Brace yourself like a man; I will question you, and you shall answer me.

"Where were you when I laid the earth's foundation? Tell me, if you understand. Who marked off its dimensions? Surely you know! Who stretched a measuring line across it? On what were its footings set, or who laid its cornerstone— while the morning stars sang together and all the angels shouted for joy?

"Who shut up the sea behind doors when it burst forth from the womb, when I made the clouds its garment and wrapped it in thick darkness, when I fixed limits for it and set its doors and bars in place, when I said, 'This far you may come and no farther; here is where your proud waves halt'?" (Job 38:1-11)

I have been silenced by God. I do not question His timing. I do not question His character when He has not responded in the timeframe I have designated. He is God. He can do whatever He wishes. It is His world. My life is His life. It is not my life anymore. He knows what is good for me. He knows my goings and my comings. He knows my shortcomings. I have committed all to Him. I have prayed for change. It is up to Him, and in His time, when He will send the full revelation of this change. I will patiently wait until my Father has executed the change in me.

Alidade Research and Furnishing the Soul

I had the wonderful opportunity while writing this book to meet Dr. Todd Hall, Associate Professor at Biola University. He is the president of Alidade Research, a center focused on psychology and spirituality. His work focuses on blending the psychological and spiritual for the betterment and improvement of one's soul and of society. The premise of his work is that we, as human beings, are psychological beings, as much as we are spiritual beings. He contends there is a marrying of the two, and if understood, it leads to significant improvement in who we are. The crux of his growth development and change instrument is to focus on who we are so we can understand who God is.

Dr. Hall's premise is how we treat God is indicative of our relationship with Him and further our relationship with those around us. He contends we are hardwired to connect with God relationally. If we are hardwired to connect with God relationally, then we are hardwired to connect with one another relationally as well. The question is not that we are hardwired to connect with God, but if we are of such nature, then how do we connect with those in our sphere?

He has created a package instrument called *Furnishing the Soul*. This packet provides a profile that will help an individual understand how they should connect with others. What intrigues me about Dr. Hall's information is it addressed the emotional intelligence, interpersonal scales, and sub-scales of empathy, social responsibility, and interpersonal relationships. Specifically, his instrument focuses on improving the interpersonal scale, but not only at the level of human-to-human, but human-to-God, as well. In Mark 12:30-31, the Bible states the greatest commandment is to *"Love the Lord your God with all your heart and with all your soul and with all your mind and with all your strength,"* and the second greatest commandment is to *"Love your neighbor as yourself."* Dr. Hall's work will not only help us improve the interpersonal relationship with one another, but help us in understanding how we should relate to God as well.

I am not endorsing this instrument as the only effective product that will help us improve relationally, but it will help us understand how to better align our desires for relational growth with the actions that are needed. His instrument focuses on five ideas:[1]

Idea 1: Hardwired to Connect—How Spiritual Transformation Works

Idea 2: Knowing God in Your Gut—How Relationships Work

Idea 3: Attachment Filters—How Relationships Shape Our Lives

Idea 4: Spiritual Tipping Points—How Soul Change Works

Idea 5: Furnishing the Soul—How We Foster Spiritual Transformation

The mere fact that you're able to harness the soul for the improvement of mankind is a noble effort and one we should all embrace.

Change and Next Step

John Kotter, the renowned Harvard Business School professor and strategist, in his book *Leading Change,*[2] cited an eight-step process for creating and exacting major change. Though Dr. Kotter's book was primarily directed to organizational change, the steps outlined can be directed at any entity, whether it is an individual, corporation, church, or any other organization. Key elements and the focus of the process can be implemented for any group. The eight steps are: 1) Establishing a Sense of Urgency, 2) Creating a Guiding Coalition, 3) Developing a Vision and Strategy, 4) Communicating the Change Vision, 5) Empowering Broad-Based Action, 6) Generating Short-Term Wins, 7) Consolidating Gains and Producing More Change, and 8) Anchoring New Approaches in Culture. The key item focused on is the sense of urgency. Until someone has informed us of the need to change, we continue to be who we are and focus on who we are. Change is at the center of the Power Step because whether we have empathy, whether we pray, or whether we yearn to have the Fruit of the Spirit demonstrated in our lives, it is going to take a serious commitment to change and to constant assessment to ensure success.

Diagram: "Obstacles to Change" wheel

- I have served God for so many years; I am a leader in the ministry; I am a leader in the organization My parents are pastors
- Who I Am — I have tried changing before I am not a failure Everybody looks at me I have created all of this
- What I Do — Oversee people; Lead people Serve the organization for so many years Everybody looks up to me People respect me
- Who I Am in My Family — Matriarch of the family; Patriarch of the family My children and their friends look up to me The main provider for my family
- Who Others Think I Am — I am the pastor; I am the leader I am untouchable; I am perfect People look up to me I am an intellectual

The questions then are "Why change?" and "Where is the urgency?" Highlighted above are the sometimes cynical and obvious reasons not to change. Each person, when confronted with the need to change, can look through the prism of who I am, what I do, who others think I am, and who I am in my family. If the need to change is analyzed through these lenses, and most of the responses are in the affirmative, the tendency to placate or ignore the need for change is extremely high. One can justify the reason not to change if everyone within his or her sphere acknowledges the great and lofty image one might have of himself.

If, however, in spite of the responses, we can challenge the status quo and believe the request to change is not just a theoretical or intellectual challenge, but rather a challenge from the Holy Spirit, then and only then can we acknowledge the need to adjust our current circumstances based on the urgency at hand. There is no guarantee you will follow though and engage in the Power Steps, but engaging at this level should cause internal reflection to begin.

The fact that a sense of urgency exists to begin change does not mean change will occur. What is needed in order to embark on the change effort and to put things into action to ensure change? The urgency for me came when I recognized my actions have led to others being hurt. The urgency came when I was informed by others that my actions did not reflect what I said and who I said I represented. The action came when I decided to deal with the shortcomings in my life hindering me from being a true Christ-follower who seeks to have his character reflective of his Savior. Anyone can experience this, but a sense of urgency will be needed to necessitate real, significant, and relevant change. Jesus stated in Matthew 18: 3, *"And he said: 'I tell you the truth, unless you change and become like little children, you will never enter the kingdom of heaven.'"* Here we are asked to adjust and be like children who are amenable to change without excuses and justification, or we will not be like Him.

As we bring this section to a close with the initial focus on change, it would not be complete if I did not contrast change with the topic of transition. William Bridges, in his book *Transitions: Making Sense of Life's Changes,* addresses the issue of transition and change. Specifically, Bridges speaks of change as instantaneous and transition as emotional, "as an inner process through which people come to terms with change, as they let go of the way things used to be and reorient themselves to the way that things are now."[3] If we are going to change, it is important for us not to rush the process, but go through the process. Too often we focus on making instantenous change. In our world of instant gratification, we do not sit down to assess what it means to make the important changes in our lives.

Transition, according to Bridges, has three specific components to be successful. There must be an ending, a neutral zone, and an actional beginning. We need to come to terms with what we are to change and what we would like to transition from. It is a conscious step to look at what you are addressing and make a conscious determination to stop any behavior, mannerism, or way of doing things to improve your general well-being. In my executive coaching efforts with clients, I usually ask them to write down all the things they will be ending in order to get to that next level. This is what is characterized as the end. It is after the ending that we would encounter the neutral zone.

The neutral zone is the time when we, for lack of a better word, feel weird or not normal about what we are going through. Neutral zone experiences are very good. It is that time when we invite the Holy Spirit to lead us from where we are to where we need to be. Too often, most change effort fails because once we encounter the neutral zone our human tendency is to revert back to our old selves because it feels more normal.

Finally, after going through the neutral zone, we encounter a new beginning—the *new us* or the *new me*. This is where we engage a new dimension of who we are and our change.

Closing the Section

1. Pause for moment. Turn to the definition of change outlined at the beginning of this chapter—to be different or radically different.

2. Ask God to prepare your heart for change and transition. Only He can change you into what He wants you to be. It is a gift to be called a child of His, so welcome His change into your life.

3. Close your eyes and meditate for a minute; then open your eyes.

4. Pray the following: "Dear Lord, you have said when I receive you I am a new creation. Old things have changed and all things have become new. God, I ask you to change me to be more like you. Let this not be a theory, but let it be a true reflection in all matters of your changing my life. I welcome change, whether the lessons come from a two-year-old or an eighty-eight-year old. Lord, use anyone to bring forth change in my life. I pray this in Jesus' name. Amen."

5. Write down what God has revealed to you.

PART VI

The Power in the Future

CHAPTER TWENTY-THREE

EMOTIONAL INTELLIGENCE IN THE WORK ENVIRONMENT

. . . .

How are you made to feel? Do you find yourself at times discouraged, alone, sad, melancholy, or frustrated? I have often wondered if people can make us feel a certain way? Yes, they can. I have seen manipulative people give others the impression they are the best people in the world, while at the same time, making them feel less than who they are. I have experienced that and I have also been the one to perpetrate such an action on someone else, either knowingly or unknowingly.

A senior executive once said, "I am an officer in a nonprofit organization. You'd think I would have no problems; however, at this point in time, I am completely and utterly depressed. I am depressed because the way in which I thought my life would be going is not exactly on track with how it actually is going nor is it in line with my expectations. Based on my work experience, I feel isolated, alone, and, even though I am at the top of my occupation, those who are higher than I, those who have the power to influence me, those who have the potential to have an effect on me have done so and I don't now know how to respond." Have you ever felt like that?

Over the past year, I have been working on improving my emotional intelligence. By working on that part of my character, I have opened myself up to the scrutiny of those who do not, nor care to, show emotions; however, it is my firm belief that if I am called into God's Kingdom then it behooves me to be more like Him. So as I try to work on myself, I have also seen areas in which I am judged, because others now see the real me who is trying to change.

Exposing the shortcomings in your life is risky. Matthew 5:48 states clearly to *"Be perfect, therefore, as your heavenly Father is perfect."* My examination of this Scripture tells me that in all I do, I should try to be like Christ. It further tells me at times, I might not feel like I am anywhere near to the character of Christ, but I should always be trying. It is this reason that caused me to want to work on improving myself, and in so doing I have surrendered my life to Christ to do with as He pleases.

Through this, I have allowed others to cast their opinions on who I am and what I am. I must be careful at this point to let it be known that I am in no way, shape, or form upset. I might be melancholy at times because no one can tell you how to feel. And as you go through the process of feeling, you might have to experience hurt and disappointment. So then as I began this section, I asked, "Can someone make you feel?" And again, yes they can. Others can make you feel based on their actions toward you. They can make you feel based on what they say about you. They can make you feel based on crushing conversation they have about you.

Experiencing hurt

Has someone said hurtful things behind your back that made you feel betrayed? Have you ever experienced others attacking your character when all you are doing is trying to be helpful? Have you ever experienced excruciating hurt because what you thought would happen in a work situation just didn't happen, and you're made to feel like a fool? Have you ever felt like no matter what you try to do and how you try to improve yourself, others have a perception of you based in the past, and you know, because of your commitment to God, you have improved? Have you ever felt others are making judgments about you incorrectly? Have you ever felt others try to put you into a box because of their own carnal experience and their own natural eyes? Have you ever felt your character assassinated based on your own attempts to remedy a situation, but others have incorrect information that makes you feel worse than those around you? Have you ever impulsively reacted the way you would have in a past situation and the others who know of it, remember it and try to make you feel as if you were still living in the past?

If you have experienced any of the above, you're not alone. We all go through this and other people might not be aware they are actually doing things that will cause you to feel disillusioned, frustrated, or even like giving up. Be aware that the way you feel is not ungodly. To the contrary, what you feel are real feelings your heavenly Father has given you. The frustration is others around you might not be aware their behavior is causing the hurt. This is real. You're not an imbecile for feeling the way you do. It is natural. Under no circumstances should you let others dictate your feelings. The question is not that you feel a certain way; the question is what do you do with the fact that you are not feeling good?

The Response

As Christian leaders, we are called to be salt and light to the world. How can we be salt and light to the world if we are hurting others or we are feeling hurt ourselves? There are three actions to be taken 1) realize the situation, 2) acknowledge it is occurring and 3) determine your reaction, whether spiritual, emotional, or a combination of both.

Realize the Situation

It is important to realize all the dynamics of what is occurring in your current occupational situation. It's not a question of the right or wrong of it. Do not shy away from it, but document what you're feeling as you are going through the pain and hurt.

Acknowledge it is Occurring

As spiritual beings, we have a Father in Heaven who is tasked with fighting our battles. In 2 Chronicles 20:15, the Lord says, *"Do not be afraid or discouraged...For the battle is not yours, but God's."* Therefore, by acknowledging the situation, you're also admitting it is occurring, and you're making sure you're not the one who is solving it. You're putting the situation into the hands of a greater power. There are potential, practical, emotional reactions and there are also spiritual reactions.

Your Reaction

You have a choice regarding how you react. You can react from a natural standpoint by lashing out at the very persons who are causing you to hurt, or you can take the matter to Christ. What happens when you take the matter to Christ and He does not instantly speak to you and tell you what you should do? What if he waits five minutes, five months or five years, for that matter? The spiritual requires you implement impulse control—the Self-control of Galatian 5:23—and wait to see what God does.

Additionally, as you wait you have to implement practical steps that are going to help you deal with the situation at hand. You could utilize and show empathy toward those who have hurt you, but according to Daniel Goleman, it is virtually impossible to show empathy when one has been hurt. You could further decide to utilize any of the fifteen sub-categories discussed in chapter 7 to help you.

CHAPTER TWENTY-FOUR

On Being Liberated

. . . .

It was the summer of 2005. My parents lived in Jamaica and I was living in the United States. My dad had suffered two stokes in the previous five years and my mother, who had been married to this man for over forty-four years, felt the stress and strain of the possibility of his death. Through the decades of trials and tribulations I could not understand why they stayed together. At times, I felt it would be in everyone's best interest if she divorced and left him. Why stay with someone if the life you live is not mutually beneficial?

The fact of the matter, though, is they truly loved one another. My mom was a Christian lady and my dad, though he might not be aware of the fact, was an alcoholic. They honored their love of home and family and the bond they had solidified over four decades ago. So during the time when my dad was suffering through the strokes, the pain was unbearable, but my mom, by then in her early seventies, endured. Imagine the thought that someone whom you have been with for so many years and with whom you have spent your entire adult life, was about to depart this Earth and leave you behind. This overwhelming pain, this feeling of impending loss, and trying to nurse someone who was partially paralyzed led my mom to have a psychotic breakdown.

I got the call from my brother Fitz who was visiting our parents in Jamaica, that our dear mom was now "not in her right mind." She was taken to the United States and admitted to St.

Francis Hospital while my dad went to be with my eldest brother Derek. As Fitz, a born-again Christian for over thirty years, and I got to the psychiatric ward, we saw all kinds of people. What a scene! There were people there who were not coherent. There were people who drooled on themselves. There were those who talked to themselves. There were patients who did not understand why they were there and why they were in strait jackets. The reality was—and the impression the Holy Spirit gave me as I entered the ward—this place is *hell*.

What does a believer do going into the realm of the demonic to console his mother? As we approached her room, two nurses were with my mother and they were not being kind to her. They shouted at her and spoke to her as if she were a child. While the turmoil was going on in the room, I looked into my mother's eyes. They were cloudier than I had ever seen them. She looked so helpless as she tried to figure out who was looking at her.

The thoughts that came to my mind were, "Why is my mother here? What has she done to deserve this? Why are people, who obviously do not know her, yelling at her? What right do they have to denigrate her and make her feel less than herself even though she's not aware of what is happening to her?"

Something rose up in me that day I would never forget. I asked the nurses who were tending to my mother to leave the room. Fitz and I went over to my mother's bed and prayed. As we prayed, God brought these Scriptures to my spirit: Isaiah 54:17, *"...no weapon forged against you will prevail, and you will refute every tongue that accuses you..."* and Genesis 1:26-27, *"Then God said, 'Let us make man in our image, in our likeness, and let them rule over the fish of the sea and the birds of the air, over the livestock, over all the earth, and over all the creatures that move along the ground.' So God created man in his own image, in the image of God he created him; male and female he created them."*

God spoke of making man is His own image and giving them

dominion over the fish of the sea, birds of the air, and every living thing. This means my brother and I had authority we were not using. I bent over the bed, looked straight in my mom's eyes, and instead of speaking to her, I addressed the evil spirit within her. I commanded that spirit to leave.

Since that day until now, even after my dad had passed away, my mom is living alone, comfortably, and completely in her right mind.

So what happened and what does this have to do with emotional intelligence? It has a lot to do with it. The fact is at times we have to dismiss the analytical and focus on the spiritual dimension I outlined in chapter 11. The spiritual dimension has to do with seeking God, understanding God, getting close to God, understanding my purpose, why I am here, and the purpose in serving Him. We are all one being. We operate in many dimensions and it would be naïve of us to think of the emotional without thinking of the other dimensions.

The emotional realm is one that has been given a lot of scrutiny over the past two decades. The emotional realm can utilize analytical means to arrive at sound conclusions as to what physiological state is and psychological state is. At times, however, we need to curtail the analytical when dealing with the realm of the spiritual.

Even though I was not knowledgeable in this area of ministry then, I did realize a few things:

1) I am a child of God.
2) God has given me rights that no one, not even the enemy, can take away.
3) God has given me authority over certain things in my life.
4) If I trust God, I can walk in that authority.

Coinciding with the extensive research in the field of emotions over the past few decades has been the rise in people's interest and participation in the realm of demonic investigation. The term used today is not deliverance, but liberation. I will use liberation in this context. Liberation is the process of confronting and expelling, through power or truth, influences of an evil nature—evil spirits—or any source or agent of evil, harm, distress, or ruin. Before I delve into this, it is important to note that even though we operate in the physical, intellectual, emotional, and spiritual dimensions, we are tripartite human beings who exist in the body, soul, and spirit. This is evident in 1 Thessalonians 5:23: *"May God himself, the God of peace, sanctify you through and through. May your whole spirit, soul and body be kept blameless at the coming of our Lord Jesus Christ."*

The body is the organized physical substance of an animal or plant, either living or dead: the material part or nature of a human. This nature is correlated with our physical and intellectual dimension. It is the natural dimension. Our spirit is our being that is bodiless, but can become visible. In Ecclesiastes 12:7: *"...and the dust returns to the ground it came from, and the spirit returns to God who gave it."* That which God breathed into us in Genesis will return to Him in the end. This nature is correlated with our spiritual dimension in which we operate and live. The soul is the moral and emotional nature of human beings, the quality that arouses emotion and sentiment, spiritual or moral force, the mind, the will. It is the expression of the self—heart, mind, will, temperament, and personality. This nature is correlated with our emotional dimension.

Your soul can be transformed to the degree that you renew the mind, change attitudes, and conform to the Word. This does not happen automatically. It does not happen because we have been saved for ten, twenty, or thirty years. It is a process that requires constant adjustment, constant re-evaluation, and constant humility. Most believers have challenges in this area often because it requires being completely honest with one's self. Romans 12:2: *"Do not conform any longer to the pattern of this world, but be transformed by the renewing of your mind. Then you will be able to test and approve what God's will is—his good, pleasing and perfect will."*

Since we operate in many dimensions and we are tripartite, the enemy of our soul has many opportunities to attack us. That attack on my mother was not natural. It was spiritual. The enemy attacked her soul. He invaded my mother's being and caused her to disassociate with her very own existence. On that day, my brother and I recognized we needed to focus not just on emotional intelligence and how I could get my mother free from what she was experiencing, but to take the authority God had given me and excise issues and challenges in my mom's life, through faith in Christ. My mom was liberated.

There are different types of liberation. They are:

- **Power Encounter:** There are times when significant authority is required to rid individuals of evil spirits. It is important not to rely on power vs. truth. It requires significant discernment to understand whether you are to use power or whether you are to use truth. This will require taking significant authority over the enemy and casting out demonic spirits based on authority in Christ. Scriptural references are Luke 10:17-20, Acts 16:16-18, and Mark 1:21-26.

- **Truth Encounter:** To utilize discernment and implement strategies through integration of the Holy Spirit to bring the human being, through dialog, to a place of understanding the spiritual realm and, in so doing, extract evil forces from his or her life. Scriptural references are Mark 5:1-20 and Luke 4:33-36.

- **Allegiance Encounter:** To utilize discernment and through questions and answers be able to ascertain where an individual is spiritually. In order to excise evil spirits from the person, the individual needs to express allegiance to

301

either God or to another. This encounter cannot continue unless allegiance is made to God. Scriptural reference is Luke 8:26-39

There are numerous books on this topic and since the incident with my mother, I have been encouraged regarding the importance of taking authority as to who I am in God. It has caused me to focus more heavily on God and on what He wants me to do. This realm is accompanied with the understanding of where someone is emotionally. It has dramatically increased my understanding of the inner man and how to analyze what might be distressing any person who comes into my sphere.

Two of the books I hold dear in my life are *When Pigs Move In*[1] by Don Dickerman and *Deliverance and Evil Spirits*[2] by Francis MacNutt. There are times when emotional intelligence cannot be adjusted through assessment, coaching, or even prayer, gauging where we are in the Fruit of the Spirit. Sometimes we need to attack the enemy at its core, which might require liberation.

CHAPTER TWENTY-FIVE

ON EXPERIENCING
INNER HEALING

. . . .

There have been many discussions regarding liberation and inner healing. In certain circumstances it has been stated that 1) inner healing comes prior to liberation, 2) liberation is done first, then there is inner healing, or 3) they can be used interchangeably. Another major belief is that inner healing is the foundation of deliverance because it breaks up the ground for attack by the enemy by dealing with forgiveness and repentance. Whatever the case may be, my approach is that I will not limit God. I will not dictate how He should set a person free. Granted, there are ways and approaches that work better than others, but it is important to know it is the Holy Spirit who accomplishes all things.

So then, what is inner healing? Inner healing is a *ministry* within the Body of Christ to enable believers to become more effective and continue on to death on the cross, and resurrection into the fullness of life in Christ. It is the *application* of the crucified and resurrected life of Jesus Christ and His blood to those parts of my heart and yours that did not fully *get the message* when we first received Jesus as Savior (see Hebrews 3:12). It is a *tool* the Lord uses to mature His people (see Ephesians 4:15). It is sincere evangelism to the unbelieving hearts of believers. It is *discovering* what practices in the old man we did not fully yield to the Cross when we first accepted Jesus as Lord and Savior. It is prayer and counsel for sanctification and transformation. It is the discipline of digging deep, under guidance from the Holy Spirit, to discover whatever roots might be springing back to life and to bring them to an effective death on the Cross.

This was extremely evident in my life. I was a believer for over twenty years, but did not recognize there were things in my life, though I had lived a life centered in Christ, that the enemy still had control over. It was the summer of 1976. We were at the wedding of our dear cousin Anthony, who was marrying a lovely young woman named June. Everything was going along fine; however, it seemed to me during the reception there was a need for my dad to say something to congratulate the bride and groom. My dad was at my table and he appeared to be uncomfortable. As the various toasts continued, it was quickly moving to the point where my dad would have to make his speech. I was looking forward to seeing him rise to the occasion and offer some warm remarks about the bride and groom to all our relatives.

Instead, my dad got up from the table and I watched as he walked across the floor to the drink servers. He appeared uncomfortable and as I continued to watch him, I kept on thinking to myself that he must be preparing for some big entrance. He took the drink from the server, drank it, and proceeded out the door.

Two minutes later, everyone said, "Rupert, Sr., it's your turn." My dad was nowhere to be found. He had left the room. He was so uncomfortable he could not stand there and make a presentation to our relatives about what he thought of our cousins. I knew exactly what had happened that day. In hindsight, my dad was so nervous about speaking in front of an audience he decided to leave instead. He suffered from anxiety and I didn't even know it. His fear of having to speak to a group of people who were blood relatives was so great he let me down. The term *let me down* turned out to be a self-serving and selfish thought until I realized just how critical it was. I remember saying to myself at that moment, "I hate my dad. He let me down. Why did he have to be so nervous? What a fool he is! I will never be like him!"

Sadly, I did not know that by saying those words, I had ventured into a world that I had not intentionally entered, but one that would have serious ramifications for my future.

Bitter-root judgment and bitter-root expectancy are terms used in the world of inner healing. Bitter-root judgment is based on historical activities that occur to us in the now or in the future, based on judgments made in the past. These judgments have the fullness of power based on the laws of God. According to Matthew 7:1-2: *"Do not judge, or you too will be judged. For in the same way you judge others, you will be judged, and with the measure you use, it will be measured to you."*

Bitter-root expectancy on the other hand, is based on historical activities we project on others relative to the future. For example, when things happen in our childhood, we think the same thing will happen to us in the future. We project on to others what we expect based on past experience, sometimes unknowingly.

Besides bitter-root judgment and bitter-root expectancy, I also dishonored my father based on my reaction some thirty years earlier. The Bible is clear in Deuteronomy 5:16: *"Honor your father and mother, as the Lord your God has commanded you, so that you may live long and that it may go well with you in the land the Lord your God is giving you."* It is clear in Proverbs 20:20, *"Whoso curseth his father or his mother, his lamp shall be put out in obscure darkness"* (KJV), and in Proverbs 30:11-12, *"There is a generation that curseth their father and doth not bless their mother. There is a generation that are pure in their own eyes, and yet is not washed from their filthiness"* (KJV).

The fact of the matter is that in one moment during a wedding, at a very young age in my life, I had unleashed powers I did not know. Take the statement from John Sanford, noted author and founder of Elijah House Ministries, "In every area where we could consciously or unconsciously honor our parents, life will go well with us. Further, in every area where we judge or dishonor our parents, life will NOT go well with us."[1]

Years later, I found myself extremely nervous in interpersonal situations. I struggled at school to make friends. I struggled on the job not be nervous. The very thing I railed against my father for was happening to me. At a going away gathering at Prudential in 1989, thrown in my honor before entering the Air Force, I was so nervous that sweat poured down my body. My shirt was soaked with perspiration. I am sure everyone there was wondering what was happening to me.

Sadly, it was not until 2009 that I discovered the key to what I had done in 1976. I had made a judgment against my dad. I had not honored him. The implications of such actions have laws rooted in the gospel and in the Bible. By doing so I became the very thing I hated in my father. At some point, I thought it was a psychological issue. At times, I thought it was a personality trait. I would speak to people who were schooled in the area of psychological dynamics, but I was not able to get a good answer.

I soon discovered I needed inner healing. Even though I was serving God since the age of eleven, I carried this with me. I had to come before God. I had to ask for forgiveness. I had to look back in my past and determine this was not good for me. I had to release and I had to come before God's holy throne and say, "God, I am so sorry for making a judgment against my dad. I ask you to forgive me because your very Word says I should honor my father and mother, as you have commanded me to do so I may live long and it will go well with me. Father, in this area it has not."

Miraculously since then, I have not suffered with this problem. It has gone. Just like that. Pills I used to take for anxiety are no longer necessary. How could this be? Is it possible to carry things for many years and not even be conscious of them, but in the split second that I do recognize my flaws, my life can change dramatically? Yes. This is the power of inner healing. It is recognizing there are things in our life that cause us to stumble— things based in our past, that we need to confront, deal with, allow God to reign, and then move forward.

There are numerous topics in the area of inner healing that affect our emotions. These topics include, but are not limited to:

- **Basic Trust:** Understanding how we should develop in a balanced life from childhood to becoming an adult. Lack of basic trust can be manifested by a lack of God's presence in one's life, a generalized anxiety in many situations and circumstances, a focus on performance, controlling by compliance or dominance that one could be socially inept, undisciplined, confused, or a conformist.

- **Failure of Forgiveness and Repentance:** There are numerous studies in literature that point to the devastating effects—physically, emotionally, psychologically, and physiologically—of not forgiving others who have hurt us or of properly seeking repentance. The results are carried forward for years and hinder growth in many areas of our lives, both professionally and personally.

- **Performance Orientation:** Have you ever seen someone who always thrives, someone who does not stop to take a breath, someone who constantly focuses on the future without focusing on the present? There is a possibility they have performance orientation issues. One has to find the root of this problem. It has to be determined what causes the individual to focus on such efforts, and even beyond that, what psychological injury in his or her past led to this? An example of a past issue driving current performance could be a parent congratulating an older sibling while neglecting the younger. The end result is once the younger sibling in the family sees that as the model of parental approval, he or she strives to be good, get good grades, possibly even in spite of great difficulty.

In my family, my dad rose at 5:00 a.m. every day and the expectation was everyone would rise at 5:00 a.m. If not, they were not worthy of being considered a Hayles. The end result is I endeavored to do that until I was in my thirties, when I realized it was unnecessary.

Some by-products of performance orientation are *pride*—a refusal to accept the fact that one is doing things for the sake of getting accolades; *approval*—the acceptance of accolades due to constant performance orientation; *fear of failure*—the constancy of increased performance due to a psychological shortfall in the area of fear; and *control*—the need to be in control, driven by the fear of failure, which in turn drives the person to constantly perform.

There are many other minor topics in the area of inner healing, such as dealing with slumbering spirits, rebellious spirits, burden-bearing, parental inversion denial, to name but a few. The key is to recognize our past does have a significant impact on our lives currently, and also has a cursory and sometimes direct impact on our legacy to the next generation.

I keep saying to myself, "If I knew then what I know now, I would be so far ahead." I must also know God will have His way. There are numerous topics in the inner healing realm that intersect liberation and emotional intelligence. There are things we need to be liberated from and healed internally of. But also we must understand how we can be emotionally intelligent about these things. Some things are related, and the process required is to go through each step. The key is to have a full life, a whole life, and a free life.

CHAPTER TWENTY-SIX

A FINAL THOUGHT

. . . .

So where do we go from here? In this material I was able to focus, for the most part, on emotional intelligence. The reason for the focus on emotional intelligence is because of my own recognition as a leader, that if I did not get control of my emotions, my leadership would be doomed to failure. I could not grow unless I had exposure in this area. The interesting thing is I thought for the most part I had arrived. I thought that as a senior leader in the church I did not need to grow any further, most people looked up to me, and therefore, I could not show any failure on my part.

On one fateful date in 2006, God showed up, and the revelation of my emotional shortfall took me by surprise and thankfully continues to take me on a never-ending journey. This journey has birthed a ministry of itself, which now more than ever convinces me that from our pain, God will launch a ministry. He uses everything. He never lets anything go to waste. This journey has now led me to do further research, not only in emotional intelligence, but the correlation and intricate dynamics between EI—emotional intelligence—and the Fruit of the Spirit. In twelve months, I will begin a three-year educational journey to query churches, seminarians, and others on the thoughts, patterns, and feelings within the emotional realm. Also, what the corresponding relationship is to how we are to be—which is to exemplify the Fruit of the Spirit. How do we do that? How do we determine our shortcomings and what do we do once we have discovered them?

Further, I have included tangential topics of liberation and inner healing. I find it very difficult to speak of the emotions without addressing the cross-section of inner healing with liberation and emotional intelligence. In the ministry of the Center for Emotional and Spiritual Development, we describe it as the Triad of Healing—liberation, emotional intelligence, and inner healing. We cannot have one without the other. It is advisable that one goes through each process because there are things to be learned, areas to improve on, and change and transition that can occur by embracing these topics.

This journey was started out of pain. I had caused others pain. I had endured pain out of hurt. When this occurs, we have choices as to how to deal with the pain. We can easily say, "This is too painful," and avoid it, or we can chose to utilize the pain to have a tremendous and cataclysmic impact on our lives and that of our generation. The key is to embrace the pain. In the book *Overcoming the Dark Side of Leadership*[1] by Gary L. McIntosh and Samuel D. Rima, the authors quote from Annie Dillard, specifically, "Ride the monster all the way down." The end result is God can intervene and make the pain we're suffering be the hallmark of healing for you, your family, and generations to come. As a result of the pain, we could easily become protective, guarded, prideful, and just ignore this very pressing thing God is showing us.

I am a very practical person. God is the Creator of the universe. I, like you, am a child of His. If we accept Him, we are brought into His family. James 1:2, states, *"Consider it pure joy, my brothers and sisters whenever you face trials of many kinds."* In other words, God is telling us not to worry about what we are enduring because He is the Creator and He will work everything together for good for those that love Him.

It is a promise from Him and I embrace it wholeheartedly. The way things are going now in our culture we need to embrace what God puts before us so He can use us as one of His own to further His work upon the Earth. Emotional intelligence is fairly new. Liberation is experiencing a resurgence. Inner healing has always been there, but in various forms. My question to you is, "Will you allow God to do something great in your life? If you will, can you imagine how much greater you could be than you are now?"

Appendix
Synopsis of EI Situations in the Bible

Synopsis of Emotional Intelligence Situations in the Bible

EMOTIONS	Passages	OLD TESTAMENT — Commentary	EI COMPONENT
Fear: anxiety, concern, fright, wariness, concern, nervousness. **Surprise:** wonder, amazement, astonishment. **Sadness:** grief, sorrow, gloom, melancholy, loniliness, despair. **Shame:** guilt, regret, contrition, chagrin	Genesis 3:8-13	**Adam** couldn't handle the enormity of his disobedience and when confronted by God on the issue he shifted the blame to his wife and to God. **Eve** followed suit and shifted the blame to the serpent.	Self-Regard, Independence
Anger: outrage, resentment, animosity, hostility, irritability. **Disgust:** contempt, aversion, distaste, repulsion. **Fear:** anxiety, concern, fright, wariness, concern, nervousness. **Love:** acceptance, friendliness, trust, affinity, agape.	Genesis 4:1-9	**Cain** was very upset with God and took his frustrations out on his brother Abel.	Emotional Self-Awareness, Empathy, Problem Solving, Stress Tolerance, Impulse Control
Anger: outrage, resentment, animosity, hostility, irritability. **Disgust:** contempt, aversion, distaste, repulsion. **Fear:** anxiety, concern, fright, wariness, concern, nervousness. **Love:** acceptance, friendliness, trust, affinity, agape. **Sadness:** grief, sorrow, gloom, melancholy, loniliness, despair. **Shame:** guilt, regret, contrition, chagrin	Genesis 16:1-6, Genesis 21:8	**Sarah** and **Hagar** did not treat each other right and were unable to resolve the conflicts that existed between them. **Ishmael** later exhibited similar attitudes towards Isaac and **Abraham** became emotionally distressed over the whole situation.	Impulse Control, Stress Tolerance
Anger: outrage, resentment, animosity, hostility, irritability. anxiety, concern, fright, wariness, concern, nervousness. **Surprise:** wonder, amazement, astonishment. **Sadness:** grief, sorrow, gloom, melancholy, loniliness, despair. **Shame:** guilt, regret, contrition, chagrin	Genesis 27:1-45	**Isaac, Jacob, Esau and Rebecca** had some major family problems and they did not resolve in a manner that was best for everyone. Favoritism, selfishness, lying, greed, deception, threats, and murderous intentions resulted.	Problem Solving, Stress Tolerance, Impulse Control
Disgust: contempt, aversion, distaste, repulsion. **Fear:** anxiety, concern, fright, wariness, concern, nervousness. **Sadness:** grief, sorrow, gloom, melancholy, loniliness, despair. **Shame:** guilt, regret, contrition, chagrin	Genesis 30:1-2	**Jacob and Rachel**. Wife stressing out the man of God about things he has no control over. As it was then, so it is now.	Reality Testing, Flexibility, Impulse Control
Anger: outrage, resentment, animosity, hostility, irritability. **Disgust:** contempt, aversion, distaste, repulsion. **Fear:** anxiety, concern, fright, wariness, concern, nervousness. **Sadness:** grief, sorrow, gloom, melancholy, loniliness, despair. **Shame:** guilt, regret, contrition, chagrin	Genesis 34	**Simeon** and **Levi** incurred their father Jacob's displeasure when they wiped out the town of Shechem in retaliation for the rape of their sister Dinah.	Adaptability, Impulse Control.

Source: R. Hayles, F. Hayles, Center For Emotional and Spiritual Development

Synopsis of Emotional Intelligence Situations in the Bible (continues)

EMOTIONS	OLD TESTAMENT		
	Passages	Commentary	EI COMPONENT
Anger: outrage, resentment, animosity, hostility, irritability. **Enjoyment:** Happiness, bliss, delight, thrill, satisfaction. **Surprise:** wonder, amazement, astonishment. **Fear:** Anxiety, concern, fright, wariness, concern, nervousness. **Sadness:** grief, sorrow, gloom, melancholy, lonliness, despair. **Shame:** guilt, regret, contrition, chagrin	Genesis 37 - 50	Joseph's life, faith, love and forgiveness are perfect examples of the right emotional response when everything negative in life (including the kitchen sink!) is thrown at you.	Self-Regard, Independence, Self-Actualization, Assertiveness, Empathy, Social Responsibility, Interpersonal relationships; Problem Solving, Reality Testing, Happiness, Optimism
Anger: outrage, resentment, animosity, hostility, irritability. **Disgust:** contempt, aversion, distaste, repulsion. **Sadness:** grief, sorrow, gloom, melancholy, lonliness, despair. **Shame:** guilt, regret, contrition, chagrin. **Surprise:** wonder, amazement, astonishment.	Exodus 32:19, Numbers 20:1-13	Moses **anger** at the sin of the Israelites after they made sacrifice to the golden calf. Moses **anger burnt** against the Israelites because they demanded that he provided water for them.	Stress Tolerance, Impulse Control.
Sadness: grief, sorrow, gloom, melancholy, lonliness, despair **Shame:** guilt, regret, contrition, chagrin	1 Samuel 15:35; 1 Samuel 16: 1	Samuel grieved and mourned for Saul even while continuing to carry out his tasks and responsibilities as God's prophet. He understood the full significance of what Saul's disobedience had cost him.	Impulse Control, Stress Management, Optimism, Reality Testing, Self-Actualization
Anger: outrage, resentment, animosity, hostility, irritability. **Fear:** Anxiety, concern, fright, wariness, concern, nervousness. **Love:** acceptance, friendliness, trust, affinity, agape. **Sadness:** grief, sorrow, gloom, melancholy, lonliness, despair. **Shame:** guilt, regret, contrition, chagrin.	2 Samuel 18:31-33; 2 Samuel 19:1- 8	David's emotions were out of place and he had to be rebuked and corrected by Joab.	Emotional Self-Awareness, Empathy, Stress Tolerance, Reality Testing, Impulse Control, Happiness, Optimism
Anger: outrage, resentment, animosity, hostility, irritability. **Disgust:** contempt, aversion, distaste, repulsion. **Fear:** Anxiety, concern, fright, wariness, concern, nervousness. **Sadness:** grief, sorrow, gloom, melancholy, lonliness, despair. **Surprise:** wonder, amazement, astonishment	1 Kings 12:1-16	King Rehoboam failed to empathize with the people (what they were feeling so strongly) and followed wrong counsel which resulted in the people of Israel revolting against his rule.	Emotional Self-Awareness, Assertiveness, Independence, Self-Regard, Empathy, Social Responsibility, Interpersonal Relationship, Stress Tolerance, Impulse Control, Reality Testing
Fear: Anxiety, concern, fright, wariness, concern, nervousness. **Sadness:** grief, sorrow, gloom, melancholy, lonliness, despair. **Shame:** guilt, regret, contrition, chagrin	1 Kings 19:1-5	Elijah after a tremendous spiritual victory becomes discouraged and depressed to the point of asking God to take his life. His emotional perspective and response though very real had to be corrected by God.	Emotional Self-Awareness, Assertiveness, Independence, Self-Regard, Stress Tolerance, Impulse Control, Reality Testing
Disgust: contempt, aversion, distaste, repulsion. **Love:** acceptance, friendliness, trust, affinity, agape. **Sadness:** grief, sorrow, gloom, melancholy, lonliness, despair. **Shame:** guilt, regret, contrition, chagrin.	Hosea 1:2:3; Hosea 3:1	Hosea the prophet demonstrates great love for his wife in spite of her unfaithfulness. (Must have been quite an emotional experience for Hosea. And we can only wonder how it was for his wife as well). This is actually a prophetic portrayal of God's love for Israel in spite of their unfaithfulness towards Him.	Emotional Self-Awareness, Assertiveness, Independence, Self-Regard, Empathy, Social Responsibility, Interpersonal Relationship, Stress Tolerance, Impulse Control, Reality Testing

Synopsis of Emotional Intelligence Situations in the Bible (continues)

EMOTIONS	Passages	NEW TESTAMENT Commentary	EI COMPONENT
Love: acceptance, friendliness, trust, affinity, agape. **Enjoyment:** Happiness, bliss, delight, thrill, satisfaction. **Surprise:** wonder, amazement, astonishment.	Matthew 15:29-38; Mark 6:32-44; 8:1-3	**Jesus** is moved with compassion for **the multitudes** and miraculously feeds them.	Emotional Self-Awareness, Assertiveness, Independence, Self-Regard, Self-Actualization, Empathy, Social Responsibility, Interpersonal Relationship, Problem Solving, Reality-Testing, Flexibility
Anger: outrage, resentment, animosity, hostility, irritability. **Fear:** anxiety, concern, fright, wariness, concern, nervousness. **Sadness:** grief, sorrow, gloom, melancholy, lonliness, despair. **Shame:** guilt, regret, contrition, chagrin.	Matthew 26:74	**Peter denied Christ.** During the denial and the disowning of Christ, he began to call down curse on himself	Emotional Self-Awareness, Assertiveness, Self-Regard, Self-Actualization, Stress Tolerance, Impulse Control, Happiness
Sadness: grief, sorrow, gloom, melancholy, lonliness, despair. **Shame:** guilt, regret, contrition, chagrin	Mark 14:32-35	Prior to his capture, Jesus went to pray in the garden of Gethsemane. The bible states that **Jesus was distressed and troubled and his soul overwhelmed with sorrow** to the point of death.	Stress Tolerance, Impulse Control,
Sadness: grief, sorrow, gloom, melancholy, lonliness, despair. **Shame:** guilt, regret, contrition, chagrin	Mark 15:33-34	**Jesus cried** out on the cross in despiration for God. He knew it was his time to be sacrificed for the sin of the world. He was seeking solace in God, but at that moment during severe stress, could not see Him.	Stress Tolerance, Impulse Control,
Love: acceptance, friendliness, trust, affinity, agape. **Sadness:** grief, sorrow, gloom, melancholy, lonliness, despair. **Shame:**	Luke 19:41	**Jesus** weeps over **Jerusalem** and her impending destruction.	Emotional Self-Awareness, Assertiveness, Independence, Self-Regard, Self-Actualization, Empathy, Social Responsibility, Problem Solving, Reality-Testing
Love: acceptance, friendliness, trust, affinity, agape. **Sadness:** grief, sorrow, gloom, melancholy, lonliness, despair.	John 11:33-38	**Jesus weeps at Lazarus's tomb.**	Emotional Self-Awareness, Assertiveness, Independence, Self-Regard, Self-Actualization, Empathy, Social Responsibility, Problem Solving, Reality-Testing, Flexibility
Fear: Anxiety, concern, fright, wariness, concern, nervousness. **Love:** acceptance, friendliness, trust, affinity, agape. **Sadness:** grief, sorrow, gloom, melancholy, lonliness, despair.	Act 7:54-59	The **stoning of Stephen** after his speech before the Sanhedrin. Stephen's reaction under stressful situation.	Emotional Self-Awareness, Assertiveness, Independence, Self-Regard, Self-Actualization, Stress Tolerance, Impulse Control, Happiness

Leadership Types and Styles

Type/Style	Demonstrated	Result/Reception	When Used	Team Affiliation
Visionary	Putting forth the big picture. Demonstrate what the new ideal and dream is.	Generally positive	When change is required. Where there is a time when immediate and rapid change needs to occur	High Capacity; Conceivers as well as Operational
Coaching	Ensuring that co-workers are on the right path. Demonstrating care and showing directional options	Highly regarded and well received	For employees that need to be challenged to move to a higher level of organizational performance. A focus on long term development over short term gain.	Works for all affiliations.
Affiliative	When there is a need for cohesiveness and harmony.	Positive with negative blindspot.	To bring team together. When emotional upheaval has occurred and needs to be mended.	Works for all affiliations.
Democratic	When participative leadership and management is necessary.	Positive with limited blind-spots.	To get consensus in terms of direction and vision. To gather input from members of the team.	Works for all affiliations.
Pacesetting	Organization in a state of rapid change.	Negative if executed improperly. Must be used cautiously and sparingly unless right support cast	When organization is in need of rapid change of direction. When organization is in constant drive and needs to attain stretch goals.	High capacity; high motivation and high energy.
Commanding	Organization/Group/Team in need of immediate direction.	Negative if executed poorly. Must be used cautiously and sparingly even with right support cast.	Used during a highly charged crisis situation. Used when situation needs fast action and high capacity leader is available to make the tough, unapologetic decisions.	Conceivers, Operational, Minders and Keepers

Source: Expanded: R. Hayles (Center for Emotional and Spiritual Development). Originally conceived D. Goleman, A. McKee, R. Boyatsis: Primal Leadership

SUBJECT INDEX

360° Assessment, 239–241
360° dimension, 123–133

A
Aaron, 76–77, 78
Abba's Child (Manning), 27, 29
Absalom, 81–82, 83, 84, 253
acceptance, 73, 130
Adam and Eve, 70, 71–72
adaptability, 206, 238
admiration, 113, 114
adulation, 113, 114
affinity, 73, 130
affirmation, 114
agape, 73, 130
Ahab, 85–86
alexithymia, 110
Alidade Research, 285
All You Ever Wanted (Green), 258
allegiance encounter, 301–302
amazement, 73
American Psychiatric Association, 113
Amnon, 81, 253
amygdala, 54–55, 264
anger, 19, 313, 314
    Apostle Paul on, 35, 145
    Biblical examples of, 313–315
    as category of emotions, 73
    childhood experiences and, 35, 36–39
    examples of relationships with others and, 23–27, 30, 38–39
    managing, 35
    Moses' example of, 76–79
animosity, 37, 73
anxiety, 71, 73, 74, 82, 87, 164, 304, 307
approval, 308
arrogant behavior, 114
assertiveness, 62, 63–64, 239
assessment, 225, 226, 235–241
astonishment, 73
attention, 113, 114
aversion, 73

]

SCRIPTURE INDEX

ENDNOTES

Chapter 1: Change: Why it is Always You

[1] Manning, B. *Abba's Child: the Cry of the Heart for Intimate Belonging*. New York, New York: Navpress Publishing Group. 2002

Chapter 3: Background of Intelligence

[1] L.M. Terman, "The Binet-Simon Scale for Measuring Intelligence: Impressions Gained by its Application," Phychology Clinic, 5 (1911): 199-206

[2] R. Herrnstein and C. Murray, *The Bell Curve: Intelligence and Class Structure in American Life*. New York: Free Press, 1994).

Chapter 4: History of Emotional Intelligence

[1] R. Bar-On. *EQi, Bar-On Emotional Quotient Inventory: A Measure of Emotional Intelligence*. Toronto: Multi-Health Systems, Inc., 1997.

[2] J. D. Mayer, P. Salovey, and D. Caruso. *Mayer-Salovey-Caruso Emotional Intelligence Test (MSCEIT), User's Manual*. Toronto: Multi-Health Systems, 2002.

[3] C. Darwin, *The Expression of the Emotions in Man and Animals*. Chicago:University of Chicago Press, 1965 [originally published 1872]

[4] R.W. Leeper, "*A Motivational Theory of Emotions to Replace 'Emotions as Disorganized Responses,*'" Psychological Review, 55 (1948): 5-21

[5] D. Goleman. *Emotional Intelligence: Why It Can Matter More than IQ*. New York: Bantam Dell, 1995

[6] P. Salovey and J.D. Mayer, *"Emotional Intelligence,"* *Imagination, Cognition and Personality*, 9(1990): 185-211

[7] S. J. Stein and H.E. Book. *The EQ Edge: Emotional Intelligence and Your Success.* Mississauga, Ontario: Jossey-Bass. 2006.

Chapter 5: The Brain and our Emotions

[1] D. Goleman. *Social Intelligence: The New Science of Human Relationships.* New York: Bantam Books, 2006.

Chapter 6: Factors Within Emotional Intelligence

[1] The basic definition of "emotional intelligence" is in Salovey and Mayer, "Emotional Intelligence," p. 189.

Chapter 7: Reuven Bar-On and Emotional Intelligence

[1] S. J. Stein and H.E. Book. *The EQ Edge: Emotional Intelligence and Your Success.* Mississauga, Ontario: Jossey-Bass. 2006.

[2] Definition adapted from R. Bar-On, *Bar-On Emotional Quotient Inventory* Technical Manual (Toronto: Multi-Health Systems, 1997), p.19

Chapter 8: Emotional Intelligence in Prior Days

[1] D. Weiss. *The Ministry of Kings and Queens: From Laity to Royalty.* New York: Discover Publishing. 2004

[2] D. Goleman. *Emotional Intelligence: Why It Can Matter More Than IQ.* New York: Bantam Dell, 1995.

[3] A. E. Nelson. *Broken in the Right Place: How God Tames the Soul.* Tennessee: Thomas Nelson, Inc. 1994.

Chapter 9: Final Note on Biblical Approach:
The Psychological and the Spiritual

[1] Ibid.

Chapter 10: Emotional Intelligence, the Church,
and Modern Society

[1] D. Kinnaman. *UnChristian: What a New Generation Really Thinks About Christianity and Why it Matters.* Michigan: Baker Books. 2007.

[2] Major news conference called by Bishop Meeks in Georgia, United States of America and capture of issues surrounding the case of Bishop Meeks and TV Evangelist and Pastor Juanita Bynum. Information recorded at the sites http://www.youtube.com/watch?v=j-I02V58TKs&feature=related; http://www.youtube.com/watch?v=yDefMmuwMNY&NR=1; http://www.youtube.com/watch?v=LdYLCROWdI4&feature=related http://www.youtube.com/watch?v=9uOgEmS_3A0&feature=related

[3] Self-awareness and empathy: see, for example, John Mayer and Melissa Kirkpatrick, "Hot Information-Processing Becomes More Accurate with Open Emotional Experience," Univesity of New Hampshire, unpublished manuscript (Oct. 1994); Randy Larsen et al., *"Cognitive Operations Associated with Individual Differences in Affect Intensity,"* Journal of Personality and Social Psychology 53 (1987).

[4] D. Goleman, A. McKee, and R. E. Boyatziz, *Primal Leadership: Realizing the Power of Emotional Intelligence.* Massachusetts: Harvard Business School Press. 2002.

[5] S. Vaknin. *Malignant Self Love: Narcissism Revisited.* Czech Republic: Narcissus Publications. 2001

[6] K. Patterson, J. Grenny, R. McMillan and A. Switzler. *Crucial Conversations: Tools for Talking When Stakes are High.* New York: McGraw Hill. 2002

Chapter 11: The Complete You - 360° Dimension

[1] R. Warren, *The Purpose Driven Life: What on Earth Am I Here For?* New York: Zondervan, 2011

Chapter 18: The Power of Empathy

[1] S. J. Stein and H.E. Book. *The EQ Edge: Emotional Intelligence and Your Success.* Mississauga, Ontario: Jossey-Bass. 2006.

[2] Ibid.

Chapter 19: The Power of Assessment

[1] D. Goleman, A. McKee, and R. E. Boyatziz, *Primal Leadership: Realizing the Power of Emotional Intelligence.* Massachusetts: Harvard Business School Press. 2002.

[2] The Bar-On Emotional Intelligence test can be administered by contact Multi-Health System in Toronto Canada or accessing the website http://www.mhsassessments.com. There are many firms that specialize in administering and coaching in the realm of emotional intelligence. Multi-Health Systems will be able to point you to those who could help you administer the self-test. Additionally, the firm Organization and People Dynamics, the firm owned by the author specializes in coaching in this realm.

[3] Definition adapted from R. Bar-On, *Bar-On Emotional Quotient Inventory* Technical Manual (Toronto: Multi-Health Systems, 1997), p.19.

Chapter 20: The Power of Prayer

[1] D. Eastman. *The Hour That Changes the World.* Michigan : Chosen Books. 1978.

[2] E. M. Bounds. *The Necessity of Prayer,* quoted in *A Treasury of Prayer*, compiled by Leonard Ravenhill. Minneapolis: Bethany Fellowship. 1961.

Chapter 21: The Power of the Fruit of the Spirit

[1] W. Green. *All You Ever Wanted.* Oklahoma: Tate Publishing & Enterprises. 2008.

[2] D. Goleman, A. McKee, and R. E. Boyatziz, *Primal Leadership: Realizing the Power of Emotional Intelligence.* Massachusetts: Harvard Business School Press. 2002.

[3] M.Wheatley, *Leadership and New Science: Discovering Order in a Chaotic World.* California: Berrett-Koehler Publishers. 1999.

Chapter 22: The Power of Change and Transition

[1] T. Hall. *Furnishing The Soul.* California: XYZ Publishing. 2007.

[2] J. P. Kotter. *Leading Change.* Massachusetts: Harvard Business School Press, 1996.

[3] W. Bridges. *Transitions: Making Sense of Life's Changes.* Massachussetts: Da Capo Press, 2004

Chapter 24: On Being Liberated

[1] D. Dickerman. *When Pigs Move In.* Florida: Charisma House. 2002

[2] F. MacNutt. *Deliverance From Evil Spirits.* Michigan: Chosen Books. 1995

Chapter 25: On Experiencing Inner Healing

[1] J. Sandford and M. Sandford. *Deliverance and Inner Healing.* Michigan: Chosen Books. 2008.

Chapter 26: A Final Thought

[1] S. Rima and G. McIntosh. Overcoming the Dark Side of Leadership. Michigan. Baker Books. 2007